Other Books by James Martin, SJ

My Life with the Saints

Becoming Who You Are:
Insights on the True Self from Thomas Merton and Other Saints

Lourdes Diary

Searching for God at Ground Zero

In Good Company:
The Fast Track from the Corporate World
to Poverty, Chastity, and Obedience

This Our Exile:
A Spiritual Journey with the Refugees of East Africa

Edited by James Martin, SJ

Celebrating Good Liturgy:
A Guide to the Ministries of the Mass
Awake My Soul:
Contemporary Catholics in Traditional Devotions

How Can I Find God?
The Famous and Not-so-Famous Answer
the Quintessential Question

A Jesuit
Off-Broadway

Center Stage with Jesus, Judas, and Life's Big Questions

JAMES MARTIN, SJ

LOYOLAPRESS.

CHICAGO

LOYOLAPRESS.

3441 N. ASHLAND AVENUE
CHICAGO, ILLINOIS 60657
(800) 621-1008
WWW.LOYOLABOOKS.ORG

Imprimi Potest Very Rev. Thomas J. Regan, SJ

Cover and Interior design by Judine O'Shea
Front Cover: © Carol Rosegg, *Back cover:* © Monique Carboni

Library of Congress Cataloging-in-Publication Data
Martin, James, S.J.
 A Jesuit off-Broadway / James Martin.
   p. cm.
 Includes bibliographical references.
 ISBN-13: 978-0-8294-2582-6
 ISBN-10: 0-8294-2582-9
 1. Guirgis, Stephen Adly. Last days of Judas Iscariot. 2. Guirgis, Stephen Adly–Dramatic production. 3. Martin, James, S.J. I. Title.
 PS3607.U49L373 2007
 812'.6—dc22

                                        2007007824

Printed in the United States of America
07 08 09 10 11 12 Bang 10 9 8 7 6 5 4 3 2

For the cast, crew, and creative team of *Judas*,
who helped me feel the sun on my face

ᏨᎧ CONTENTS ᏨᎧ

DRAMATIS PERSONAE ∽

Eric Bogosian .... Satan

Maggie Burke ....Second Henrietta Iscariot

Elizabeth Canavan ....Second Fabiana Aziza Cunningham

Liza Colón-Zayas .... Mother Teresa

Jeffrey DeMunn ....Judge/Caiaphas the Elder/Saint Matthew

Yetta Gottesman .... Mary Magdalene

Craig "Mums" Grant .... Saint Peter

Stephen Adly Guirgis .... Playwright

Stephen McKinley Henderson .... Pontius Pilate

Philip Seymour Hoffman .... Director

Salvatore Inzerillo .... Bailiff/Simon the Zealot

Trevor Long ....Understudy for Jesus and Judas

Abby Marcus .... LAByrinth Company Manager

Adrian Martinez ....Sigmund Freud/Saint Thomas

Monica Moore .... Stage Manager

Mimi O'Donnell .... Costume Designer

John Ortiz .... Jesus of Nazareth

Sam Rockwell ....Judas Iscariot

Elizabeth Rodriguez .... Saint Monica

Brian Roff ....Assistant Director

Deborah Rush ....Henrietta Iscariot

Kohl Sudduth .... Butch Honeywell

Callie Thorne ....Fabiana Aziza Cunningham

Yul Vázquez ....Yusef El-Fayoumy

ix

FOREWORD

Have you ever wanted to cross-examine a Priest? I did. Over many lunches and dinners and coffees and late-night phone calls and even-later-night calls, and then during early-morning meetings *after* late-night dinners and phone calls. I forcefully, aggressively, and desperately cross-examined Father Jim on anything and everything having to do with Scripture, Catholicism, The Priesthood, Jesus and Judas, Heaven and Hell, God's Plan and the Nature of Man—and then followed up my questioning with more questions that had little, if anything, to do with ANY of the above. I asked many questions that, perhaps, one is not supposed to ask, and, on occasion, Father Jim would reply with answers that perhaps he was not supposed to give. I tried to—and needed to—leave no stone unturned, and Father Jim, secure in his faith and his priesthood, never did anything but supply direct answers to pointed questions. And he did so kindly, thoughtfully, and with both a passion for the subject and a wealth of *com*-passion for me—his confused, often irate and disconsolate lapsed Catholic Interrogator. In short, he was everything I think a Priest should be: kind, caring, thoughtful, strong, unimpeachable—and up for the challenge. In short, I have no doubt that Father Jim is one of Jesus' true soldiers. And trust me: I'm not the doubt-free type. I drown in doubt, and to the degree that that's true, Father Jim, from our first meeting and right up to today, is slowly teaching me to swim.

So anyway, what was it like to work with a Priest on a piece of Theater? Not weird at all. What was it like to bring a Priest to rehearsals and encourage him to speak freely and mingle with the cast? It was common sense. Was it weird during Performances to have a Priest hanging around backstage? It was completely normal. Why was Father Jim made a member of our theater company? Because he serves a useful purpose and because we all fell in love with him. So was it all just peaches and cream? No, writing and putting up any kind of play is difficult. This play was especially difficult to write, direct, act, and produce. There were problems all the time. All kinds of problems. In fact, there were so many problems to tackle that having a Priest around was the least of our worries. The reason things worked out so well with Father Jim was that he took off his collar (not literally) and picked up a shovel. He became a worker among workers—and very quickly a friend among friends. The play—and more important, the Experience—could never have been the same without him. And along the way, Father Jim accomplished that thing that I hoped, and hope, to accomplish with the play itself: he got good people thinking about God again, and even got some back to the church. Even me.

Lastly, I remember often asking Father Jim about the Celibacy thing. He would say that, yes, there were times when it felt lonely not to be able to have the experience of sharing his life and heart with another person. But he went on to explain that abstaining from a single, intimate relationship allowed him the time and freedom to be of greater service to others and to the community at large. To be part of a larger family. Celibacy was not a sacrifice, but rather an Opportunity.

As I write this and reflect on what Father Jim has given just me and my theater company alone, I feel a deep sense of gratitude for his embracing that sometimes lonely road. And having seen him in action, I know that his time with us was only one part of his day. We were not nearly the only community being served.

One last thing: I haven't really read this book. I don't know why, but I just can't. It's hard to be a character in someone else's story. I have read all his other books, though, and I recommend them highly. He tells a very good story, has an honest and clear voice, and there's always plenty of gentle humor and well-balanced food for contemplation and thought. I'm sure one day I'll sit down and read this one all the way through. But for now, I am content with my own memory of the experience of meeting and working with and being befriended and ministered to by Father Jim. I will always remember that, more than just a "theological adviser," he was a cheerleader, a rabbi, and a friend during the creation of *The Last Days of Judas Iscariot*. And I will never, ever forget that when I found out my mom had terminal cancer, I called him and he was there in thirty minutes. He gave my mother last rites (twice), counseled her, visited her, listened to her, was there for me and my family, and he booked the church and conducted her funeral Mass when she passed. I took care of my mom in many ways—but none better than by having a friend like Father Jim to see her through her Last Days.

P.S. Don't be afraid to talk to Priests about serious stuff. And if the first guy you reach out to doesn't really get it, then ask another. And even another. My mom used to always say that back in the day, Priests were our friends. Things may be a little different now, but perhaps not so much. The best Priests, like Father Jim, are here to serve, and to expand their communal life by expanding our spiritual lives. So reach out and speak your heart. You have a right to expect answers and assistance. And you may even make a friend.

—Stephen Adly Guirgis
Author, *The Last Days of Judas Iscariot*
May 19, 2007

PROLOGUE

Until a few months ago, what I knew about the theater—playwriting, directing, acting, dramaturgy, set design, and all the rest—wouldn't have filled a paper cup. When the playwright Stephen Adly Guirgis and the actor Sam Rockwell contacted me to help with a new Off-Broadway play called *The Last Days of Judas Iscariot*, I wondered how much I could contribute to their production. On the other hand, after sixteen years as a Jesuit, I thought that I might be able to help the two learn something about what happened in first-century Palestine to the itinerant preacher and the man who betrayed him.

I didn't know then that I was about to learn quite a lot myself—about acting, about the theater, about hard work, and even about the spiritual life.

The Last Days of Judas Iscariot, which ended a sold-out run at the Public Theater in New York City in April 2005, examines the fate of one of the most reviled men in history. The play was coproduced by the LAByrinth Theater Company, of which both Rockwell and Guirgis are longtime members, and the Public Theater. Guirgis, a successful playwright, had wondered about Judas's fate ever since childhood, when he was taught in his Catholic school that God had consigned Judas to hell for his sins. Despite what the nuns told him, Guirgis never regarded Judas's fate as a fair one. His play, which put Judas on trial in a courtroom in purgatory with a host of witnesses (including Mother Teresa, Sigmund Freud, Simon the Zealot, Pontius Pilate, and Caiaphas), considered whether or not the betrayer of Jesus deserved eternal damnation.

Guirgis provided a sophisticated theological treatment of the issue, all in the slangy (and sometimes foul-mouthed) urban argot for which he is known among theater aficionados. In this case, the streetwise lingo represented the playwright's attempt at what theologians call an "inculturation" of the Bible—that is, a translation of the Gospel texts not simply into a different language but for a specific culture.

For Guirgis, that culture is contemporary urban life. Hence, his saints and apostles speak (and often shout) as if they were standing on a crowded subway platform at rush hour. Freed from the need to provide historically accurate quotations for his characters, Guirgis deploys such language to reveal the essential nature of his characters in surprising ways.

For example, when the defense attorney in *Judas* faces difficulty in getting Judas's case heard before a judge in the afterlife, she appeals to Saint Monica, the fourth-century woman whose relentless prayers are credited for the conversion of her wayward son, Augustine. In the biography *Augustine of Hippo*, church historian Peter Brown describes Monica as an "all-absorbing mother, deeply injured by her son's rebellions."

In Guirgis's world, a fiery Monica is a self-described nag who encourages the audience to seek her intercession: "I got a calling, y'all—you should try giving me a shout if ya ever need it, 'cuz my name is Saint Monica . . . and ya know what? My ass gets results!"

Among some Jesuits, Guirgis's approach got results, too. After one performance, a friend said to me, "Maybe I should start praying to Saint Monica again."

Saint Monica was one of the first characters included in the early drafts of *The Last Days of Judas Iscariot*, a play that was still being written when I was asked to serve as what would eventually be called a "theological adviser."

The prospect of a Jesuit priest working alongside an Off-Broadway acting troupe is not as odd as it might seem. The image most people have of the daily life of the Catholic priest is a prosaic one: celebrating Mass, baptizing babies, marrying couples, presiding at funerals, and hearing confessions, all the while knowing little about the larger culture—except maybe where to buy the best brand of single-malt scotch—and certainly nothing at all about popular culture.

If priests are seen in a positive light—an increasingly rare phenomenon in the wake of the church's sexual abuse scandals—they are imagined as leading a hidden, almost monastic existence. But in my experience, the lives of most Catholic priests bring them into contact with more suffering, more craziness, more humanity—in short, more *reality*—than do the lives of many of those with other, "real-world" jobs.

Since its founding in 1540, the Society of Jesus (the formal name of the Catholic religious order to which I belong) has been training its members for a surprising variety of jobs, many quite unorthodox, both in the church and in the world. Today, Jesuits are probably best known as educators. In the United States, members of the society founded, and still work in, dozens of high schools, colleges, and universities—including Georgetown University, Boston College, and Fordham University.

But the Society of Jesus was not created simply to run schools. Its original goal, as articulated by its founder, the Basque lover-turned-soldier-turned-mystic-turned-writer, Saint Ignatius of Loyola, was much broader than that. The fundamental goal of the Jesuits is to "help souls."

Simply put, this means that for more than 450 years Jesuit priests and brothers have taken jobs that were both expected (running parishes, retreat houses, and high schools) and unexpected (exploring uncharted rivers, overseeing observatories, and cataloging newly discovered indigenous languages.) Among its members have been theologians and philosophers, to be sure, but also physicians, poets, politicians, and peace activists. (You can read a fuller history of the Jesuits in the back of this book, in the chapter "Who Are the Jesuits, Anyway?") So working with a theater company is a fairly tame venture for a Jesuit, and very much in keeping with the mission to help souls, even if they happen to be actors, directors, and playwrights.

This book is the story of my time with the cast and crew of a new play. Like any tale worth telling, it is something of a journey—for me a journey into unfamiliar territory. My navigation would not take me down the Amazon River or into an obscure province of China, as it did for some of my Jesuit brothers in past centuries, but into the Public Theater in Lower Manhattan. In a way, this book is a kind of modern version of the reports, called the *Relations,* that the seventeenth-century French Jesuits were asked to send to their religious superiors in the Old World, who were fascinated by what was happening in the New. But instead of writing about the religious ceremonies of the Hurons and Iroquois, I'll relate something about how a new play is created: the writing of the script, the readings, the castings, the rehearsals, the previews, the opening and closing nights, as well as what goes on backstage, what happens when the reviews (both good and bad) hit the papers, and so on. All this was new to me, and I'll share my reactions to the surprises I experienced.

Along the way, I'll address topics that were familiar to me but not as familiar to the cast and crew, and perhaps not as familiar to readers: life in first-century Palestine; what the great spiritual masters said about despair, detachment, and poverty of spirit; whether one can rely on the historical accuracy of the Bible; who was responsible for the death of Jesus; the real-life histories of saints such as Peter and Thomas and Mary Magdalene; the accuracy of films such as Mel Gibson's

The Passion of the Christ and novels such as Dan Brown's *The Da Vinci Code*; and even the long-forgotten history of what was called "Jesuit theater." I will also introduce you to the remarkable men and women with whom I worked, and I will share with you the stories of their own journeys—spiritual, emotional, professional, and otherwise.

One final aside before we begin in earnest. Stephen Adly Guirgis's script was written in a slangy style that included the occasional obscenity. That never bothered me; I found his writing fresh and alive. The cast and creative team sometimes spoke that way as well. That didn't bother me either; I considered it a compliment that they felt comfortable being themselves around me. However, some of the language bothered my Jesuit superiors, and it may offend readers unused to seeing certain words in a book written by a Catholic priest. So what to do? In the end, hoping to be faithful to the spirit of the play, and wanting to quote accurately those with whom I worked, I have elided some of the more piquant profanities with dashes. It's not a perfect solution, but it preserves the flavor of the play and my interviews with the cast, and it satisfies the desire for the book to be accessible to a wider readership.

⟪⟫

My journey with the cast of *The Last Days of Judas Iscariot* was actually a short one, beginning and ending in the space of just six months. Like many memorable trips in one's life, it wasn't one I had planned on making.

ACT 1: INTO THE DEEP END

October to December

Judas called first.

In late October 2004, I got a phone call from Sam Rockwell, who had just been cast as the title character of Stephen Adly Guirgis's new play. He left a polite message on my answering machine: I'm an actor who is working on a play about Judas. Would you be willing to talk with me about him?

As an associate editor of a Catholic magazine and a Jesuit priest, I spend most of my time editing manuscripts, proofreading galleys, writing books and articles, lecturing on spirituality and religion, celebrating Mass, and hearing confessions. Until I got the call from Sam, I had no experience working with actors, directors, or playwrights (unless you count my unfairly forgotten turn as Hugo F. Peabody in Plymouth Whitemarsh High School's 1978 production of *Bye Bye Birdie*).

I didn't know what to expect, particularly with someone of Sam Rockwell's caliber. Besides *Confessions of a Dangerous Mind*, *Matchstick Men*, *The Green Mile*, *Galaxy Quest*, and *Charlie's Angels*, he had also starred in lesser-known indie gems such as *Box of Moonlight*, where he played an off-the-wall, off-the-grid loner who teaches John Turturro's uptight electrical engineer a thing or two about life. Would the actor arrive at my Jesuit residence with his handlers? His posse? Would fits be pitched if I didn't have his favorite brand of bottled water?

1

Sam arrived on a cold Sunday afternoon, the last day of October, wearing a nylon sweat suit and talking on a cell phone. "Hey, man," he said with a broad smile. "I'm Sam." He pulled off his wool cap, and his staticky brown hair stood straight up from his head. He explained that the few days' growth of reddish beard was part of his look for the new character.

When we sat down in the musty library of my Jesuit community residence, Sam told me about his background. Both his mother and his father were actors and had met while studying at the American Conservatory Theater in San Francisco. When Sam was five, his parents divorced. Though he remained with his father in California, during the summers he visited his mother in the Latino neighborhood where she lived in Harlem. Years later, that background would enable him to feel comfortable in the LAByrinth Theater Company, then a company for Latino actors in New York. "I was one of the first gringos they ever accepted," he said. "Definitely the first Irish-German guy."

Sam got an early start in his profession, appearing with his mother onstage when he was ten. While still a student in high school, he won a leading role in a horror movie, a job that gave him the confidence to move east. After graduating from San Francisco's School of the Arts High School, he left for New York, initially boarding with his mother and stepfather. A variety of restaurant jobs, including a stint delivering burritos by bike, enabled the actor to save enough money to move "from sublet to sublet" in Brooklyn. He took almost any job to make ends meet. "I even was an apprentice to a private investigator," he said with a laugh.

Once settled in New York, Sam began studying with the acting teacher William Esper, a follower of the Sanford Meisner technique, which emphasizes the importance of relating to the other actors onstage. It was at Esper's studio that he met several future members of the LAByrinth Theater Company, including Stephen Adly Guirgis, the playwright of *Judas*. Sam studied with Esper for two years and began finding more work and landing bigger parts.

In time he was cast in a few television commercials (Burger King), found work in a television series (*Law & Order*), and began landing some film roles, including a part in the 1989 movie *Last Exit to Brooklyn*. He counts his role in *Box of Moonlight* as his big break. In 1997, he won a Best Actor award at the Montreal World Film Festival for his role as a troubled young man in *Lawn Dogs*, which led to roles in several more mainstream films. All told, Sam had been acting for more than twenty-five years.

"I like acting because it's cathartic," he said. "When it's at its best it's pretty therapeutic, and even spiritual. There's a kind of release that comes with it, almost like an exorcism, as you let go of a part of yourself that you've kept locked away."

"But it's hard, too," he added. "I have this kind of love-hate relationship with acting. It gives me a lot of anxiety—all that performing and auditioning and traveling takes a lot out of you. And the business part of it . . . well, it's just mind-boggling how crazy that can be sometimes."

If I didn't know what to expect from our meeting, neither did Sam; he didn't know any priests. Casting about for someone to speak with about his part, he had gotten my phone number from one of his mother's friends who worked at a local Jesuit parish where I celebrate Mass on Sundays.

Eventually Sam got around to describing his religious background. "My grandmother was Irish Catholic and used to try to bring me to church, but I used to squirm around and hide under the benches," he explained sheepishly. "I went to Catholic school, too—but just for a month. I was too rebellious. So I wasn't raised religious, and I don't know anything about religion." His exposure to religious topics, to the Bible, and to the story of Jesus had come almost exclusively from film.

As for his own faith, he said, "Well, I pray to God when I'm having an anxiety attack or am panicked about a performance. God's there when I need him, but I'm still not sure if I really believe or not."

It appeared that both of us were in unfamiliar territory: I with theater and Sam with religion.

But religious topics provided enough common ground for a free-wheeling conversation that lasted until sunset. With Sam's small tape recorder placed before me, I launched into a sort of Introduction to Christianity, scribbling notes on stray sheets of paper, summarizing the history of the Hebrew people in the Old Testament, sketching a crude map of Judea in the first century, describing the ministry of Jesus of Nazareth, listing the twelve apostles, and outlining how the various Christian denominations had grown apart over the centuries.

Sam followed my mini-lecture attentively, squinting and cocking his head when something wasn't clear. When something made an impression he would stare intently, nod, and say, "Yeah, yeah, yeah . . ."

The actor had already screened several films about Jesus and was in the process of listening to Gregory Peck narrate the Gospels on tape, and in fact he knew more about the Bible than he suspected. He enjoyed the 1969 movie *Jesus Christ Superstar*, in particular for the passionate and very physical performance of Carl Anderson, the actor who played Judas. "It helped me to see some of Judas's point of view," he said. But it was *Jesus of Nazareth*, the six-hour film directed by Franco Zeffirelli in 1977, which still appears regularly around Easter and Christmas on cable television, that was his favorite of all the Jesus films.

It was my favorite, too. *Jesus of Nazareth*, which stars the British actor Robert Powell as Jesus, is the film that, at least for me, most effectively conveys the sweep of the Gospel narratives. Certain scenes have imprinted themselves so deeply onto my religious consciousness that whenever I hear, for example, the story of the raising of Lazarus, it is not any Renaissance painting or fresco that comes to mind, but Robert Powell, clad in his white robes, standing before an open tomb and shouting in a booming voice, "Lazarus, come *forth*!"

On the other hand, Zeffirelli's film adheres to the cinematic doctrine that while the twelve apostles are to be portrayed as simple men who speak plainly, Jesus himself must speak with a plummy British accent, as if the Messiah divided his time between Galilee and Oxford.

Sam had a terrific memory for scenes from Zeffirelli's film. The gentle way in which Jesus treated the adulterous woman, quickly silencing the crowd intent on stoning her, made a marked impression on him. It was an account that he referred to again and again. "Even if you forget about the miracles," said Sam, "what Jesus said and what he was trying to do were pretty extraordinary."

Each answer I gave to one of Sam's questions prompted a digression that led to yet another question. We jumped from the book of Genesis to Charlton Heston's performance in *The Ten Commandments*, from the origin of the phrase *doubting Thomas* to Martin Luther and the Reformation, from the rosary to Saint Peter's betrayal of Jesus, from the work of a Jesuit priest to Christian fundamentalism, from Mary Magdalene to Mel Gibson's film *The Passion of the Christ*, from the Eastern Orthodox Church to the contradictory accounts of the Resurrection in the Gospels.

At one point Sam asked about the Our Father. When the actor learned that it was a prayer that Jesus taught to his disciples, he asked me to dissect it for him, line by line. We talked about its underlying structure—the traditional praise to God, the expression of hope for God's "kingdom," the petition for one's daily needs, the desire for forgiveness, and the offer of forgiveness for others. Each phrase provoked more questions from Sam. For all his lack of formal religious training, he posed queries that would have challenged even the best theologians: "I want to go back to something you just said: 'Thy kingdom come.' Your kingdom come? Does that mean I'm coming to your kingdom in heaven, or is heaven coming to me?"

After we dipped into random passages from the Bible, Sam and I started to focus on what he was most interested in for the purposes of the new play: the story of Jesus of Nazareth and the man who betrayed him.

As it happens, the study of what contemporary theologians term the "historical Jesus" has long been an avocation for me. This branch of New Testament scholarship uses modern scholarly methods—archaeology, text criticism, and research into the social and cultural life of first-century Palestine—to understand Jesus of Nazareth and his circle of disciples. Almost twenty years ago, when I entered the Jesuit novitiate, I was given a slim book called *Jesus before Christianity*, by a Dominican priest named Albert Nolan. Nolan describes daily life in ancient Galilee, Jewish practices and beliefs at the time of Jesus, and the real-world events that lay behind some of Jesus' most famous stories and parables. Nolan's fascinating study launched me on a quest to read as much as I could about the Jesus of history.

Sam was on his own quest—to learn everything he could about his character. I could see how important this kind of preparation was for him. And I was happy to discover that the actor was an open and self-effacing fellow—anything but the stereotypical movie star.

The more Sam and I talked, the more enthusiastic I grew about the play. Over the next few months, Sam would put me to the test with a barrage of questions: What was life like for the apostles? What do we know about Judas Iscariot? Why did he betray Jesus? Could Jesus have forgiven him? Sam's curiosity astounded me.

When I mentioned this to a Jesuit friend, he said, "Aren't you glad you paid attention in your New Testament classes?" Then he paused and asked, "What do you know about Judas anyway?"

About Judas

Very little is known about Judas. The Reverend John Meier, a professor of New Testament at Notre Dame and the author of a multivolume study on Jesus called *A Marginal Jew*, is one of the leading contemporary scholars on the "historical Jesus." In the third volume of his work, entitled *Companions and Competitors*, Meier notes that only two basic things are known about Judas: Jesus chose him as one of the twelve apostles, and he handed Jesus over to the Jewish authorities.

Those "two bare facts," Meier writes, "are almost all that we know about the historical Judas. Beyond them lies theological speculation or novel writing, with the dividing line between the two activities not always clear-cut."

In other words, many of the standard traits of the Judas who appears in films and onstage, such as his reddish hair color (Harvey Keitel in *The Last Temptation of Christ*) and his fiery disposition (*Jesus Christ Superstar*), as well as various "facts" that appear in supposedly historically minded narratives (Judas is the first disciple called by Jesus in *The Greatest Story Ever Told*), are almost purely speculative, invented primarily for artistic purposes.

Many of these artistic speculations can be traced back to varying interpretations of a single word in the New Testament: Judas's last name, Iscariot.

According to John Meier, there are four main theories about the name. From these interpretations came two millennia of artistic representations of Judas. In turn, these representations have influenced how Western culture has come to think about the man and his actions.

First, the name is said to derive from Judas's membership in the *Sicarii*, or "dagger wielders," a band of religious terrorists of the time. In this speculation, Judas was aligned with the Zealots, a fanatical group that included another apostle, Simon. As a result, Judas is sometimes portrayed, as in *The Last Temptation of Christ*, as an apostolic hothead. But, as Meier notes, the *Sicarii* did not emerge until around AD 40 or 50, well after the death of Jesus of Nazareth. Also, if Judas was a *Sicarius*, then he would have been more likely to assassinate Jesus by stabbing him in a crowded place—the approved method among the *Sicarii*—rather than hand him over to the detested authorities.

The name Iscariot is also said to have come from the Semitic root verb *sqr*, meaning "to lie." But here the problem is subtler: Judas is not portrayed throughout the New Testament as a liar as much as a betrayer. (An even more tenuous linguistic connection is to the Semitic verb *skr*: "to hand over.")

Others see in the name a link to a Semitic word describing the man's occupation, a red dyer, or a reference to his supposed reddish hair color. (Near the end of the play, Sam Rockwell would sport a full reddish brown beard, a feature that prompted one of my Jesuit friends to ask if he had dyed it for the part.)

Finally, Iscariot may refer to a place of birth, a village named Kerioth in Judea. Therefore, Judas Iscariot would be, in Hebrew, "a man of Kerioth" (*'ish qeriyyot*). In this construct Judas would have been the only apostle not from Galilee, a tantalizing possibility: it would make the Judean Judas an obvious outsider among the Galilean apostles. Unfortunately, it is not clear that a town called Kerioth ever existed.

The best explanation may be the simplest: Iscariot was the name that Judas took from his father, who is identified in the Gospel of John as Simon Iscariot. Where the father got his name, however, remains a mystery. And whether John's narrative is authoritative on the matter is also doubtful. In the end, says Meier, "the nickname, like the person, remains an enigma."

The lack of historical information on Judas would be—to borrow a line from the Old Testament—both a blessing and a curse to the play's creative team. It offered the playwright, the director, and the actors a great deal of creative freedom with the story. On the other hand, it made research into the title character's motivation more difficult. As one character in the play says, referring to the sparse record: "Not a lot to go on—especially when we're meant to rely on facts." Especially when even the "facts" come from writers intent on convincing us of the underlying truth of their story.

There was one thing I could tell Sam unequivocally: Judas was not always as villainous as he has appeared historically in art and literature. Judas Iscariot was, after all, chosen to be one of the twelve apostles. This means that Jesus, supposedly a shrewd judge of character, must have seen some redeeming qualities in him. Likewise, Judas identified Jesus as someone worthy of following and initially accepted the sacrifices required to become his follower.

This alone argues for a more sympathetic portrayal of Judas. In other words, how could someone so irredeemably evil decide to give up everything to become a follower of Jesus? And if any of the traditions have any factual basis, and Judas was indeed a passionate man, we can speculate that he could have been one of the more devoted followers of Jesus of Nazareth.

Needless to say, the writers of the Gospels would have been unlikely to include any material in their narrative that would cast Judas in a positive light. Evidence of Jesus' early affection for Judas or any stories showing Judas's initial devotion to Jesus would probably have been set aside by the evangelists in their writing and editing. Consider one of our more recent villains, Benedict Arnold. Because we know that he turned traitor in the end, we may have less interest in knowing what positive things he might have done for the American cause earlier in his life. In a way, we can allow the later sins to obliterate the earlier graces when we are forming opinions—or writing histories—of people.

Consequently, the generally accepted understanding of Judas begins with sources that painted him in the darkest tones possible. And the writers of the four Gospels were also good storytellers who knew that, for simple dramatic effect, the story of Jesus required an arch villain: a divine protagonist needs the wickedest of opponents.

Later Christian traditions built on such presentations were, unfortunately, also influenced by nascent anti-Semitism, as the early church distanced itself from its Jewish roots. Writing in the fourth century, Saint John Chrysostom, patriarch of Constantinople, used Judas as an example of the wickedness of Jews in general. Chrysostom was one of several saints whose writings were tinged with—and contributed to—the virulent anti-Semitism common at the time. In Chrysostom's view, Judas was evil not only because he betrayed Jesus but also because he was Jewish.

Chrysostom sees the suicide of Judas as foreshadowing the suffering of the Jews, and he comments on this approvingly. In his *Homilies on the Acts of the Apostles*, he writes: "This desolation [his fate] was a prelude to that of the Jews, as will appear on looking closely into the facts." That one of the most influential figures in the patristic era could write so cruelly shows the rapid assimilation of anti-Semitism into Christianity and the hardening of the Christian heart against Judas.

These characterizations, which influenced the medieval Passion plays, continued to color the work of the early and late Renaissance writers and artists. Dante, for example, places Judas in the lowest circle of hell in his *Inferno*, where the arch sinner is torn apart by a three-headed Satan. Kim Paffenroth, a religious studies professor at Iona College in New York, writes in his wide-ranging historical study *Judas: Images of the Lost Disciple*: "For Dante, Judas is the worst example of the worst sin possible, betrayal, and therefore he places him at the center of hell, the worst of human sinners."

Virgil, the poet's guide to the underworld, identifies the man who is being chewed upon by one of Satan's mouths while his back is being "raked clean of its skin":

> "That soul up there who suffers most of all,"
> my guide explained, "is Judas Iscariot:
> the one with head inside and legs out kicking."

As Paffenroth notes, most of the Passion plays popular throughout Europe in the fourteenth and fifteenth centuries accentuated the ties between Judas and the Jewish people. The development of the most famous of these plays shows how central that identification was.

In the seventeenth century, the Bavarian town of Oberammergau vowed to stage an elaborate Passion play every ten years as a sign of thanksgiving for being spared the ravages of a terrible plague. From 1634 until the mid-eighteenth century, writes Paffenroth, the Oberammergau play was similar to other European versions, with its crowd-pleasing depictions of many devils tearing Judas apart for his perfidy. But in 1811, a rewrite excised the devils and prompted what Paffenroth calls an "amazing transformation."

The new version of the Oberammergau play blamed the Jews exclusively—instead of devils or the devil—for the death of Jesus, thus "elaborating and accentuating Jewish evil as completely human but utterly and irredeemably evil." The Oberammergau Passion continues to be staged; according to Paffenroth, only in 2000 were any "substantial" changes made to the script regarding anti-Semitism.

Over time, then, the stereotype of Judas as the wickedest of all human beings, as well as layer upon layer of anti-Semitism, made it difficult if not impossible for later generations to gain any distance from Judas's story and to understand his motivation. The historical Judas was buried under the artistic representations of him. As Graham Greene wrote in his novel *The End of the Affair*, "If we had not been taught how to interpret the story of the Passion, would we have been able to say from their actions alone whether it was the jealous Judas or the cowardly Peter who loved Christ?"

An edgier interpretation comes from David A. Reed, a Scripture scholar writing in the *Biblical Theology Bulletin*. Perhaps, says Reed, one could see in Judas a kind of offbeat heroism. Reed suggests that in the first century, Judas's suicide would have been understood as a calculated decision to shame the Jewish religious leaders for refusing to take back the money they had given Judas in payment for his betrayal, as well as a means for Judas to atone for his sin.

"Like many figures in the Hebrew Bible," writes Reed, "he has experienced atonement in the best sense of the word, though it shocks us that his atonement came about by suicide."

In lengthy conversations, Sam and I explored some of these insights into the life of his character. Without a real understanding of Judas's history, Sam would not be able to portray him accurately or compellingly onstage, and so he was interested in learning anything he could about his character. For example, once Sam saw Judas as initially supportive of Jesus' ministry, he was able to portray him as something more than the monster described by most Christian writers. Over time, the actor's questions also helped me see a familiar story from a fresh perspective.

Eventually, we had to sift through the traditional explanations for, and biblical descriptions of, Judas's betrayal of Jesus. One Saturday afternoon, I made my way to Sam's apartment downtown. Fortified by a few cups of strong tea, we turned our attention to the act that defines Judas in the popular imagination. Unfortunately, as Meier points out in *A Marginal Jew*, the four canonical Gospels (Matthew, Mark, Luke, and John) offer confusing and even contradictory explanations for his motives.

The Gospel of Mark gives no motivation for Judas's sudden betrayal. John's Gospel has Jesus telling Judas at the Last Supper, "Do quickly what you are going to do," implying coercion on the part of Jesus. Matthew, writing a decade or so after Mark, attempts to clarify things in his account by introducing the motive of greed: "What will you give me?" Judas asks the Jewish chief priests.

This theme is taken up by the Gospel of John as well: long before the Last Supper, Judas is depicted by the evangelist as the greedy keeper of the common purse. When, shortly before his crucifixion, Jesus is anointed with costly perfume by a woman in the town of Bethany, John's Gospel has Judas complain, asking why the money was not given to the poor.

In an aside, John says to the reader, "He [Judas] said this not because he cared about the poor, but because he was a thief; he kept the common purse and used to steal what was put into it." So John paints Judas as exceedingly greedy and a thief as well. Finally, Luke's Gospel tells us that at the Last Supper, "Satan entered into Judas." Daniel J. Harrington, SJ, a New Testament scholar, told our class in graduate school that for the interested reader this phrase from Luke explained "either everything or nothing."

There is another hypothesis that sometimes remains unstated by Scripture scholars: the evangelists simply concocted the entire story of Judas's betrayal for dramatic purposes. Some have posited that the one who betrayed Jesus could have come from outside the circle of the Twelve and that Judas was simply a convenient fall guy. Similarly, Judas may have been invented as a generic "Jewish" character in order to lay the blame for the Crucifixion on the Jewish people.

But this wholesale invention is unlikely. By most accounts, Mark wrote his Gospel around AD 70, only forty years after the death of Jesus. Luke and Matthew wrote some ten to fifteen years later. The early Christian community would have still counted among its members those who were friends of Jesus, those who were eyewitnesses to the Passion events, and those who knew the sequence of events from the previous generation. We can assume that these followers would have criticized any wild liberties taken with the story. Rather, as Father Harrington told me recently, "Judas's betrayal of Jesus was a known and most embarrassing fact." In other words, the ignominy of having Jesus betrayed by one of his closest friends is something that the Gospel writers would most likely have wanted to *avoid*, not invent. Overall, though, none of the four Gospels provides a clear or convincing reason for why one of Jesus' inner circle would have betrayed the teacher he esteemed so highly. Greed, for example, fails miserably as an explanation. After all, why would someone who had traveled with the penniless rabbi for three years suddenly become consumed with greed?

One Scripture scholar, the late William Barclay, former professor of divinity at the University of Glasgow and author of the widely used multivolume Daily Study Bible, suggested that the most compelling explanation is that in handing Jesus over to the Romans, Judas was trying to force Jesus' hand, to get him to act in a decisive way. Perhaps Judas expected the arrest would prompt Jesus to reveal himself as the long-awaited Messiah by overthrowing the Roman occupiers.

Barclay noted that none of the other traditional explanations (greed, disillusionment, jealousy) explains why Judas would have been so shattered after the Crucifixion that he committed suicide. Only if Judas had expected a measure of good to come from his actions would suicide make any sense. (The recently discovered *Gospel of Judas*, written in the fourth century, more or less takes that same approach.)

"This is in fact the view which best suits all the facts," Barclay concluded.

After we had batted around Barclay's theory for a while, Sam thought for a moment and remarked, "Maybe Judas was throwing Jesus into the deep end of the pool, hoping he'd swim." I liked his analogy so much that I used it in a homily at Mass the following Sunday at a local Jesuit church. After Mass, one of the parishioners approached me on the steps of the church and said, "That was a great insight about Judas. Where did you get that from?"

Sam's insight would eventually find its way into Guirgis's play, on the lips of Simon the Zealot, one of the twelve apostles, who provides the main defense for Judas: he hoped to help Jesus fulfill his destiny. "I think Judas was trying to throw Jesus into the deep end of the pool," says Simon. But the playwright doesn't let Simon off easily. Through the Egyptian-born prosecutor, he provides a trenchant rejoinder to Barclay's hypothesis: "[Judas was] there to lend zee helping hand, yes?" says the prosecutor sarcastically. "Yes, I think you are correct. . . . I'm sure [if I were Jesus on the cross] my first thought as I gasped for air and bled to death would be, 'Really, that Judas—what a *helpful* guy!'"

The Birth of a God-Haunted Play

Stephen Adly Guirgis's theological interests were even more wide-ranging than Sam Rockwell's. As the playwright, he needed to know not only about Judas but also about all the events leading up to the Crucifixion, including the roles of Pontius Pilate, the Jewish leader Caiaphas the Elder, and the apostles.

Like Sam, Stephen had gotten my name from a Catholic church in Manhattan, called Corpus Christi, his childhood parish. When we first met, the play was still being written, although it had been performed in readings at the past two annual summer workshops of the LAByrinth Theater Company. As Stephen would later explain, "Lab," as he called it, had been his creative home for almost a decade. Working with close friends afforded him a measure of comfort in the midst of the otherwise stress-inducing venture of staging a new play.

And this play would certainly be a challenge: not only was it new, but it would also be staged in a larger venue and before a wider audience than any of Stephen's previous works. *The Last Days of Judas Iscariot* was slated for a run at New York City's prestigious Public Theater, also the coproducer of the show. Founded in 1954 by the impresario Joseph Papp, the Public Theater was the originator of the popular Shakespeare in the Park series, as well as the source of some of the most successful Broadway plays in the past few decades. Shows as diverse as *That Championship Season, Hair, A Chorus Line, The Pirates of Penzance, Take Me Out,* and *Bring in 'Da Noise, Bring in 'Da Funk* all began their profitable lives at the Public. Over its fifty-year life, the theater has staged plays that have won 40 Tony Awards, 135 Obies, 38 Drama Desk Awards, and 4 Pulitzer prizes. The Public, therefore, would give Guirgis's play instant attention. But wider visibility and a larger audience would also mean an increased risk of failure, and a very public one at that.

At my first meeting with Stephen, in early November, over dinner at a Greek restaurant around the corner from my Jesuit community in Manhattan, the affable and voluble playwright handed me a book of his plays. Stephen was an unlikely looking intellectual: sleepy eyes hung at half-mast, a few days' growth of beard, gray-tinged black hair flopped over his collar, layer upon layer of T-shirts and sweatshirts, and a crumpled pack of cigarettes at the ready.

He was also a natural conversationalist, every once in a while offering an observation so insightful and clear-eyed that I realized why he was a successful playwright. Though I had heard of two of his most successful works—*Our Lady of 121st Street* and *Jesus Hopped the "A" Train*—I was embarrassed to admit that I had seen neither. But I read through these two plays over the next few nights.

Stephen's writing revealed a playwright who seemed, in the words of the theologian Johannes Baptist Metz, "religious 'by nature.'" Underneath many of his foul-mouthed characters were men and women, usually poor and unlucky, who had nonetheless not given up searching for meaning, for answers, and for a modicum of faith. I thought of a quote from Saint Paul's second letter to the Corinthians, "We are afflicted in every way, but not crushed; perplexed, but not driven to despair; . . . struck down, but not destroyed." While Stephen might have blanched at the description, the two plays I read were deeply theological.

They were also wildly profane, full of the kind of vulgarity heard not in church sacristies (at least not most church sacristies) but in locker rooms, bars, and traffic jams. That kind of in-your-face language not only reflected the milieu of the characters but also prevented the presentation of religious themes from becoming either cozily conventional or piously sentimental, and probably helped open a window into theological questions for those normally put off by such topics.

Jesus Hopped the "A" Train, or *Jesus*, as Stephen called it, tells the tale of Angel Cruz, a young Puerto Rican in New York jailed for shooting a born-again Christian who has brainwashed his best friend. "All I did was shoot him in the ass," explains Angel, an essentially good-hearted man. But the minister dies, condemning the young man to his fate. While in jail, he meets Lucius, a born-again serial killer intent on conveying his religious worldview to Angel.

It is an incendiary work, written in the playwright's slangy style, with the two main characters arguing over questions of free will, personal responsibility, the nature of evil, and faith. "If prayer don't mean s——t," says Lucius to Angel, "then how come I was awoken the other night to hear a sorry little bitch stutterin' over some prayer in between chokes 'n' sobs 'n' snorts from inhaling his tears on the damp little prison pillow?"

Even reading the script in the quiet of my office, I felt the play's passion and intensity. *Jesus* garnered Stephen a good deal of attention and received nominations for several dramatic awards. In 2002, it was nominated for the prestigious Olivier Award for best new play in London. Writing in the *New York Times*, Ben Brantley said, "Plays of this ilk automatically raise the body—and mind—temperature of New York theater."

Our Lady of 121st Street, Stephen's next work, paints an affectionate group portrait of the former students of a much-loved Catholic sister, whose funeral they are attending in their old, and poor, neighborhood. The police are also investigating why the nun's body has disappeared from the funeral home. "What did Rose ever do till the day she died but be a . . . living saint on earth to deserve . . . this sacrilege?" says one character in the first scene.

At the heart of *Our Lady* is the way in which the tough-talking characters—Anglo, Latino, African American—are forced, through direct conversations with one another, to accept responsibility for their lives. As in *Jesus*, questions of faith take center stage: characters talk about confession, the story of Jonah and the whale, and Saint Paul's letter to the Corinthians. Like *Jesus*, *Our Lady* was greeted enthusiastically. It received nominations from the Drama Desk and the Outer Critics Circle for best play. In a review of the original production, Bruce Weber said in the *New York Times* that the playwright had "one of the finest imaginations for dialogue to come along in years."

After glancing at the back jacket of the book, I was further embarrassed by my ignorance. A writer in the *New York Times Magazine* stated that Stephen Adly Guirgis "may be the best playwright in America under forty." Other reviewers compared him to Tennessee Williams, David Mamet, Joe Orton, and even Fyodor Dostoyevsky. Subsequent conversations with theatergoers at my parish pointed up my sorry lack of theatrical knowledge. One woman active in our parish told me that she had seen all of his plays.

"You're working with Stephen Adly Guirgis?" she said. "He's God-haunted, I think."

Stephen admitted as much in a later conversation. "In the final scene of *Jesus*," he explained, "Angel listens to his conscience, a way of entering into relationship with God. In *Our Lady*, it is ultimately a priest who gets through to the main character. My last few plays have been about exploring my conflicts with the spiritual side of life as well as what continues to draw me to it." *Judas* was a natural next step.

The Making of a Playwright

Before my first meeting with Stephen, his new play already had a long history. In a way, it had begun when Stephen was in third grade. That year, one of the Dominican sisters teaching at Corpus Christi told his class the story of Judas. Stephen was horrified. He believed in a loving God, and the idea that God had consigned Judas to a place called hell "just stopped me in my tracks." He loved and respected the nuns in his school but wondered about what they were telling him. How could God not feel sorry for Judas?

The third grader had stumbled upon a theological conundrum that has challenged theologians, philosophers, and saints for centuries. Doesn't God, who is kind and merciful, as the psalms say, forgive every sin? How could a merciful God create hell? In the Gospel of Matthew, Jesus of Nazareth repeatedly forgives sins, but he also tells his followers that they will be judged at the end of time, with the "sheep" being separated from the "goats." How does one reconcile justice with mercy? Saint Thérèse of Lisieux, the nineteenth-century French Carmelite nun, solved this dilemma for herself by saying that she believed in hell but also believed it was empty. How could anyone in heaven, wondered Thérèse, be happy if there were still souls suffering in hell? (Tertullian, one of the most influential early Christian writers, disagreed—which is putting things mildly. He predicted that one of the chief joys of heaven would be thinking about the torments of the sinners in hell.)

It would have been unfair to expect Stephen's teacher to present her third-grade class with a sophisticated presentation of the Catholic understanding of hell, a topic that prompts even the best theologians to scratch their heads.

There is obviously no earthly way of knowing what awaits sinners and the "elect," but that has not prevented Christians from reflecting on what the soul might face after the death of the body. And it is a difficult topic to avoid, not only because of our innate curiosity (and fear) but also because Jesus of Nazareth alluded to what is called the "Last Judgment" in his preaching, most famously in his parable of the sheep and the goats. For the "sheep"—the good souls, the faithful—there is the reward of heaven, eternal life, or, in Christian terminology, the "beatific vision": the direct seeing and knowing of the divine.

But from as early as the late fifth century, the church has also recognized punishment after death for the "goats," those who die in a state of "mortal sin," or serious sin. Popes and ecumenical councils have wrestled with the topic until the present time, striving to arrive at a definition that preserves God's justice while not understating God's mercy. In 1979, the Vatican's Congregation for the Doctrine of the Faith, in its "Letter on Certain Questions concerning Eschatology," reaffirmed the belief that some sinners are punitively "deprived of the sight of God."

But beyond this—and contrary to popular belief—the church has never affirmed that any individual human being has been consigned to hell. Not even Judas.

The general understanding of ordinary Christians, however, is slightly different. What theologians call the *sensus fidelium* ("sense of the faithful") can be summed up as follows: there is a hell, and Judas is probably there, along with, say, Hitler and Stalin and a few other evildoers. (Most Catholics, perhaps being forgiving sorts, or perhaps trying to hedge their bets on their own sins, don't like to go further than the most notorious sinners.) This view seems to be what Stephen's teacher imparted to his class.

For the young boy, though, the notion of a vengeful deity was shocking, disturbing his previously benign image of God. He explained his reaction to me over lunch one day.

"It's like I'm getting to know you," he told me, "and all of a sudden someone says to me, 'Hey, Father Jim is a murderer!' And I go to you, and you say that you *are* a murderer, and there's nothing wrong with that." Harboring questions like these made Stephen feel guilty for having a viewpoint different from that of his teachers and, by extension, different from how God viewed the world. He felt that he was a bad person for believing these things. This was the beginning of his problems with faith.

But the boy with the questions about faith would spend most of his childhood in Catholic schools, first at Corpus Christi and then at Xavier High School, a Jesuit school in Manhattan, until eleventh grade. During that time, his mother, a devout Irish Catholic, and his father, an Egyptian immigrant who was baptized in the Coptic Church, taught him to pray and encouraged him to go to Mass. And he would go—sometimes. "My mother would give me money for the collection in an envelope, but sometimes I would skip Mass, take the money, and play pinball."

This only added to his guilt. "I felt that it should be easier for me to do the right thing—to pray, to go to church, to be more into all of it." Stephen grew into an intelligent young man prone to misbehavior: he became proficient at shoplifting, mainly to keep up with his neighborhood peers, whose families were wealthier than his. "I got really good at it, too."

In tenth grade, Stephen underwent back surgery to correct a childhood curvature of the spine, which put him in a full body cast and kept him out of school for six months. Afterward, his limited ability to walk meant leaving Xavier for a school nearer home; he enrolled at the Rhodes School, which he characterized as being less disciplined than his previous schools. Aimless after graduation, he was a bike messenger for a time and then applied to state universities. Albany State University accepted him, and Stephen described seven years of working toward his degree while partying, battling depression, and teetering on the edge of expulsion, until he discovered the drama department.

"For me, it was a chance to escape and to dream and to play make-believe," he said. Stephen still acts and recently appeared in Todd Solondz's movie *Palindromes* and Kenneth Lonergan's *Margaret*. "I love acting, and if I go too long without acting, I get pretty sad, and then I realize that it's because I haven't done any acting for a while, and then I try to find a way to do some, and then I immediately feel better."

His spirituality—even in the midst of doubt—was always a part of his life, and it became part of his profession. "Whenever I perform, I pray to God and ask him for help. I pray to Mary, because I figure she'll help me more because she's a woman. And I pray to the Holy Spirit to move through me as I act."

More confident of his direction in life, he finished his degree in 1991 and almost immediately founded a small theater in the Bronx with a friend. He left after a year, upon realizing that it was acting, not managing, that he wanted to do most. After a year in Santa Fe (where he founded another theater), he returned to New York and heard that a friend from Albany State, John Ortiz, had cofounded the Latino Actors Base, the precursor of the LAByrinth Theater Company. Stephen auditioned and was accepted. Around the same time, he began taking acting lessons at William Esper's studio, where he met Sam Rockwell.

In 1993, Ortiz asked his friend to write a one-act play for LAB. The fledgling company was having a hard time finding scripts to produce. *Francisco and Benny*, Stephen's first play, was a success. "Everyone laughed at the funny parts and was quiet at the serious parts," he said. "After that, [the company members] kept pestering me to write something for their summer workshops."

A number of successful full-length plays followed, directed by Philip Seymour Hoffman, a friend and fellow company member. Stephen the actor had become a playwright.

In the summer of 2003, John Ortiz called Stephen again and said, "You're writing something, right?"

At a loss, Stephen blurted out, "*The Last Days of Judas Iscariot*." His last three plays had focused on religious topics, and since Judas had been his original stumbling block with religion, he figured, "Why not go back to the source of my problems and see where it takes me?"

For the first workshop, he brought in a twenty-page script. During the following year, Stephen landed acting roles in two movies, while the play percolated through his unconscious. In the summer of 2004, a few months before I met Stephen, the play, now twenty pages longer, had another reading at the LAB summer workshop. Stephen also began to cast a few members from LAB, including Sam. Hoffman agreed to direct *Judas*, and the play was scheduled for the next season. After that summer, Stephen's research began in earnest. So did his resistance.

"I discovered that there was a *reason* I hadn't written it before," he told me not long after the play closed. "The subject was terribly daunting for me, in almost every way. It not only touched on all my spiritual struggles, but it seemed too big a topic for someone like me to tackle." A visit to the pastor of Riverside Church, where Stephen had attended kindergarten, gave him the courage to continue. Another conversation, with the pastor of Corpus Christi Church, who also gave him my phone number, further encouraged him. His doubt had led him back to his kindergarten and childhood parishes.

Stephen's spiritual life at the time was also beginning to deepen. "The last several years have been about trying to reconnect and get closer with whatever it is that God is," he said. "This play about Judas is part of that journey."

Still, he faced inner resistance. "So I'm trying to write this play about avoidance in Judas's life—and I'm avoiding it! One day I had lunch with Sam, who said that he had met this young priest and that I should call him. It's a manifestation of a general spiritual problem that I have: I always think I need to do everything by myself. But the reality is the exact *opposite*! So I knew I needed to talk to someone about all this theology."

I asked him whether he believed that his lunch with Sam was a kind of providence.

"Well," he said, taking a drag off his cigarette, "I took that as a sign of providence, and I took it as a sign that I should get up off my ass and call you."

Theological questions were indeed foremost in the playwright's mind, and our conversations ranged from broader questions about grace, forgiveness, and despair to more detailed inquiries into the history of the individual characters in the drama.

Stephen came to our first meeting armed with an impressive knowledge about his new protagonist. His initial preparation had included reading several books and screening a wide variety of movies about Jesus. "When I had trouble reading about Judas, I went to the video store and bought every Jesus movie I could find."

While this research provided some useful background, it left some key questions unanswered.

Shortly after our first meeting, I lent Stephen a few favorite books and copied some articles I had kept from my graduate studies in theology. These he squirreled away in his cramped, West Side apartment, a fourth-floor walk-up whose front door was a riot of stickers, posters, and photos from previous LAB productions, and whose chaotic interior—the floor was littered with books, clothes, CD covers, loose pages from his scripts, even a dinner plate or two—made locating the books he borrowed a challenge after the play closed. Stephen's apartment reminded me of the saying that while Jesuits *take* the vow of poverty, there are others who actually *live* it more fully than some of us do. But while Stephen eagerly accepted any and all of the books and articles I gave him, it was conversation and debate that seemed to engage him most.

"Okay," he said one night over the phone, "give me the case *against* Pontius Pilate." I told him what would lead people to conclude that Pilate was the man responsible for the death of Jesus. After an hour of that, he said, "Okay, now give me the case *for* Pontius Pilate." What most surprised me about these late-night sessions were not the questions Stephen asked but what he did with the answers, quickly transforming the raw material of our conversations into monologues and dialogues in his streetwise style.

Early on, for example, Stephen asked a provocative question about Pontius Pilate: "What do you think he thought about his time in Judea?" As it happened, I had recently read Ann Wroe's superb biography *Pontius Pilate*, in which the author tries to answer that question. Wroe, a former literary editor of the *Economist*, based her book on the limited evidence about Pilate himself and the more available history of the time.

Her biography speculates that the procurator of Judea was, above all, a thoroughly Romanized man, a man who believed firmly in the Roman gods and the ethical code of the empire, and who held Rome to be the center of the world. Pontius Pilate most likely spent many years as a Roman soldier before being assigned to his post in Palestine. Judea was not the first place a Roman soldier would choose for a home. "His job was not a plum appointment," she wrote. "It was a junior officer's billet; more experienced men got Syria or Egypt."

As a citizen of the great Rome, Pilate would almost certainly have viewed the hot and dusty Judea as a backwater, with little of the cultural amenities available in faraway Rome. "Armpit of the empire," I suggested to Stephen over the phone.

The next morning, the playwright e-mailed me a scene based on our discussion. In this scene, Pilate, on the witness stand, lays out his opinion of the region he had been sent to govern on behalf of Caesar. During the run, Pontius Pilate was played by Stephen McKinley Henderson, an actor with a booming voice and a commanding presence.

As Pilate, Henderson was casually dressed in golfing attire, including plaid socks, as if to communicate his disdain for the proceedings. In the following scene, he has just described his role as procurator of Judea to Fabiana Aziza Cunningham, the defense attorney.

CUNNINGHAM. I see. And you governed or procurated over Judea from twenty-six to thirty-six A.D., correct?

PILATE. Longest ten years of my life.

CUNNINGHAM. Why do you say that?

PILATE. You ever been to Judea, missy? It ain't Paris, France—believe that.

CUNNINGHAM. I see.

PILATE. Yeah, that Moses musta read the map backwards— misplaced his bifocals, sumpthin'—'cuz if that was the "promised land," . . . them Jews shoulda held out for a better Promise.

CUNNINGHAM. You didn't care for Judea much?

PILATE. Care for it? Armpit of the Empire, if you ask me. No atmosphere, nuthin'. Hot. Dirty. Dusty. Flies everywhere. Complete lack of Culture and Amusements. . . . But Augustus ordered me to keep the peace there, so I obeyed my Emperor, and did my duty.

CUNNINGHAM. And kept the peace?

PILATE. The Pax Romana, baby, the prime directive—dass right.

Pilate's dismissive responses to Cunningham always elicited laughter from the audience. But Guirgis was interested in more than simply getting laughs or making Pilate a risible figure. Ultimately, the play-wright wanted to help the audience appreciate the complicated mix of motives that led to the crucifixion of Jesus of Nazareth.

Who Killed Jesus?

Examining responsibility for the death of Jesus was critical for the pur-poses of Stephen's play. The controversy surrounding the implication of Jewish responsibility in Mel Gibson's blockbuster movie *The Passion of the Christ* made Stephen see that the treatment of Roman governor Pontius Pilate and the Jewish high priest Caiaphas would need to be carefully written. In our conversations, Stephen and I probed the more reasonable explanations for the Crucifixion in recent books and films and discarded the less reasonable ones. Stephen was careful to repeat to me, however, that he had purposely avoided seeing Gibson's film, to prevent him from writing a "response" to it.

The Passion of the Christ raised fresh controversy over the ques-tion "Who killed Jesus?" (Almost entirely overlooked was the more interesting question of why.) Mel Gibson's film generated coverage in every major magazine and newspaper as well as hours of face time for a variety of expert (and not-so-expert) commentators. Critics of the movie contended that by making Pontius Pilate appear as a thoughtful and conflicted official, the movie tipped the balance of responsibility to the Jewish leaders at the time. The movie's supporters, on the other hand, contended that any attempt to remove guilt from the Jewish leaders amounted to a whitewashing of history.

One problem with the public conversation that surrounded *The Passion of the Christ* was the frequent presentation of a dichotomy between reason and faith. Some on the secular left argued that reli-gious faith blinds a person to the need for serious historical scholarship.

That is, religious people are willfully ignorant of facts—or they're just idiots. Some on the religious right countered that appeals to historical evidence betray a lack of faith. That is, academics are prejudiced against religion—or they're just atheists.

This is a false dichotomy. The majority of Christian denominations have long recognized the importance of serious Scripture scholarship, as well as the need for using historical tools to understand the Bible. Underlying this recognition is the belief that Scripture is one of the primary means through which God is revealed. In the early 1960s, the Catholic bishops who convened at the Second Vatican Council to consider contemporary theological issues wrote in *Dei Verbum* ("Word of God"): "Sacred tradition and Sacred Scripture form one sacred deposit of the word of God." This reemphasis on serious Scripture scholarship (long the domain of dedicated Protestant theologians, philologists, and historians) led to a flowering of Catholic biblical scholarship during the past few decades.

Today most mainstream Christian scholars rely on what is called the historical-critical approach to Scripture, a way of studying biblical texts that considers their original historical settings and what the texts would have meant in those contexts. For example, in studying the parables of Jesus, which include references to farmers, crops, and planting cycles, it helps to know something about agriculture in first-century Palestine, a topic we can understand more deeply with the help of independent historical sources and studies. This kind of approach is essential when trying to understand something as complicated as the death of Jesus.

From as early as the second century, for example, a handful of Gospel passages have been used to support the charge of "deicide" (literally, God-murdering) against the Jewish people as a whole. Used most often is a passage from the Gospel of Matthew, where "the people" say, in response to Pontius Pilate, "His blood be on us and on our children!"

Until recently, the history of Christian-Jewish relations has been largely a record of Christian hostility, persecution, and cruelty. Throughout European history, Jews were exiled from their homes or murdered in the name of the church. Both anti-Semitism and anti-Judaism were also, as noted before, given expression and encouraged by medieval Passion plays sponsored by Catholic churches and organizations. This was the last thing Stephen Adly Guirgis wanted to emulate in his new play.

Eric Bogosian, the actor and writer who would play Satan in Stephen's play, offered an example of how anti-Semitic sentiments may operate in subtle ways in the film and television industry. Though a Christian of Armenian descent, Eric told me that because of his olive complexion, aquiline profile, and dark curly hair, many people assume that he comes from another ethnic background. "I look Jewish," he said bluntly. "And in the real world that seems to make me a natural bad guy: my black curly hair, and so on, is a quality equated with evil." As a result, the actor is often offered the role of the heavy in films. "It's part of the continuing vilification of the Jews."

More tellingly, almost every review of *The Last Days of Judas Iscariot* would celebrate Eric's performance as Satan. He hoped that it was because of his acting skills but suspected that something else might be involved. "I found it interesting that many of the reviews said, 'Bogosian is perfect as Satan.' I wondered how much of that had to do with the way I look. Did the fact that I have Semitic looks make me 'perfect' to play Satan?"

It could be argued that all of this is a by-product of the way that the story of Judas, the Jews, and the Crucifixion has been told over the centuries. Indeed, the long history of Christian anti-Semitism and the horrific fate of the Jews during the Second World War are in themselves reason enough to consider carefully the ways in which

Christians understand and present the Passion story. In one of its most important decisions, the Second Vatican Council, after decades of work on Catholic-Jewish relations, published its document *Nostra Aetate* ("In Our Age"). Echoing the statements of Saint Paul in his letter to the Romans, the council reaffirmed the role of the Jews as the "people to whom the covenants and promises [of God] were made." *Nostra Aetate* also repudiated the ancient accusations that the Jewish people as a whole were responsible for the death of Jesus: "True," the council wrote, "the Jewish authorities and those who followed their lead pressed for the death of Christ; still, what happened in His passion cannot be charged against all the Jews, without distinction, then alive, nor against the Jews of today."

More recently, Pope John Paul II worked diligently on Catholic-Jewish relations. Apologizing for the church's role in Jewish persecution throughout history, he stated, "Erroneous and unjust interpretations of the New Testament regarding the Jewish people and their alleged culpability [for the Crucifixion] have circulated for too long, engendering feelings of hostility toward this people."

The historical-critical approach to interpreting the biblical accounts also makes sense intellectually. Put simply, a completely literalistic or fundamentalist interpretation is impossible. The proof for this is plain: the Gospels are not always consistent.

A few examples will suffice. The adult Jesus makes only one journey to Jerusalem in the synoptic Gospels (Matthew, Mark, and Luke), while he makes several in John. The story of Jesus' birth in the Gospel of Matthew describes Mary and Joseph as living in Bethlehem, fleeing to Egypt, and then moving for the first time to Nazareth, while Luke has the two living originally in Nazareth, traveling to Bethlehem in time for the birth, and then returning home again. Mark and John have nothing of such traditions. More serious still, in terms of basic tenets of the Christian faith, some of the Resurrection stories are substantially different. In some accounts, the risen Christ appears as a material being; in others, he can walk through walls.

The various ways of telling Jesus' story reflect the different views and concerns of the Gospel writers (and, in the case of the Resurrection, the difficulty of fully expressing what the earlier witnesses had experienced). Despite what many fundamentalist Christians contend, the Gospels are not to be treated as strictly historical chronicles.

This points up the need for a careful approach to even the most familiar of New Testament stories, such as the betrayal of Jesus by Judas. The first-century writers of the Gospels presented different views of Jesus Christ, and they did so with different communities, concerns, and readers in mind. So when arguing about historical accuracy, it is not enough simply to say, "It's in the Bible."

Likewise, when believers raise questions about the accuracy of certain historical contexts, unearth inconsistencies in the narratives, or critique a reliance on literalistic interpretations, they are not trying to "water down" the Gospels, as some of their critics accuse them of doing. They are engaging in an important aspect of the life of faith. Theologians call this adopting a stance that is "historically conscious." And in mainstream Christian theology, reason and faith are not opposed to each other; both are seen as expressions of God's leading human beings in the search for truth. Indeed, one of the most venerable definitions of theology, from the eleventh-century saint Anselm of Canterbury, is *fides quaerens intellectum*: faith seeking understanding.

Stephen Adly Guirgis's own "historically conscious" questions into what really happened to Jesus and Judas were therefore an important part of his own spiritual journey. And once put on stage, they would become part of the journey of the audience—at least for a few hours.

After all his research, Stephen wanted to hear what I thought about who killed Jesus. The responsibility for Jesus' death was the underlying theme of his play, and the answer to the question of who was responsible would help us unlock the riddle of Judas Iscariot. "So who do you think was responsible?" he asked me one evening a few days before Thanksgiving. "Caiaphas or Pilate?"

The most notable recent effort to answer Stephen's question is a sixteen-hundred-page, two-volume work, *The Death of the Messiah*, written by Raymond E. Brown, a Catholic priest and one of the leading New Testament scholars of the late twentieth century. He points out that while it is clear that some of the Jewish leaders were opposed to Jesus, it is also clear that only Rome had the power to condemn and crucify a man.

Brown also reminds us that as the early Christians began to move away from Jewish traditions and to embrace non-Jews into their movement, strains of anti-Judaism crept into their writings—the accounts that would become our New Testament. Because the early church sought to distance itself from its Jewish roots, it encouraged readings of the events of the Passion that would cast the Jewish authorities in a poor light. The writers of the Gospels were not immune to this. Contemporary scholarship therefore treats this issue with justifiable care and attention.

No matter how fine the scholarship, one has to remember that we are dealing essentially with reconstructions of what happened to Jesus. Those reconstructions were written by his followers, anxious to tell an inspiring tale. The Gospel accounts are not necessarily eyewitness accounts.

In an essay entitled "Who Killed Jesus?" New Testament scholar Daniel J. Harrington, SJ, answers the question simply: "Pontius Pilate, with cooperation from some Jewish leaders in Jerusalem, killed Jesus."

The key point is that Jesus was executed by Romans for a Roman crime: sedition. "Jesus was, in fact, executed by the Romans," writes D. Moody Smith, professor of New Testament at Duke University, in an essay in *Harper's Bible Commentary*. Still, some Jewish religious leaders were likely angered by what they saw as Jesus' blasphemous utterances, as well as actions that threatened their understanding of their religious duty—among other things, his claim to have the power to forgive sin, his violent expulsion of the money changers from the temple grounds, his association with people considered "unclean," and his followers' declaration of their teacher as the Messiah.

But the Gospels are murky about precisely what lay behind the death of Jesus. For the evangelists were not as concerned with providing a historically accurate picture as modern readers might assume. "From the outset," writes Raymond Brown about the Passion narratives, "we must be cautious about the NT [New Testament] reports." Here is a blunt warning against simplistic interpretations of the Gospel narratives, coming from one of the most accomplished scholars of those Scriptures.

What Matthew, Mark, Luke, and John were intent on providing was not historical truth but something more elusive, and far more important for the early Christians: the religious meaning of the events in question. As a result, the descriptions of the last days of Jesus differ from Gospel to Gospel. For example, the Gospel of John has Jesus speaking at length to Pilate, and the other three Gospels present him as virtually silent during his Roman trial.

In another of Brown's books, *An Introduction to the New Testament*, the author notes that only one Gospel tries to give a more or less complete explanation for Jesus' condemnation: "Only John explains clearly why Jesus was brought to Pilate (. . . the Jews were not permitted to put anyone to death) and why Pilate rendered a death sentence even though he knew that Jesus did not deserve such a punishment (. . . he would be denounced to the Emperor for not being diligent in punishing a so-called king)."

It is critical to note that the use of *the Jews* in the Gospels as a description of the opponents of Jesus is not meant to convey "all Jewish leaders" any more than "the Jewish people." Unfortunately, phrases such as *the Jews* in the Gospel of John have been used to foster anti-Semitism. That particular phrase has been used to blame all Jews for the decisions of a few specific religious leaders who have been dead for almost two millennia. As D. Moody Smith notes, "Certainly the Evangelist could not have foreseen the awful implication and effects of his words as they have resounded through the centuries."

This is one reason Mel Gibson's *Passion of the Christ* proved problematic for so many theologians and biblical scholars. *The Passion* focuses on the last several hours in the life of Jesus, beginning with his betrayal by Judas in the Garden of Gethsemane and ending with his crucifixion and resurrection. It was both exceedingly popular and exceedingly violent, sparing viewers little of the blood and gore of Jesus' execution.

While Gibson's film superbly portrays the utter brutality of the Crucifixion and the emotional responses of the disciples, and does so in the language of Jesus and his circle—Gibson's brilliant use of Aramaic neatly avoids the problem of the Oxford-educated Jesus—it does a poorer job in handling the complicated question of Jewish and Roman responsibility. For all his emphasis on historical accuracy, Gibson presented a story that was far from what most biblical scholars would call historically conscious.

The Passion of the Christ contains dialogue and scenes that, in general, make the Jews look worse and Pilate look better. For example, the Gospels are unclear about the number of Jews in the city of Jerusalem who demanded the Crucifixion. The movie, however, shows a large mob, visually implying that the city's entire Jewish community wanted Jesus dead. Some scholars point out that Jesus likely had many Jewish supporters in Jerusalem; one reason that the Romans arrested him at night, as mentioned in the Gospel of Mark, was probably to minimize angering those supporters. New Testament scholar John Dominic Crossan has suggested that the pilgrims at the temple were much taken with Jesus' teaching on Monday, Tuesday, and Wednesday, and that there is every reason to believe that by Friday the authorities would have been reluctant to take the popular teacher by daylight.

In addition, what are called the Palm Sunday narratives present Jesus entering Jerusalem the week before his death to the adulation of a celebratory crowd. That the Jewish population as a whole would have flip-flopped from adulation to publicly calling for Jesus' execution seems unlikely.

In many ways, *The Passion of the Christ* was a needed corrective to the saccharine and bloodless portrayals of the Crucifixion we see in many mainstream movies about Jesus. But the movie subtly shifted the burden of responsibility for the death of Jesus away from Pontius Pilate and to the Jewish leaders. Mel Gibson's film thereby overlooks some of the insights of modern Scripture scholars and may frustrate the desire of many mainstream Christian denominations to avoid precisely this kind of misrepresentation.

Any artistic retelling of historical events must take liberties with the original story for dramatic purposes. Some events will have to be omitted for the sake of time; conversations will have to be invented to convey information; and characters will have to be eliminated for the sake of simplicity. But those who tell the stories and produce the films and plays must discern how many liberties they can take and whether these liberties fundamentally alter the underlying history.

Even the most rigorous of historians would accept the validity of the question of how much liberty an artist can take in a retelling of history. In 1997, Edmund Morgan, one of the most admired historians of colonial and early America, wrote an appreciative review of the film version of Arthur Miller's *Crucible*, starring Daniel Day-Lewis, Joan Allen, and Winona Ryder. Based on Miller's successful stage play of the same name, which was written at the height of the anti-Communist crusades of Senator Joseph McCarthy in the mid-1950s, the film takes as its subject the ghastly Salem witchcraft trials that took place in late-seventeenth-century Massachusetts. The trials resulted in the executions of nineteen people.

Morgan's provocative essay is included in a collection entitled *The Genuine Article: A Historian Looks at Early America.* "A playwright dealing with historical figures can scarcely ignore what is known or knowable about them. . . . The only question is how closely a playwright must be tied to what is known, for he cannot be tied so closely that his play or film becomes merely a documentary. He is surely entitled to make up things that did not happen. Indeed he must make them up if he is to give us more understanding of what did happen than historians have been able to do in confining themselves to proven facts."

Though the artist and the historian draw from the same well of historical data, they use the material for different ends. The central weakness in the presentation of the last days of Jesus of Nazareth in Mel Gibson's movie is, therefore, not that it is one man's artistic representation of the Crucifixion, but that it substantially tips the balance of responsibility to the Jews in ways unsupported by historical evidence—and does so while asserting its historical accuracy.

In tackling essentially the same story, and in trying to achieve the delicate balance between historically accurate material and artistically compelling action, Stephen Adly Guirgis knew what a difficult task he was taking on.

One morning in early December, Stephen e-mailed me a scene that placed an arrogant Pontius Pilate on the witness stand to be examined by the defense attorney. Neither the Jewish nor the Roman tribunals of the time offered attorneys for defendants, but the device would help the modern-day audience better understand the facts of the "case" before them. (Besides, courtroom dramas like *Twelve Angry Men* and *A Few Good Men* seem always to make for good theater.)

A few days later, I read a scene in which a patient but weary Caiaphas, the Jewish high priest, is similarly questioned. I was astonished to see how well Stephen had incorporated our conversations into the dialogue between the two witnesses and the attorneys. In the prosecution's cross-examination of Caiaphas, Stephen even leavened the scene with a measure of historical irony. Early on, the prosecution asks Caiaphas whether he is certain that Judas approached him. When the high priest says he is, the prosecution expresses his doubt: "Because I saw in a film once . . . where it was *you* who approached *him*."

By using the trial method, Stephen's treatment would show the complexities involved in placing blame for the death of Jesus. When Pilate is summoned to the witness stand, his situation is first laid out for the audience. As Roman prefect, or procurator, of Judea, he was charged with preventing violence from breaking out; he was trying to keep the peace and was adamant about being loyal to Augustus Caesar. The historian Edith Hamilton notes in her book *The Roman Way* that ingrained into the Roman soldier was what she calls the fundamental idea of discipline. "However fierce the urge of their nature was," she writes, "the feeling for law and order was deeper, the deepest thing in them." Palestine had to be kept under control, which dictated quick and savage responses—including mass executions—to movements that were seen as potentially revolutionary. In addition, Pilate could have argued that he was only doing what the Jewish leaders in Jerusalem apparently wanted: keeping the peace.

But Stephen presented a strong case *against* Pilate as well. The defense attorney reveals him to be a ruthless dictator who had no qualms about killing a Jew he knew nothing about. Moreover, only the Roman governor had the authority to put someone to death. Any innocence that had accrued to Pilate was the result of the historical attempt to blame the death of Jesus on the Jews. He was the man ultimately responsible.

The Last Days of Judas Iscariot would therefore reject the notion of the conflicted and thoughtful Roman governor who appeared in Mel Gibson's film. "You didn't wash your hands, Pontius Pilate," says the defense attorney in Stephen's play, referring to Pilate's famous action after announcing Jesus' death sentence. "History did it for you."

In the play, Caiaphas, the Jewish high priest, doesn't get off easy, either. One night Stephen asked me to assume the role of Caiaphas and speak in his defense. This was not hard, because I felt that I knew something of how devoted he must have been to his religious traditions. The high priest would have been forced to safeguard not only his deeply held religious beliefs but also his people. The prophet Jesus could easily be seen as an insurrectionist and a blasphemer. In *The Death of the Messiah*, Raymond Brown lists the actions of Jesus that would have angered the religious authorities of that time and then concludes, "I see little reason to doubt that his opponents would have considered him blasphemous."

And blasphemy (from the Greek, "speaking evil")—the utterance of contemptuous language to or about God—was a capital offense. In the Hebrew Scriptures, the prescribed punishment was stoning.

In Stephen's play, the defense attorney questions the high priest about his decision to hand over Jesus to the Roman authorities. Caiaphas responds with growing impatience:

> CAIAPHAS. Our Torah has six hundred thirteen Sacred Laws—I
> can't even count how many Jesus broke or treated
> with wanton disregard and disdain! He broke the
> laws that came from the God of Abraham, Isaac,
> and Jacob! He violated the word of God. He violated
> the Laws of Moses. He consorted with the Unclean,
> and women, and prostitutes. He performed Miracles
> on the Sabbath, He proclaimed himself Messiah! He
> forgave sin! *Who was he to forgive sin?!* Only God
> can do that! If that's not crossing the line, then I
> don't know what is!!

So controversial was this question of responsibility that Jeffrey DeMunn, who would play Caiaphas, said that taking on the role scared him, though he had worked as an actor for more than thirty years.

"I felt a tremendous pressure to do nothing but present Caiaphas in the most honest and unbiased manner possible," he said. "Nor did I want to offend any Jewish theatergoers by presenting a demeaning portrayal of the man, or a demeaning portrait of the Jewish people." Philip Seymour Hoffman, the director, told Jeffrey that, despite his trepidation, the role of Caiaphas would probably be one that he would eagerly anticipate doing every night. Hoffman was right.

"Sometimes," explained Jeffrey, "I would feel such rage on his behalf. Rage to the point of tears. Having to answer questions from the lawyers that suggested that Caiaphas was less of a man, less of a human being, and even suggesting that he was evil."

The defense attorney takes pains to underline Caiaphas's role in the drama of the Crucifixion: How, she asks, could he have condemned a fellow Jew, and someone called, at least by his followers, "Rabbi"? How could he have mistaken an obvious prophet, a holy man who had done nothing but heal and help others? How could he have handed him over to the Romans, knowing that they would certainly put him to death? Caiaphas counters that if he hadn't taken action, the Romans would have turned on the whole Jewish people, resulting in a bloodbath. "I determined that it were better to have one man dead than a thousand," he says.

Stephen's use of the trial device would show the audience not only how but also why the death of Jesus occurred, shedding light on a notoriously dark topic. As I watched Stephen deal with the demands placed upon these scenes—the requirement to sort through so much history, the artistic need to keep the interest of the audience, and the sordid history of Passion plays always lurking in the background—I was impressed with what he was able to accomplish. And amazed at how quickly he was able to do it. As artists have done for centuries, Stephen was aiming to present his own interpretation of the story of Jesus, for his own time. Sal Inzerillo, a LAB member who was cast as Simon the Zealot, said, "Stephen is trying to bring all this into the culture and world we live in. It's like it's this little Gospel, a self-contained Gospel for today."

A Study in Despair

Around the middle of November, and after a few conversations with Stephen and Sam, I began to realize how much work the play might require of me. When they had first contacted me, I had expected a few meetings and a couple of hours of flipping through some old theology books, with perhaps a handful of free tickets thrown in for my efforts. But the more Stephen and Sam and I talked, the more I saw how much good could come from their creative efforts, the more I found myself taking a personal interest in the project, and the more of my free time I spent researching their questions.

In just a few weeks, I found myself wanting to help Stephen's play to be as accurate as it could be, and Sam's performance to be as compelling as it could be. Simply put, I started to care about their play.

I must admit, too, that I was having fun. Sam and Stephen were, in very different ways, friendly and inquisitive guys. I was being drawn into relationship with creative people who cared about their work. And, unlike many of my Jesuit friends who had worked in high schools or colleges, I had never before spent any time as a teacher. For the first time, I was seeing how satisfying teaching could be, especially when the material was already so meaningful in my own life.

The playwright's burning interest in the questions about the last days of Jesus of Nazareth had thrown me back into a topic I hadn't studied seriously since graduate school. I had to create my own crash course in historical research on Jesus, Pontius Pilate, and Caiaphas. At night, after work, I would plow through my old theology notes and, for good measure, haunt my Jesuit community library to see what books on the Gospels I might have overlooked during grad school.

Yet there were other, broader theological and spiritual questions that arose during this early stage in the development of the play that even the best Bible commentaries could not answer. Nearing midnight one evening, Stephen called to ask me about a complicated theological concept that was central to the play: despair. In traditional Christian theology, Judas was condemned to hell not simply because of his betrayal of Jesus but also because of the despair that led him to suicide. Traditional Catholic theology has maintained that suicide is a sin.

While the *Catechism of the Catholic Church* states that some "grave psychological disturbances" can diminish the responsibility of the person who commits suicide, it is nevertheless an act that, for several reasons, is "contrary to love for the living God."

The first of those reasons is that our life is not ours to take. "We are stewards, not owners, of the life God has entrusted to us," say the authors of the *Catechism*. The act also goes against the "natural" inclination to preserve life; it offends the "just love of self," and it even marks an offense against the love of one's neighbor, since it "breaks the ties of solidarity with family, nation, and other human societies to which we continue to have obligations."

This view was most likely what the parochial-school nuns who taught Stephen had themselves been taught and believed. Judas was reprehensible as a suicide, as well as for the despair that led him to that act. "You were right to be afraid, Judas," wrote Saint Augustine in his *Exposition on the Psalms*, "but your fear ought to have been accompanied by hope in the mercy of him whom you feared."

Stephen saw it otherwise: Why couldn't God have saved Judas? Was it fair that despair should cause someone to be condemned? Our conversation grew heated, with Stephen refusing to accept my initially glib answers.

The playwright had stumbled into another thorny theological dilemma. Why do some people—in Scripture and in real life—seem to have an easier time leading a spiritual life? And why are others seemingly unable to avoid despair? Does it spring from their psychological makeup? And if so, is this a form of predestination? Liza Colón-Zayas, a LAB member who would appear in the play, made the same point in a later conversation.

"Look," she said, "if I make a car with a certain malfunction or something, why blame the car if it's not running right?"

From a certain vantage point, the fate of Judas, if based solely on his despair and resulting suicide, seems unfair.

Despairing of answering Stephen's questions on my own, I reached over to my bookcase and pulled off a book by the Trappist monk and writer Thomas Merton. A brilliant and erudite man, Merton had, after a desultory religious upbringing and dissolute youth, converted to Catholicism in 1938. In a nice twist, Merton had been baptized in Corpus Christi Church, Stephen Adly Guirgis's childhood parish, and the place where Stephen had been given my phone number.

Shortly after his conversion, Merton had, to the astonishment of his friends, entered the Trappists, one of the most austere of all Catholic religious orders, in a monastery tucked away in the hills of Kentucky. For the next several decades, until his death in 1968, Merton was one of the most influential American Catholics of the twentieth century, writing books, articles, and essays on a host of topics, from contemplative prayer to the renewal of monastic life to nonviolence to Zen Buddhism. His books, including his popular autobiography, *The Seven Storey Mountain*, had initially guided my own interest in the priesthood and in religious life. Except for Jesus of Nazareth, there was no other person as influential in my becoming a Jesuit priest.

"Despair," I said, quoting Merton in his book *New Seeds of Contemplation*, "is the ultimate development of a pride so great and so stiff-necked that it accepts the absolute misery of eternal damnation rather than accept that God is above us and that we are not capable of fulfilling our destinies by ourselves."

Merton's insight on despair made a deep impression on me when I first came across it as a young Jesuit novice. Like many Christian spiritual writers, Merton believed that despair, when reduced to its essentials, can be understood as a form of pride. The person in despair (though he or she may not feel the capacity for pride) denies that anything can change: Things are hopeless. I am convinced—more accurately, I *know*—that things will not and cannot ever change. In other words, I know better than God.

Stephen initially found Merton's explanation unsatisfying. If human despair is so powerful, does that mean that God is powerless over it? And if that's the case, does that mean that God is not all-powerful? Stephen and I talked briefly about the concept of free will. As Saint Augustine held in the fourth century, God does not take away a person's free will. While Augustine admits that a certain "force of habit" may make a person more likely to gravitate toward one course of action over another, in the end a person always has the freedom to choose. And that includes the freedom to "choose" despair.

Stephen remained unconvinced. Why was Judas incapable of seeking forgiveness? Why was he condemned to hell for his sins when others who had also betrayed Jesus were not? Saint Peter betrayed Jesus too (by denying—three times—that he even knew Jesus). But after Jesus' resurrection, Peter sought and received forgiveness from him. What made Peter able to do this, but not Judas?

"Why couldn't God just break through his despair?" Stephen asked.

Frustrated, I shouted into the phone: "No! That's not the way it works! You have to *participate* in your own salvation!"

The next day, one of the Jesuits in my community asked, horrified, "Who were you shouting at last night? That's no way to talk to someone in despair!"

Eventually, I admitted to Stephen that while Merton's approach was appealing to me, it had its flaws. For one thing, it seemed pitiless to blame the victim of despair for despairing. Moreover, Merton's approach seemed primarily an intellectual one. Perhaps this understanding made sense for someone like Thomas Merton, who lived in the relatively protected atmosphere of a cloistered Trappist monastery, whose physical needs were more or less provided for, and for whom despair would have represented mainly a spiritual crisis.

And I wondered how others with whom I had worked—for example, the desperately poor refugees in East Africa who had seen their families slaughtered, who had languished in overcrowded refugee camps in the deserts of Kenya, and who were trapped in a life of degrading poverty— would have responded if told that despair was a form of pride. For those facing starvation, or the prospect of years of hardship, despair might not be the result of pride but the human inability to face a future characterized primarily by suffering. And yet—something that was always a source of amazement to me—these refugees were often the very people who seemed least likely to despair, so firm was their faith in God.

So perhaps Judas and others who face despair deserve more of our pity. Perhaps Judas deserves the pity that Christians normally afford Peter for his denial of Christ. At one point I suggested to Stephen that Judas might have wondered why Peter got a basilica named after him in Rome, but Judas was condemned to hell. (Secretly I hoped that this line would make its way into the play, but it never did.)

In time, Stephen decided that the best way to handle these complex questions would be to have an "expert witness" address the topic of despair, to speak about it from personal experience. After batting around some possible names, we settled on Mother Teresa. One night, I gave Stephen a thumbnail sketch of the recently beatified nun. Having just finished writing an essay on her for an upcoming book on the saints, I was familiar with her life. I was especially intent on telling Stephen the story of Mother Teresa's own battle with despair, of which only a few people (including her spiritual director) had had any knowledge. After her death in 1997, when her private letters and journals were being read in preparation for her canonization process at the Vatican, it was discovered that Mother Teresa had gone through what Saint John of the Cross, a sixteenth-century Spanish mystic, referred to as a "dark night."

Mother Teresa had initially entered the Sisters of Loreto, an Irish-based religious order, while a teenager. A few months later, she was sent to work with the order in a convent school in India. But a profound religious experience convinced the young woman that her ultimate vocation was to work with the "poorest of the poor" on the streets of India. This she did for the rest of her life, founding the Missionaries of Charity, whose hospices for the sick and dying are now scattered around the world. She was deeply committed to her faith—which is why most of her admirers would be surprised to learn that Mother Teresa struggled with belief in God.

Not long after leaving the Sisters of Loreto, Mother Teresa privately described to the archbishop of Calcutta an extended period of terrible doubt and intense despair. In an open and honest letter, she wrote that she had been experiencing "a terrible pain of loss, of God not wanting me, of God not being God, of God not existing."

Upon hearing this, Stephen decided that he had found the perfect expert witness on despair, and he set about writing a scene for her. He did this, literally, overnight. The next morning he faxed me a scene that incorporated nearly all of what we had discussed over the past several evenings.

Early in the play, a Hispanic-accented Mother Teresa is asked by the prosecution to elucidate the concept of despair. Before offering her testimony, the hard-of-hearing nun asks for a set of earphones to enable her to hear. A few minutes later she compares despair to throwing away one's earphones: "One must participate in one's own salvation," says Guirgis's Mother Teresa. "In order to hear, one must be willing to listen. When you turn off God, you are saying, 'I know better than you.' No good, boy. No good."

And, for good measure, she quotes Thomas Merton on despair.

Several months later, Callie Thorne, the actress who would play Judas's defense attorney, spoke about the workings of despair in her own life. Among the cast, she had one of the more unusual religious upbringings: her mother, who raised Callie outside of Boston, was both a Christian and a professional astrologist. Callie found solace in the way her mother presented spirituality to her. "She talked to my sister and me about God and Jesus of course, but she also used astrology as a kind of spiritual therapy for people. And in my own life I've been able to see how these astrological patterns work. When she describes what a Scorpio is like, for example, it fits me like nobody's business."

But her acceptance of her mother's belief system was hard won. "When I was growing up, all the other mothers in our neighborhood were soccer moms—very preppy and white-bread," she said. "And in junior high, when the other kids found out what she did, they started calling her *gypsy* and *witch*. It's awful to say this, but I felt so ashamed. After that, when she tried to talk about astrology I would just shut down." It wasn't until beginning undergraduate studies at Wheaton College that Callie encountered greater tolerance. "As soon as I told my friends about my mother they all asked when they could have their charts done!"

Callie still turns to her mother's astrological charts, and to God, during times of confusion and pain. But she laments that her belief in God doesn't prevent her from falling into despair. And she is sometimes prone to dark moods. "When I'm in despair I find it hard to believe that there even *is* a God. Of course, when things are wonderful, I'm suddenly thanking God and believing in him. But when I'm melancholy, there's a kind of egomaniacal pity that makes me ask why God would let me go this far down. And, boy, when I'm in that state I can't hear what *anyone* is telling me."

"I Don't Know, Man . . ."

After several meetings with Sam and Stephen, I was invited to attend a reading of the play, still in an unfinished form. All along, I had been following the news of the casting as Stephen labored over selecting the right actors. Philip Seymour Hoffman, a close friend of Stephen's who had directed the playwright's last four plays, was busy acting in the film *Capote* and had given Stephen the freedom to make any decisions about casting. "Phil gave me his confidence," he said, "so I feel a tremendous responsibility to get the right people." Roughly half of the actors, he predicted, would come from LAB, and the other half from open auditions.

"They're looking for Jesus now," I told a Jesuit friend.

He laughed. "Who isn't?"

The cast and creative team of *Judas* met in Sam's place downtown on a bright and windy November afternoon a few weeks before Thanksgiving. As we entered the apartment, Sam asked his guests, perhaps thirty in all, to remove their shoes and make themselves at home. At first I felt out of place—knowing no one but Stephen and Sam—but I was quickly welcomed by the assembled actors, writers, and directors, many of whom introduced themselves as members of LAB. The scene had a decided air of expectation: many of those present had been in one or another of Stephen's plays and were looking forward to hearing the latest version of his newest work.

While we got settled on an overstuffed sofa and a few random folding chairs, our host padded around in his socks, making sure everyone had enough soda and potato chips. As with many of the actors, Sam's humility and self-effacement would make a lasting impression on me.

Stephen, I noted, seemed excited by the reading, but also worried.

"The scope of everything in this play is just bigger," he said to me. "You know, we started out my last three plays almost anonymously, in a seventy-seat theater. But so many people already know about this one. The cast is going to be larger, there will be lots of actors from outside the company to integrate into the group, and so overall there's more pressure to deliver. And the subject material is just overwhelming."

As those of us gathered flipped through the script, we could see that Stephen's play had taken on a distinct shape.

The Last Days of Judas Iscariot would focus on the trial of Judas. The play would consider whether or not Judas deserved his fate, the question that Stephen had first asked in third grade.

The mother of Judas would be the first to appear, on a darkened stage, speaking about the painful experience of burying her son. An angel would follow to explain the play's setup: we were in Hope, just across the tracks from Purgatory. Judas would begin the play in Hell, in a state of almost catatonic despair, turned in on himself, unable to communicate with anyone.

The judge presiding over Judas's case would be a bilious Civil War veteran, himself languishing in Purgatory as the result of his own suicide. The judge would be assisted by a bailiff, who would keep the case running smoothly. After initially being denied the right to present the case before a jury, Judas's defense attorney, Fabiana Aziza Cunningham, would appeal for help to Saint Monica, who would approach God on Cunningham's behalf.

Once God had relented and a writ could be produced, the trial would begin before a jury. The defense attorney and the prosecutor, an Egyptian man named Yusef El-Fayoumy (Guirgis himself is half-Egyptian), would present their cases, making use of a variety of historical witnesses such as Simon the Zealot and theological figures such as Satan in order to adjudicate the question of whether Judas deserved his fate. Flashbacks from the life of Judas—a scene from his childhood involving a young friend, a meeting with Satan after the Last Supper, and a confrontation with Pontius Pilate—would offer insights into the man's actions as well as his character.

Two "expert" witnesses, Mother Teresa and Sigmund Freud, would speak about two topics key to understanding the actions of Judas: despair and suicide. Caiaphas and Pilate would be called to explore the question of who was ultimately responsible for the death of Jesus. From time to time, some of the disciples—Peter, Matthew, Thomas, Mary Magdalene—would appear to offer their own perspectives on Judas's fate. The apostles would speak directly to the audience, removed from the proceedings, in monologues placed between the scenes. An Everyman character, a jury member named Butch Honeywell, would at some point relate his own experience of betrayal in a monologue, as a way of inviting the audience to reflect on how the play's themes might relate to their own lives. The script was leavened with Stephen's characteristic salty language and humor but was crafted to lead the audience into meditation upon some timeless questions.

After we had finished the read-through, several participants, including a few well-known actors and a film director, offered their opinions. Judas was underwritten, said one. Satan needed to be stronger, said another. Seated on the floor, Stephen listened carefully, scribbling notes on his script atop a large coffee table.

In the midst of the freewheeling conversation, Sam sidled up to my chair and whispered, "You should say something, man. Everyone wants to know what you think." Tentatively, I offered that I enjoyed the play, particularly its human portrayals of the saints, but wondered where it was all going. Even with the official readings and casting about to begin in a few weeks, Stephen's play remained half-finished, with many crucial questions unanswered. Sheepishly, Stephen admitted that arriving at the first reading with a half-completed play was unusual, but it was also his characteristic way of working. Worried glances from veteran company members and subsequent delays would confirm both facts.

Chief among the unanswered questions was how the play would end. Stephen knew that Jesus needed to confront Judas in the final scene. But to say what? To forgive him? To condemn him? And how would Judas respond? It was perhaps the most important scene in the play, for it would communicate, more than any other, the playwright's theological worldview. Is forgiveness possible for even the most unrepentant of sinners?

The play's ending (as well as myriad other unfinished scenes) began to torment Stephen. Even the normally patient Sam started to confess growing concern about the incomplete script.

"I don't know, man . . ." he said to me that night over the phone.

ACT 2: TEASING THE MIND INTO ACTIVE THOUGHT

January

On a cold and windy morning in the first week of January 2005, I took the subway to the Public Theater, located near Astor Place in downtown Manhattan. It was the first day of readings for *The Last Days of Judas Iscariot*, and I was both excited and anxious. Outside I met Sam and Stephen, bundled up against the freezing weather and standing with two other men. Stephen, with an orange wool cap pulled low over his unruly hair, stood against the red brick building taking desperate drags off a cigarette and talking to a young man with dark curly hair and a scruffy beard.

Gesturing to the other man beside him, Stephen tilted his head back and exhaled a cloud of smoke. "This is Jesus," he said. The man smiled and reached out to shake my hand.

Over time, I realized that the producers had cast an excellent Jesus: John Ortiz enjoyed great respect among the other actors thanks to his impressive acting skills, his distinguished career, and his long history with the LAByrinth Theater Company. (He had played the lead role of Angel in *Jesus Hopped the "A" Train*.) His soft-spoken presence would often prove a balm for tired actors and overworked crew during the production. And it was a testimony to his humility that I wouldn't learn until long after I met him—from a stray comment from a cast member—that John was not only a member of LAB but also one of its original founders, and now its codirector.

The LAByrinth Theater Company

John Ortiz had grown up "just above the poverty line" in the Bedford-Stuyvesant section of New York City. After high school he attended Albany State University, where he met Stephen and Liza Colón-Zayas, who would play our Mother Teresa. Studying to be a teacher, John decided almost on a lark to audition for a professional play called *De Donde?* which would be produced in Cincinnati during the university's winter recess.

To his surprise, he got the part. "They told me I was making $540, and I thought they meant for the whole play. When they told me it was for one *week*, I thought I was the richest guy in the world!"

He had also discovered what he wanted to do. "I saw how lucky I was to be acting, and how happy the other actors were. It was a real calling. And so I decided not to go back to Albany."

In 1992, news broke that the Broadway production of Ariel Dorfman's *Death and the Maiden*, a play that featured Latino characters, would not employ Latino actors. The Latino community was outraged. At the time, John Ortiz, now living in New York City, read a news account in which the director admitted that he had looked for Latino actors but didn't know where to find any. Along with three actor friends, John decided to found a company to help create a supportive environment where Latino actors could hone their skills—and make themselves known to directors and producers. They called it the Latino Actors Base, or LAB.

LAB began modestly, making its home in an abandoned theater space owned by another theater company. The fledgling company had such a difficult time finding scripts to produce that the actors themselves began writing plays. (Stephen Adly Guirgis was originally an actor with the company.) In a few years, LAB grew into one of the most inventive and productive theater companies in the city. Over its fifteen-year life, it has been home to a number of award-winning Off-Broadway plays, including nearly all of Stephen's, who calls the company his "artistic home."

As the company admitted members from a variety of cultural backgrounds, LAB changed its name to the more inclusive LAByrinth Theater Company, though the company remains largely Latino, and it is not uncommon to hear company members joking in Spanish in the dressing rooms.

All of the company members are encouraged to expand their talent far beyond their comfort level: actors write, directors act, writers direct. As the company's mission statement says, "It is our goal, as an ensemble, to take on all the roles involved in the collaborative process of creating new theater." Even as LAB grew and company members became more successful and well known, it remained faithful to its original vision, and a relaxed, almost familial atmosphere characterizes the working environment. Some of the actors, thanks to their long association with the company, have worked with one another on dozens of plays and know each other very well. I was touched to hear several actors refer to another company member as "my best friend" or "my girl."

At the same time, cast members who are not officially members of LAB are welcomed into company productions as if they have been with LAB from the beginning. (Some are later invited to join.) This is one reason the company is so esteemed by New York actors, whose profession can be both competitive and lonely. And it is esteemed by theatergoers as well: a 2007 article in the *New York Times* called LAB "one of the preeminent downtown theatrical ensembles in New York."

"A lot of people in this business spend a lot of time giving you compliments," said John Ortiz. "For me, LAB is a place of brutal honesty, where I'm going to be pushed, and where it's okay to fail. In fact, it's more than okay. It's expected."

Each summer, LAB members gather for a two-week intensive workshop, typically held at a college or university in a bucolic setting. The "intensives" serve a number of purposes: company members plan for the next season, attend professional workshops, stage newly written plays, and just enjoy one another's company. For some veteran LAB members, busy professionals whose schedules shuttle them around the country, the intensives are an opportunity to reconnect with old friends. LAB also invites guests to the summer intensives, typically actors and directors who have worked with the company on a project during the past season and writers whose plays-in-progress are under consideration for the next season.

The two-week-long retreats are called intensive for good reason. Mornings are given over to a variety of workshops and seminars: on any given day, one might attend a seminar on acting techniques, voice work, movement, meditation, Shakespearean dialogue, or even juggling. After lunch, the writers, directors, and actors gather for rehearsals of the new plays that will be read that evening in front of the whole company.

Three new plays are read and staged in the evenings, and these often continue well past midnight. The writers are sometimes seeing their work performed for the first time; the actors know that if they do well, they could be cast in the actual performance. It can be nerve-racking, but the audience roots for everyone to do well. The summer intensives were where *The Last Days of Judas Iscariot* first began to take shape—the few scenes that Stephen had written proved so compelling that the company decided to produce it based on just ten pages of dialogue.

In between readings and stagings of the full-length plays are occasional one-man shows and, recently, performances from the classics. So a gritty prison drama or a play about a young woman who finds herself working in porn movies might be followed by a selection from *Romeo and Juliet* or *Miss Julie*. Typically wired after the evening readings, company members relax with a few beers, some impromptu singing, and long, often raucous late-night conversations about the day's events. The next morning, bleary-eyed, everyone starts again, discussing the previous night's offerings over breakfast, lots of coffee, and lots of cigarettes.

During the summer intensives, interns and apprentices, some of whom are acting students still in college, are often given roles in the readings and are welcomed as much as the founding members are. The summer after *Judas*, I was invited to the intensives at Bennington College and was surprised to discover myself cast in a role in Stephen's latest play. (I received rave reviews for my six-line part as "Young Male Visitor" opposite John Ortiz.) The graceful welcoming of members and guests, the relaxed atmosphere, and, especially, the heartfelt encouragement to use one's own gifts made me think that LAB had a few things in common with the circle of disciples that Jesus drew together in Galilee. For example, company members work together for a common purpose with little or no promise of financial or worldly success, often under difficult physical conditions. (Minimal sleep and bad food characterize a typical theatrical run.) There is also little apparent competition and much rejoicing over the successes of others.

LAB members seem also to appreciate that each person has a unique set of skills that helps the company grow. These varied gifts—in acting, directing, and writing, as well as stage design, costume design, and lighting design—combine for the good of the whole. That aspect of LAB reminded me of a quote from Saint Paul's first letter to the Corinthians: "Indeed, the body does not consist of one member but of many." This is Paul's famous comparison of the Christian community to a body that lives only because it can rely on each of its individual parts. "If all were a single member, where would the body be? As it is, there are many members, yet one body. The eye cannot say to the hand, 'I have no need of you,' nor again the head to the feet, 'I have no need of you.' On the contrary, the members of the body that seem to be weaker are indispensable. . . . If one member suffers, all suffer together with it; if one member is honored, all rejoice together with it."

The religious imagery, in the case of LAB, doesn't seem all that far-fetched. Eric Bogosian thinks that LAB is distinguished among theater companies for its warmth. "And perhaps that leads us naturally to spiritual matters."

Like any human group, of course, the company regularly faces the usual stresses and misunderstandings and arguments, and company members sometimes have to deal with frustration and anger. But during my time with them, this multicultural collection of artists seemed genuinely to enjoy one another's company.

"We have our beefs and our brawls," Liza Colón-Zayas admitted. "But LAB is like another family for me. I couldn't imagine not being a part of the group."

A lot of churches—my own included—would be happy to embody the ideal of Christian community the way that this sometimes foul-mouthed, sometimes chain-smoking, sometimes hard-partying Off-Broadway acting troupe tries to do.

Readings

When I arrived at the Public Theater for the first day of readings that cold January morning, I knew little about LAByrinth and its approach to theater. Despite my growing friendship with Sam and Stephen, I was apprehensive. My experience with these two LAB members should have left me more open-minded, but several well-meaning friends had warned me to expect long sessions of name-dropping, grandstanding, and general misbehavior. So I had braced myself for a few weeks of drama, and not the good kind.

That cold January morning, Sam Rockwell leaned against the Public Theater, wearing a black peacoat, with his arms clapped around him for warmth. Snaking out from under his wool cap were two white iPod wires. As I approached, he laughed and said, "Hey man, I'm listening to you!" He removed his earphones and placed them over my ears, and I was surprised to hear my own disembodied voice on the tape from our first meeting: "Blessed are the poor in spirit . . ."

Inside the Public Theater complex, I climbed three long flights of stairs to black metal double doors that opened into Martinson Hall, a cavernous space with black-painted walls punctuated by ornate metal columns. Under its high, vaulted ceiling, a series of plastic tables were set up on the concrete floor. Seated around the tables on cheap folding chairs were the newly chosen cast members of *The Last Days of Judas Iscariot*. The fifteen young and middle-aged actors, dressed mainly in jeans, corduroys, sweatshirts, scarves, and wool caps, waited to begin. The cast of *Judas* was unusually large for an Off-Broadway show. Because of the cast's limited availability, the show was scheduled for a brief run, perhaps four to five weeks.

I was somewhat nervous, because there were several well-respected actors seated around the table. Eric Bogosian, the author, film and television actor, and celebrated monologist, was playing Satan. I had seen him in the films *Talk Radio* and *Ararat*. Philip Seymour Hoffman, who had appeared in numerous Broadway productions and several well-received films, and who had been dubbed by some the greatest actor of his generation, was the director. Just before the readings began, he had completed a starring role in the movie *Capote*.

The prospect of spending time with Hoffman made me especially nervous. He had long been one of my favorite actors. Whenever I spied his name in the opening credits of a movie, I knew there would be at least a scene or two that I would enjoy, because any scene with his character was bound to work well. Chameleonlike, he slipped into roles that one would say he was born to play, were it not for the fact that the roles were so varied: a besotted porno-movie cameraman in *Boogie Nights*, a duplicitous preacher on the lam in *Cold Mountain*, a spoiled preppy who sees what no one else sees in *The Talented Mr. Ripley*, and a coolly manipulative and talented writer in *Capote*.

Meeting Hoffman also raised a strange question of etiquette that had first come up when I met Sam. Long before meeting the two, I had been a fan of their work. I had enjoyed several of Sam's films, and Hoffman's as well. Should I say so? I was concerned that expressing my admiration for their work would make it seem as if I was trying to curry favor. On the other hand, saying nothing might seem rude. And most people like to be complimented on their work. Unfortunately, I never found a good time to tell either of them that long before getting to know them, I had admired their work. They'll find out when they read this.

I was also apprehensive about whether I could be useful in this kind of environment. Would the rest of the cast be as open as Stephen and Sam had been to a Jesuit priest talking about the Gospels? Or would I be met with hostile stares, a response Christians have been conditioned to expect from some "secular" quarters? I wondered if they would suspect me of using the opportunity simply as an excuse for proselytizing.

Entering the vast space of Martinson Hall, I was introduced to the cast by Stephen. I took my seat at the table and was surprised at how eagerly the actors greeted me—asking about my background, about how I had gotten to know Sam and Stephen, and, even before we began the first reading, about the Gospels. Phil Hoffman greeted me cheerfully and thanked me for joining them.

I felt at home instantly. This was the first of many revelations.

"You Wanna Do This Role?"

A few days into the readings, I bumped into Sal Inzerillo, who was playing Simon the Zealot. Sal is a tall, burly, good-natured New Yorker who always greeted me with a friendly "Hello, brother!" Sporting a few days' growth of beard, he looked tired. When I commented on this, he rubbed his eyes and said that he had been sleeping on the floor of his brother's apartment; that was all he could afford at the moment. Though Sal had appeared in several television shows and plays (including one of Stephen's plays for several months in London's West End), occasionally he had to go on unemployment until more work came his way.

Before his acting career began, Sal worked as a cook and as a professional mover and owned a commercial piping business. In the late 1990s, he studied with William Esper in New York, where he met Stephen. "Before I started acting, I felt very limited in my life. Now I have the opportunity to express myself and to explore all sorts of areas of people's lives."

A strong work ethic undergirded his life as an actor. Sal described a typical week: "There are usually rehearsals for readings, some auditions for different parts, whatever keeps me in front of the material. All along, you're trying to get little gigs and land your next part and hope that something will open up."

Did he ever get discouraged? "Yeah, sure," said Sal, smiling. "But I isolate the discouragement for a day, and then just try to let it go. I mean, I love acting."

I admired the company members' perseverance. All but the most well-known actors must search constantly for work. One might assume—as I had—that an actor who has landed a part in a production at the Public Theater written by a popular playwright and directed by a talented director would have it made, at least financially. Except for a big-budget Broadway show, how much higher could a stage actor hope to rise? But many of the actors in *Judas*, though well respected for their work on stage and in television and movies, still struggled, worrying about their next job, their next review, and their next paycheck.

Early on, Eric Bogosian explained a bit about salaries for theater actors during an average run and asked me, "Guess how much we're getting for this show?" I shook my head. "Four hundred dollars a week." Hardly enough to live on in New York. Few of the actors could survive on theater pay; most of them had to supplement their earnings with frequent spots in television series.

Adrian Martinez had been cast as both Saint Thomas and Sigmund Freud. A stocky man with a mop of curly black hair, he had a quick smile and mordant sense of humor. A few months after the play closed, Adrian shared his approach to the challenges of how work ebbs and flows. "It's a combination of faith and hard work. When things weren't going well, I have to admit, I would scream and cry and curse and was impossible to live with. And then I would just pray and pray, and put one foot in front of the other—just keep calling my agent, keep researching, keep networking, and keep auditioning, doing all this almost on blind faith. But every time I thought about quitting, an opportunity would come up."

Adrian, who attended parochial school as a young man and then the Jesuit-run Fordham University in New York City, realized when he was a senior in college that acting was something he could do well. After studying for some time at the HB Studio with the legendary Uta Hagen, he asked his teacher, "Do you think I could do this professionally?"

Hagen answered, "Of course, you idiot!" That was just what Adrian needed to hear. His career was launched.

That these actors struggled wasn't the only thing that surprised me. Their humility was also a constant revelation. None of the cast members tried to impress me, or one another, with their résumés, with the people they knew, or with the television series or films they had appeared in. The most they would say was "Yeah, I just finished a film in Toronto," or "I'm up for a part in a movie." Sam had a movie that would soon open, *The Hitchhiker's Guide to the Galaxy*, but he rarely referred to it. And Hoffman referred not at all to his time in *Capote*, the role that would win him an Academy Award.

Though Saint Ignatius of Loyola counseled Jesuits to pray for humility from the day they entered the novitiate, I thought that I could learn a lot about that particular virtue from the men and women seated around the table during readings. It was only after the play began its run that I started to discover how accomplished and well known many of these people were.

"You didn't tell me that Poet from *Oz* was in this," said one friend after seeing the play.

"Who?" I asked.

"Mums Grant," he said, mentioning the saturnine African American actor who played Saint Peter. "He's my favorite character!" Even my mother, it turned out, knew Craig "Mums" Grant. "That's cool," Mums said with a chuckle, when I mentioned my seventy-five-year-old mother's interest in the HBO prison drama.

"Callie Thorne?" said my sister, a successful businesswoman and inveterate student of pop culture. "Make sure to tell her that I love her on *Rescue Me.*" A striking young actress with large liquid eyes and long brown hair, Callie spent her first week of *Judas* fighting a miserable winter cold that had her reaching constantly for Kleenex and throat lozenges. Although she could barely speak, she gamely croaked her way through pages and pages of dialogue, a wool cap crammed on her head. As Judas's defense attorney, Fabiana Aziza Cunningham, Callie would be in nearly every scene of the play.

Callie, who had acted since graduating from Wheaton College in 1991, was not a member of LAB, though she was a longtime friend of both Sam and Phil. Her audition with Hoffman and Stephen Adly Guirgis, just a few days before rehearsals began, proved surprising for her. "Well, I was excited about working at the Public and just *crazy* about the idea of working with Phil and Stephen. So I worked like a maniac on preparing," she said. "After the audition, Stephen and Phil walked out of the room, and a few minutes later both of them sort of shuffled back in, and Phil turned to me."

She dropped her voice several octaves for an impressive imitation of Hoffman: "Yeah, you wanna do this role?" It was the first time she had been offered a role on the spot. "I had to ask Phil, 'Is this for real? Can I tell people?' Phil just laughed and said yes, I could tell people." That Callie still evinced surprise when she related the story belied her professional credentials. Besides a leading role on *Rescue Me*, she had appeared as a regular on *Homicide* and *The Wire*, and after *Judas* ended, landed a recurring role on *ER*.

In my early days with the cast, I wasn't entirely comfortable being around people who were so accomplished. It helped to remind myself that, in the past, I had sometimes felt the same around writers whose work I esteemed. Initially I would be tongue-tied when I told them how much I liked their books; then, as we got to know each other better, I grew less nervous. As they got to know me, I became comfortable around them, and, finally, we became friends. Gradually, I started to look forward to meeting my favorite writers, finding myself less nervous around them. Knowing them also helped me understand that their Amazon rankings and their position in the best-seller lists did not mean that their lives were any less human than mine.

In a strange twist, one writer who had become a close friend of mine, Ron Hansen, let me in on some good news the same month as the readings were taking place. Ron had authored one of my favorite novels, *Mariette in Ecstasy*, about the religious experiences of a young nun in New York State in the early 1900s. Ron told me that one of his first novels was going to be made into a film. *The Assassination of Jesse James by the Coward Robert Ford* was set to star Brad Pitt in the title role. A few weeks later, just after *Judas* opened, I met Sam downtown for coffee. He mentioned that he was trying out for a role in an upcoming film and needed to scout around for a hat to wear for the audition. "What's it called?" I asked. Sam said that he didn't know the exact title, but it was the story of Jesse James and his assassination. I couldn't believe it. What were the odds?

"Is it by Ron Hansen?" I asked.

"Yeah, it is!" he said. "How'd you know that?"

"I know him. We're good friends."

"Wow! No kidding!" said Sam. "Could you ask him a few questions about the book? There are a few things I'd love to know for my audition." I agreed to do so and called Ron that day, who laughed at the coincidence. When I called Sam and told him what I had learned, he laughed. "Man," he said. "You're not just a priest; you're an *agent*!" Sam went on to play Charley Ford, a member of Jesse's gang.

The Gospel According to Phil

During the first two weeks in January, the cast traveled painstakingly through the text of *Judas*, with Phil Hoffman offering, like any good teacher, insight, encouragement, and direction when needed.

A week or so into the readings, I mentioned who was directing *Judas* to a writer friend. "Philip Seymour Hoffman?" he said, and then paused. "You make sure to tell him that I think he's a *genius*." The next day I greeted Hoffman and said, "Okay, so my friend told me to tell you that you're a genius." He blushed for a moment and then laughed. "I like your friend!"

Clad in rumpled jeans, a faded sweatshirt, and a wool cap, Phil, as everyone called him, projected an easygoing intensity. While he approached the text with an almost Scholastic seriousness, attending carefully to every line in Stephen's script, he was nonetheless a relaxed presence among the cast. I learned in time that Phil's style was something of a rarity. A friend from my parish was an actress, and I asked her, "Are directors normally that relaxed with the cast?" She laughed and said, "You're very lucky."

From time to time, to illustrate a thorny point, or to describe the emotion that might underlie a scene, Phil would offer a story from his own life. "Did you ever have this experience?" he would ask, and then he would recount a tale illustrating despair or hope or joy or betrayal or trust.

It began to dawn on me that Phil was providing something like contemporary parables for the cast. In the Gospels, the parable form is one of the primary ways in which Jesus communicates his understanding of elusive but important concepts. In Luke's Gospel, for example, Jesus tells the crowd that one is to treat one's neighbor as oneself. But when someone asks him, "Who is my neighbor?" Jesus does not offer a precise definition but instead spins out the story of the Good Samaritan. When asked to explain what he means by the "kingdom of God," the central message of his preaching, Jesus likewise talks about mustard seeds, wheat and weeds, and seeds falling on rocky ground.

C. H. Dodd, the great Scripture scholar, defined a parable as "a metaphor or simile drawn from nature or common life, arresting the hearer by its vividness or strangeness, and leaving the mind in sufficient doubt about its precise application to tease it into active thought." In other words, parables are poetic explanations of concepts that are otherwise impossible to comprehend fully.

The concept of the kingdom of God is too rich to be encompassed by something as simple as a definition. And the notion of radical forgiveness is impossible to explain in a few words, no matter how carefully chosen. Jesus grasped the benefit of telling a story about, say, a father's reconciliation with his prodigal son and allowing the hearers to tease out the underlying meaning for themselves. Besides, if Jesus had given a philosophical lecture to the predominantly peasant community, they probably wouldn't have understood him anyway.

Where a strictly worded definition can be somewhat shallow and actually close down a person's thoughts, a story is endlessly deep and more likely to open one's mind. Jesus' stories carried meaning without having to be converted into a concept, and the power of his parables was that they always went against the expectations of the audience, as when the Samaritan, hailing from a hated ethnic group, was ultimately revealed as the good guy who cares for the stranger. "The deep places in our lives—places of resistance and embrace—are not ultimately reached by instruction," wrote the Protestant theologian Walter Brueggemann. "Those places of resistance and embrace are reached only by stories, by images, metaphors and phrases that line out the world differently, apart from our fear and hurt."

Phil's direction embodied this insight. Until this point, I expected that a director would say, "Say your lines like this," or "Move your arms like this." (During a break one day, I mentioned this to Yul Vázquez, and he laughed and began flailing his arms around.) Instead, Phil provided the actors with a deeper level of understanding. One actor said that Phil's direction enabled him to understand the script on a more personal level. This was what a parable did for the disciples whom Jesus had gathered around him.

A few months after the play ended, when I asked Phil about his directing style, he readily agreed with the inherent strength of the parable—or, in his words, the personal anecdote—in its ability to communicate more than a strictly worded directive. "It's the way I normally direct," he said. "The anecdotes and stories spark a discussion with the actors, and it starts a give-and-take about the character or the scene. And the more personal, the better. If I can be open with my life, then the actors usually feel more comfortable expressing themselves through the work."

I asked if he ever felt the need to be more specific in his direction. "Sometimes you have to tell someone exactly what you want, but you can't dictate," he said. "You have to keep suggesting. Otherwise the person becomes a sort of empty shell, and they end up performing in a way that's not at all, well, spiritual." He offered another illustration. "It's like if I were to tell you onstage that your character had to mix a bowl of oatmeal. I could tell you how to hold the pot and the bowl and the spoon, but unless you made the act your own, it would be just my way of doing it."

In a sense, his approach mirrored the way Jesus preached. One of my theology professors said that apart from the initial calls of the apostles, which seem peremptory, brooking little dissent ("Follow me," he says to Peter), much of Jesus' preaching involves *inviting* his listeners to consider something new ("Consider the lilies . . ."). Or, to use Phil's words, Jesus was always *suggesting*, in order that the decision to follow or not to follow was that person's own decision.

Phil's strength as a director was also a result of his interest in, and familiarity with, the raw material of the play. From the beginning, he encouraged the cast to ask questions about the Gospels and the story of Jesus and Judas. Some of his comfort with the material had to do with his religious background.

As a boy growing up in a town outside Rochester, New York, Phil attended Sunday classes in preparation for confirmation in the Catholic Church, though his parents were not especially religious. "My parents were pretty liberal people who didn't talk about God much in the house," he said. "It was nothing like Stephen's family."

Early on, religion was uninviting for him. "Those Masses really turned me off," he said. "Lots of rote repetition, pretty boring, and sometimes really brutal."

His perspective changed when one of his two sisters became active in a Christian evangelical movement, to which she still belongs. She encouraged her brother to accompany her to meetings with her friends, and Phil went along happily. "There was something that was so heart-felt and emotional. Nothing about it felt crazy at all. And my sister was certainly the sanest person you could ever meet. It all felt very real, very guttural, even rebellious."

The idea that a young person could be sane, generous, intelligent, and Christian held out great appeal for Phil. So did the palpable sense of community that he felt with his sister and her friends. Still, he held back from the sort of total commitment his sister had made. "It was a little too much for me," he said. "And by that time I was more into partying and acting."

Phil, who describes himself as a believer who prays from time to time, carried this positive approach to Christianity with him into

Martinson Hall. "My time with my sister and her circle of friends is something I still think about today." He remarked that he is often defensive about the way many actors react to the idea of evangelical Christians. I asked him if there is a bias against that kind of person in the acting community.

"Absolutely!" he said. "It pisses me off that there is this knee-jerk reaction against them. There is certainly an antipathy to them in the acting world, just like there is an antipathy in the politically liberal world. As a result, the liberal Christian is not heard from as much. And, you know, a liberal person who has a deep belief in Christianity can be a very powerful influence on things."

Phil's natural curiosity prompted him to further study the Gospel narratives. Consequently, he was often the most animated person at the table, especially when we talked about Jesus. "My image of Jesus is someone who is exciting," he said in December, eight months after the show closed. Though that word is too infrequently used to describe Jesus, I agreed with him. He added, "Were he alive today, he would be causing *havoc!*"

I laughed when he said this, but he was right. The tame, doe-eyed, unthreatening Jesus is not the Jesus who is found in the Gospels. (Nor is it likely that he would have attracted many followers.) More often it is the Jesus who, in upending the status quo, proves a threat to those around him. Phil recounted seeing an episode of Fox's conservative talk show *The O'Reilly Factor* in which Bill O'Reilly and a commentator on the show discussed the recent capture of a Christian man during the Iraq war. The commentator told O'Reilly that the Christian hostage had forgiven his captors, and then she asked the host, to his discomfort, whether he thought that Jesus would have invaded Iraq. O'Reilly evaded the question, so she answered: he wouldn't.

Phil loved that. "That's exactly right! Jesus forgave his persecutors. If he were around today, he would be doing things that would be so . . . *unwieldy*!"

Searching for God, Jesus, and the Buddha

It was during these early readings that I felt I had the most to contribute—when the play was still being written, the direction was still being considered, and the actors were still creating their characters. Unlike many playwrights, Stephen presented the cast with an unfinished script that would mature during the following weeks: scenes would come and go; lines would be changed; even whole characters would be added and then eliminated. In a sense, the play was still being born. Stephen himself would joke about his habit of unfinished plays in the early stages. During these first days and weeks, we would read through scenes that would trail off and end with the words "More later."

Over the course of just a few weeks, we covered almost every topic in Scripture and theology. "I feel like I'm in grad school," Stephen said one day. And perhaps because many of the actors had shared long histories with LAB, no one seemed bashful about offering an opinion or asking a question.

At times, the freewheeling theological discussions reminded me of what in Saint Thomas Aquinas's day were called *quodlibetales*. In the thirteenth century, students at the University of Paris sometimes engaged in an academic free-for-all, during which they could lob any theological question at their professors.

At other times, I felt as if I were once again facing my examiners during comprehensive exams for my master's degree in divinity, with questions ranging rapidly from topic to topic: Who was Saint Matthew?

Why was his being a tax collector so bad? Did Jesus know he was God? Who was responsible for the death of Jesus? Did Pilate want him dead? Did Caiaphas? What does the "Lamb of God" mean? Why is forgiveness so important in Christian theology? Was Mary Magdalene really married to Jesus, like *The Da Vinci Code* says? How much of Mel Gibson's movie is true?

Discussions with the cast also revealed a variety of spiritual paths, which meant that my answers would need to be geared toward a wide audience. Some of the actors were self-described lapsed Catholics, like Stephen. Some were lapsed Christians. Others, like Yetta Gottesman, came from a family of mixed religions. A few, like Sam Rockwell, had grown up in a family with little or no religious interest.

Jeffrey DeMunn, a veteran actor with white hair and impressively dark eyebrows that hover above piercing eyes, played three roles in the play: the judge, Caiaphas the Elder, and Saint Matthew. During his long career he has appeared in many movies, including *The Green Mile* and *The Shawshank Redemption*. The week after I met him, I noticed him on an episode of *Law & Order*, where he had a recurring role.

Jeffrey had been raised in a Christian family. As a teenager, he joined a group called the Liberal Religious Youth, sponsored by the Unitarian church in Buffalo, New York, after his sister told him that he needed to see that there was more to life than simply how it appeared to be. "Basically," said Jeffrey, "she told me to wake up." The group, which brought Jeffrey into contact with African American youths in the early 1960s, emphasized the social-justice aspect of Christianity and solidified for him the value of faith, focusing more on the idea of God and less on the person of Jesus.

Jeffrey's perception of God fit into some classical philosophical notions, though not in an obvious way. He and his wife spend much of their time in a cabin a few hundred miles north of New York City, and, perhaps not surprisingly, it is easy for him to find God in nature.

"I'll be in the woods sometimes and I'll stop, and there it is—all around me. It's hard for me to label it," he said, and stopped to find the words he wanted. "The closer you get to it, the more you drop your needs and anxieties. It's like getting closer to this enormous perfect force, this ineffableness that you can connect with and that says that, ultimately, nothing is needed. It says that if you take a step forward, there's nothing to worry about, because there will always be something underfoot. But, you know, I don't think I want to put a name to it."

There is a long history to this kind of discourse about the transcendent: describing without wanting to describe. Saint Thomas Aquinas, the Scholastic philosopher of the Middle Ages, wrote that if one can label it or name it or define it, what one has labeled or named or defined cannot be God, because God is by definition unknowable. And the sixteenth-century Spanish mystic Saint John of the Cross spoke of God as *todo y nada*, everything and nothing.

Eric Bogosian, a man of impressive intellect and wide-ranging interests, was well versed in the Bible. My prejudicial image of actors as unfamiliar with Scripture or religion was challenged after hearing a learned disquisition one day by Eric on the history of his character, Satan. (I'm not sure why I believed that actors wouldn't be well read: perhaps I imagined them reading scripts more than books.) A few days into the readings, he told me about his interest in the world of late antiquity, which had led him to an archeological expedition in Egypt. Had I known more about Eric's intellectual background, I might not have been so surprised by his acumen: he is not only an actor but a playwright and novelist as well, and he won a Guggenheim Fellowship in 2004.

Raised outside of Boston in a religious family that belonged to the Armenian Apostolic Church, Eric had read widely in biblical literature and the history of world religions. Early on, he offered a witty image of what Jeffrey DeMunn was referring to: God's ineffability. "Here's what I would call my Empire State Building theory of God," he said with a smile. "Let's say you were to take a dog to the front door of the Empire State Building and say, 'Well, here it is.' The dog could look at it, and see it, and smell it, and even go up and down in the elevators, but no matter how hard he tried, he'd never be able to understand it. To understand how it was built, what its purpose is, and what the goal of its builders was would be beyond him. How could he possibly begin to understand it?"

For some members of the cast, the theological discussions at table readings brought back memories of childhood experiences with religion. "Starched habits and polished mahogany floors and school uniforms," said Deborah Rush, neatly summing up a lost world of Catholic girls schools run by no-nonsense sisters. Deborah, who was part of the original New York production of the comedy *Noises Off*, was the product of fourteen years of Catholic education, including the Academy of Saint Elizabeth, a high school run by the Sisters of Charity of Saint Elizabeth in suburban New Jersey. A petite, elegant woman with fine features, ash-blond hair, and near-perfect diction, Deborah was cast in the role of Judas Iscariot's mother.

"I was very devoted to Mary, of course," she said, recalling her girlhood. "She was so pure and holy and never yelled—at least that's how she was presented to us. But I also like Saint Joseph, who I thought was rather overlooked. I used to pray at his altar in church to give him equal time. And when I was lying in bed at night and worried about anything, I got great comfort from the guardian angels."

early success in his career, before that success (coupled with too much money) led him into some dark and depressing times in his personal life. Though raised Christian, he had come to identify Christianity with a punitive God who had Jesus as a "right-hand man." As a result, Kohl developed a largely antagonistic relationship to Christianity. It was Zen that helped him regain his equilibrium, and he now calls his spirituality the most important thing in his life.

"Life with Zen becomes all about practice," he said, "and about seeing each moment of the day as an opportunity to experience reality with your whole body and your whole mind. The mundane becomes something else entirely."

During his Zen retreats, Kohl spends eight hours a day meditating, or "sitting," as he said, a feat that made my own annual retreats seem lax by comparison. Kohl is also a fan of Thomas Merton. We had plenty of conversations about Merton, who was himself interested in Eastern spiritualities and died during a trip to Thailand.

✦

While Kohl was firmly grounded in his spiritual practice, other members of the cast had traveled a circuitous spiritual path and were still on a quest to find something hat worked for them. One such cast member was the understudy to Jesus and Judas, a friendly actor named Trevor Long. His path reminded me of Saint Augustine's intellectual quest in the fourth century, which led him from Greek philosophy to Manichaeism—a religious doctrine that dismissed the Old Testament and stressed a dualistic approach to good and evil forces in the world—to, finally, Christianity, after a dramatic experience in a garden, during which he overheard a children's song telling him to "take and read." What was on hand for Augustine to read was the New Testament. Opening it at random, he chanced upon a line from Saint Paul that

urged the young libertine to "put away the cares of the flesh." It would
be the answer to Saint Monica's prayers for her son's conversion.

With his long dark hair and scruffy beard, Trevor looked like a
Renaissance artist's version of Jesus. Born into a desultory Episcopalian
family, Trevor drifted away from even the moderate religious practices
of his parents when he entered Brown University in 1993. After completing his master's degree in acting at Rutgers University, he moved to
Los Angeles to begin an acting career. It was there that the articulate
actor began what he calls his quest for meaning. Trevor had recently
gone through an intensely painful breakup with his girlfriend and felt
himself weighted down with guilt and regret. "I needed something to
center me," he said, "and to get me out of myself." In response, he did
what Augustine had done: he took up books and read.

His reading tour took him from Hermann Hesse's novel *Siddhartha*
to Norman Vincent Peale's *The Power of Positive Thinking* to the
Foundation for Inner Peace's *Course in Miracles*. Around the same time,
he started to practice meditation. Ernest Holmes's book *The Science
of Mind*, which suggests that positive results can accrue in one's life
from a positive relationship with God, deepened Trevor's interest in a
more personal God. So did Christian mystics such as Saint John of the
Cross, Meister Eckhart, and Thomas Merton, whose book *Thoughts in
Solitude* held great appeal for Trevor. "Merton spoke like a Buddhist,"
said Trevor, "but had a traditional Christian faith." Trevor's hope to
meet "the God that I came to know through Merton, Eckhart, and
John of the Cross" moved him from meditating to praying more specifically to God. Ultimately, he was led to services at the Hollywood
Presbyterian Church. He also started reading the Bible, particularly
the Psalms.

"This is going to sound really corny," he said apologetically, "but I
had a vision of reading a really old, really worn King James Version of

the Bible. And I went into this bookstore one day and found one just like the one I had envisioned. Anyway, I bought it and—"

Embarrassed, he stopped, and I had to urge him to finish the story. "On the inside I wrote: 'To Trevor, from God.'"

In 2002, while doing a show in New York, Trevor went into the Marble Collegiate Church, where Norman Vincent Peale had preached. There Trevor had a powerful religious experience. Still searching for a release from his guilt and seeking a direct experience of God, he entered the church and sat down in a pew. "I went inside and immediately became emotional," Trevor said. "I started to cry and felt this deep sadness coming up from the depths of me, and then this extreme sense of release. It was very frightening and overwhelming, and I was self-conscious about crying in church, but I felt that there was someone *there* with me. As if someone there had put an arm around me and said, 'Everything is going to be okay.' I felt very happy and so relieved and thought, *I need to go back to church.*"

Trevor's experience at Marble Collegiate mirrored that of some of the Christian mystics, which begins with the onset of what Saint Ignatius of Loyola called "consolation without prior cause," the unexpected feeling of the closeness of God. Such feelings are often accompanied by a fear of this transcendent reality, a natural reaction that is described as early as the New Testament. (After seeing one of Jesus' miracles his disciples are typically *both* amazed and afraid.) Finally, Trevor experienced the comfort that the English mystic Julian of Norwich described when she wrote, "All will be well, all will be well and all manner of things shall be well." Trevor's experience in church had a distinguished heritage, and it offers an example of why "mysticism" is more common than most people may believe.

Trevor's journey has not ended. His interest in Christianity led him to begin practicing explicitly Christian meditation. Recently, he has slowly gravitated toward Buddhism. "I was afraid that I would use a personal God as an excuse to help me and babysit for me," he explained. For Trevor, Buddhism now best expresses his relationship to the world. But he admits he is still searching, and one day I suggested that the personal God he had been searching for had found him in the pews of Marble Collegiate. He paused and said, "I never thought of that. I'm going to have to think about that."

The Jesus of History

Every actor, no matter what his or her religious background, was interested in questions of religion and, especially, the story of Jesus of Nazareth. And everyone—even those with no religious background at all—seemed to have brought his or her own Jesus to the reading table.

Chief among the cast's questions was the issue of historicity. Bluntly put: how do we know which parts of the Gospels are accurate and which may not be?

As John Meier makes clear in *The Roots of the Problem and the Person*, the first volume of his monumental series on Jesus called *A Marginal Jew*, there were two distinct stages to the writing of the Gospels. First was the oral tradition, when the story of Jesus of Nazareth was passed by word of mouth from person to person. During this period there would have been little need for written records of the story of Jesus: his disciples and eyewitnesses were around to offer firsthand, and no doubt vivid, accounts of their encounters with Jesus. (And, in any event, many of the early disciples were likely illiterate.)

As those men and women died, the second stage began, which required the editorial work of those people generally known as the "evangelists," who compiled the Gospels for the early church. Each evangelist wrote for a different community and therefore might stress different parts of the story, perhaps leaving out what another writer would think important or adding what another writer would consider inconsequential. This is one reason for some of the variety in the four Gospels. As an aside, the term *gospel* is an Old English derivation of the word for "good news." Likewise, *evangelist* comes from the Greek *euangelion*, "good news," or "good message." (The word *angel* derives from the same Greek root.)

Daniel J. Harrington, SJ, my New Testament professor in graduate theology studies, once told our class that it is reasonable to think of the four evangelists (Matthew, Mark, Luke, and John) as sitting at their desks with scraps of paper scattered about them, on which were written favorite sayings from, and stories about, Jesus of Nazareth. Father Harrington suggested that the Gospels they wrote offer us a "general outline" of the life, death, and resurrection of Jesus.

The editing decisions (or "redaction," as scholars say) of the evangelists ultimately determined what made it into their Gospels and what didn't. During the editing process, however, these authors inserted various comments and emendations for the purpose of explanation or exhortation. (An author like Luke, writing for a Greek community, might feel it necessary to explain some Jewish practices.)

Three of them also relied heavily on one another. While there are competing theories about how Matthew, Mark, and Luke borrowed material from one another, it is clear that they did. Most scholars posit that Mark came first, writing to a non-Jewish community around AD 70. Matthew's Gospel, written around 85 or 90, addressed to a primarily Jewish audience, is an expanded and revised version of Mark, supplemented with other stories, most famously the narrative of the birth of Jesus. Luke, though most likely a Gentile, or non-Jew, nonetheless knew a great deal about Jewish traditions when he wrote his Gospel around the same time as Matthew. Both Matthew and Luke relied to a great degree on an independent source of sayings—nicknamed "Q" by scholars, after the German *Quelle*, for source.

And while Matthew, Mark, and Luke each carefully designed their books to appeal to a specific community of readers, their three Gospels are so similar that they are often referred to as the synoptic Gospels, because the story seems told with a common vision. The Gospel of John, on the other hand, was written later, for Christians in the Eastern Mediterranean in the late first century, and is markedly different from the synoptics. John introduces several key characters who do not even appear in the other three Gospels, including the man born blind, Nicodemus, the Samaritan woman, and Lazarus. Few of the episodes during Jesus' public ministry that are recorded in John mirror those in the synoptics. Jesus himself seems different. No longer the earthy spinner of parables, John's Jesus is an omniscient sage who speaks solemnly, even oracularly: "I am the way, and the truth, and the life." The Jesus of John often seems far more divine than human. As Joseph Fitzmyer, SJ, expostulates in his book *A Christological Catechism*, "What a picture of Jesus we would have, if we had only the fourth gospel!"

But the question remains: how can we tell what comes from the time of Jesus and what comes later, from the writers of these four Gospels?

In *A Marginal Jew*, Meier lays out the ways that one can discern the most authentic material from what may be a later addition. His presentation of these historical criteria is the simplest and most direct I've seen anywhere. It is also the one I offered the cast of *Judas* as a way to understand what things needed to be taken at face value in the story, as well as the way in which Scripture scholars have attempted to understand the texts that lie at the heart of the play.

First is the criterion of "embarrassment." There is no reason to believe that the writers of the Gospels would have gone out of their way to insert something new into the story that would have embarrassed or "created difficulty" for the early church. "Rather, embarrassing material coming from Jesus would naturally be either suppressed or softened in later stages of the Gospel tradition," says Meier.

Meier uses the example of the baptism of Jesus by John the Baptist. Though it's a familiar story, in many ways it would have made little sense to the early church. After all, why would Jesus have to be baptized? If anything, shouldn't it have been the other way around? Shouldn't the Son of God be doing the baptizing? It's such an odd story that the Gospel of Matthew has Jesus actually explain to John why he needs to be baptized.

For the early church, eager to prove Jesus' divinity, this story would have proved problematic. Reading backward, we can see that the evangelists were stuck with an event that would clearly have been hard to explain to newcomers to the religion. There is little chance that they would have consciously made up something like this, which argues for the essential historicity of the event.

The second criterion is "discontinuity." You might also call this the criterion of "originality." If a word or an action attributed to Jesus is seen nowhere else in the Hebrew Scriptures or early Christian writings and seems fresh and innovative, chances are it originated with Jesus. For example, his eating with "sinners" and having women among his close followers might have been anathema to some devout Jews of the time. On the other hand, since we will never know everything about life in first-century Palestine, there is the possibility that what seems idiosyncratic was actually a common practice or saying. Still, thinking about what might be, in Meier's phrase, "strikingly characteristic" of Jesus is a helpful tool in trying to get at the accuracy of the texts.

Third is the criterion of "multiple attestation." If a saying or deed of Jesus is attested to in more than one source, it can be seen as more likely to be authentic. For example, Jesus speaks frequently of the "kingdom of God" in Mark, Matthew, Luke, and John, and we even find echoes of the phrase in the writings of Paul. Meier points out that the phrase appears in many of the various literary genres in the Gospels (parable, beatitude, prayer, aphorism, miracle story). "Granted this wide sweep of witnesses, in different sources and genres, coming largely from the first Christian generation, it becomes extremely difficult to claim that such material is simply the creation of the Church."

The fourth of Meier's criteria is "coherence," which on its face may seem to contradict "discontinuity." This criterion requires that scholars consider parts of the Gospel that would be coherent or in conformity with other parts already seen as "historical." In other words, if we assume that John the Baptist baptized Jesus, what other sayings and actions in the Gospel (that is, later references to the event) conform to this? We must keep in mind, however, that Jesus himself was not always a "consistent" preacher, as Meier reminds us: ancient Semitic thought "delighted in paradoxical statements that held opposites in tension." And in addressing different audiences, Jesus may have stressed different facets of his message.

Finally, we have the criterion of "rejection and execution." Since what Jesus said and did led to his execution, we can identify as authentic those words and deeds in the Gospels that fit with this pattern. A bland Jesus or a harmless thinker, says Meier, would not have posed a threat to the Roman authorities or to some Jewish leaders. This is the Jesus that Phil Hoffman described as "causing havoc." As Meier writes, "A Jesus whose words and deeds would not alienate people, especially powerful people, is not the historical Jesus."

Taken together, these criteria, along with other historical tools (archeological research and the study of other sources of the time), can help one gradually come to understand more about the "historical Jesus" and gain a more realistic appreciation for his life and times.

I had long accepted the underlying historicity of the Gospels; whether the actors and creative team of *Judas* did was another matter. "I still don't really know how much of the story is true, or if any of it is true," said Stephen one day, with refreshing bluntness. "I can't honestly say that I know it happened, but what I've found out after these readings is that underneath it all is Jesus' worldview, which is beautiful and inspiring and feels like the right way to go."

At the end of the first week of readings, on a blustery January afternoon, the cast met uptown at the Metropolitan Museum of Art. We were scheduled to take a brief tour of the museum's vast collection of medieval art. The show's costume designer (and Phil's partner), Mimi O'Donnell, hoped to examine some medieval paintings to spark ideas for her work. The cast, for its part, was encouraged to meditate on Christian religious art, in the hope that artistic representations would open yet another window into the life of Jesus and his followers. Phil and Stephen asked me to be on hand to answer any questions that came up about the subject matter in the paintings.

The actors seemed to appreciate the break from the intensity of the readings, and there were plenty of jokes, some at Sam's expense ("Hey, Judas, man, look what you did!" said one cast member, pointing to a gruesome crucifixion scene). The museum's comprehensive medieval art collection included portraits of almost all the characters in the play, from Peter to Mary Magdalene to Thomas. At dusk, Sam and I ambled over to a nearby Jesuit church to study the stations of the cross—a series of images depicting the trial, crucifixion, and death of Jesus. Walking "through" the stations of the cross—that is, meditating on these events while walking from image to image—is a tradition practiced in many Christian churches during the season of Lent. It occurred to me that we were about to enter the Lenten season, and as I recounted the story told by the fifteen bright mosaics that lined the wall, I could see that Sam was listening intently. Because he was unfamiliar with the story's particulars, I became even more aware of them, even though I had gone through the story hundreds of times; the inherent violence of the scenes became more vivid for me. Members of the LAByrinth Theater Company were discovering, in new ways, the gutsy story of Jesus. But I was making discoveries, too, and encountering the ancient events in new ways.

Essentially, I was starting to realize that, after almost twenty years as a Jesuit, I had grown so accustomed to the story of Jesus that it had become overly familiar. Seeing the Gospel stories through the eyes of people like Sam reminded me of the inherent shock of the story, and how difficult it must have been for the first hearers of the tale to comprehend it. After all, St. Paul mentions in his letters that the story of Jesus was a "scandal," that is, a stumbling block, to some of the Jewish people in his time, particularly the notion that God would assume a human form and then be brutally murdered. But over the past two millennia we have tamed Jesus, so thoroughly domesticating his story that his remarkable sayings are no longer surprising and his astonishing deeds appear familiar, even bland.

But if you were a Jew living in Roman-occupied Palestine, listening to Jesus upend some of the social conventions of the time would have been shocking. Seeing a person you had known all your life healed from a lifelong illness would have been astonishing. Watching Jesus die in agony on the cross, especially if you had been following him for three years, would have been appalling. And encountering a person who had been raised from the dead would have been life-changing.

There was a reason that Jesus, and later his story, and later his disciples, caused such havoc. My time with the theater company was reminding me of this essential truth of Christianity.

Living with the Saints

Over the month of January, I continued to bring in reams of scholarly materials for the cast. The actors were serious about incorporating the background material I presented to them—in the form of books, articles, and essays—into their performances. I gave Sam and Stephen almost every volume on my bookshelf about the historical Jesus, Mums Grant an essay by the Franciscan writer Richard Rohr on Saint Peter's humanity, and Jeffrey DeMunn a long article on the Sanhedrin, the Jewish priestly council at the time of Jesus. By the time the play closed, I would give Liza Colón-Zayas three books on Mother Teresa.

The role of Mother Teresa was a key one for the play. As played by Liza, a diminutive and vibrant actor with a ready smile, Mother Teresa would explain to the audience not only her straightforward understanding of the life of faith, but also the corrosive way that despair works and how it led to the suicide of Judas.

The part could easily have degenerated into caricature. Perhaps because of Mother Teresa's immediately recognizable face and costume, or her participation in what could be called "extreme Christianity," she has become a favorite character in several recent plays and movies, showing up either as a visual punch line or as an emblem of selfless compassion. For example, in *Jeffrey*, Paul Rudnick's play (and, later, movie) about gay life, Mother Teresa arrives to comfort the title character after he has been mugged.

Liza, with her light brown face framed by the familiar blue-and-white habit of the Missionaries of Charity (and a small crucifix provided by her "theological adviser"), made a strikingly improbable Mother Teresa.

Liza's personal history made her donning of Mother Teresa's persona all the more remarkable. Born and raised in the Bronx in a Catholic family and the product of Catholic schools, Liza stunned her family by joining a Christian cult called the Church of Bible Understanding when she was sixteen. At a time when she felt lonely and was frequently high on pot, the "happy and welcoming" group of young people she encountered one day on a Bronx street corner appealed to her. After several weeks, when they asked, "Do you accept Jesus?" she said yes and joined the group.

Soon after entering the cult, she moved to Philadelphia with the group, which made her family "hysterical." There she lived in a residence where thirty to forty members worked full-time jobs and returned home in the evenings for intensive Bible study. Most of the work on behalf of the cult was recruiting. "They told us that we were supposed to save as many of Jesus' lambs as we could, since he was coming back real soon."

Liza described the atmosphere of the house as "no music, no television, nothing worldly. And, of course, no boyfriends and no sex. They said the devil puts those things in the world to tempt us."

Though Liza soon became one of the group's "top earners," bringing in new recruits for an approving leadership, she left because the cult's grueling schedule exhausted her and the daily life made her miserable. Liza returned to her family in the Bronx after one year. For many years afterward, she was a self-described atheist.

Aimless for a time, Liza eventually enrolled in a local college, transferring to two other schools before graduating from Albany State. Her initial interest in economics, though, quickly gave way to a passion for drama. She had done some acting during high school and returned to that love. "I always liked the fact that acting lets you escape, and I had a lot to escape from—having grown up in an environment of violence and sexual abuse and addiction." Acting, she says, gives one the permission to pretend in the way that one does during childhood. "And I never wanted to give up that permission."

After graduation, she moved to New York City, where she found work in a group called Hospital Audiences, performing skits promoting AIDS awareness in hospitals. A chance advertisement in *Back Stage* magazine prompted her to attend an audition for "Excellent Latino Actors."

She laughed when recalling this. "Well, I didn't know if I was *excellent*, but I went anyway."

While standing outside the audition space, she heard a familiar laugh emanating from the room. It was John Ortiz, with whom she had studied at Albany State, and the audition was for the LAByrinth Theater Company. Stephen Adly Guirgis was another classmate from Albany. "But I still had to audition with them," she added quickly. "Three times!"

For Liza, it was worth the effort. "I've worked in television and film and in other theater companies, and working with LAB is the most fun you could have. You get your ass kicked, and have to be honest and truthful as an actor, but it's so much fun!"

During those January readings, Liza talked to me about her religious beliefs in the wake of her experience with the Church of Bible Understanding. "I would say now that I believe in something, but I'm not sure what. But the longer we talk about Jesus and the more I read all those books and watch all those documentaries, the more his life is put into a perspective. When I was in the cult, I swallowed everything I was told: you were taught not to question anything. Now I see that it helps to have a context about things. And that's helped me take another look at the Bible."

Given Liza's experience with organized religion, the role of Mother Teresa would be an unusually challenging part for her. She read several books on the woman and screened a documentary about her work in Calcutta. While she admired Mother Teresa's work with the poor, Liza was skeptical about Catholicism and strongly disagreed with Mother Teresa's opposition to abortion.

"Look, I'm pro-choice, okay?" Liza said. "But I have respect for Mother Teresa for going out to the sick and the poor and trying to make their last days beautiful. I mean, some people who say they're religious don't do anything like that. You have to come from a position of pure love to be able to do what she did."

When I asked Liza how she admired Mother Teresa's work among the poor while disagreeing with her stance on abortion, she offered a surprising answer. "Well, the Bible was filled with all sorts of dichotomies, right? So are people. And, look, if I cared for thousands of dying people, I figure I should be able to say what I want about anything!"

Liza's reading and thinking about Mother Teresa obviously informed her performance. Whatever she thought about Mother Teresa's opinions, as soon as Liza stepped onstage she immediately assumed the tough, no-nonsense attitude of a woman who had battled despair and now sought to help others find comfort and spiritual support. In the play, Mother Teresa is initially flattered by the prosecutor, who happily listens to her criticizing Judas for giving into despair. Then the defense attorney grills her about some of her own decisions, as a way of casting aspersions on her expertise in spiritual matters and discrediting her as a witness. Did she blame the wars of the world on abortion? Yes, she says. Did she take money from dictators and other shady men? Yes, she says.

After the defense attorney asserts that she has had two abortions, Mother Teresa says, "I will pray for you and your children."

A back-and-forth of retorts ensues, with Cunningham saying finally, "Must be nice to have all the answers."

Mother Teresa faces the attorney and says sadly, "Must be hard to have only questions."

In the cast's eagerness to learn everything they could about their characters, they also welcomed images of the saints and other religious figures in the play. I was always on the lookout for prayer cards, photos, drawings, and paintings of the characters in *Judas*. In time, reproductions of works by the Old Masters, which I hoped would help provide fresh insight into the characters, lined the white walls of the dressing rooms.

Michelangelo's *The Martyrdom of Saint Peter*, for example, helped reveal the consummate humility of the man Mums Grant would be portraying. Michelangelo depicts Peter being crucified upside down; according to tradition, he considered himself unworthy of being executed in the same way Jesus had been. While Roman soldiers hammer Peter's hands to the cross, the gray-bearded saint stares directly out at the viewer. It is a striking image, and it made an impression on Mums.

Likewise, Caravaggio's painting *The Incredulity of Saint Thomas*, in which the risen Jesus guides Saint Thomas's hand to the wound on his side—made by a centurion's spear at the Crucifixion—probably said more to Adrian Martinez, the actor who would portray Thomas, about doubt and faith than I could in a year of readings and rehearsals.

Our study and appreciation of these characters as flesh-and-blood human beings also made some traditional artistic representations of the characters shocking. One portrait I brought was Giotto's famous *Kiss of Judas*. In it, an angry mob surrounds a serene Jesus, who is being embraced by Judas. The betrayer throws his arms around his master, covering him with his saffron-colored cloak. Giotto painted Judas with narrow, slitlike eyes, a protruding jaw, matted red hair, and a hardened expression. Judas looks like an ape. The artist's approach typifies the traditional Renaissance portrayal of Judas, and the Jews, as something less than human.

"That's Judas?" said Sam when he saw the painting. The actor seemed wounded, as if the artist had unjustly described someone he had come to know well.

Quite by accident, I stumbled upon a cache of artistic representations the week before opening night. I was in Los Angeles for a conference, and before it began I paid a visit to the new Cathedral of Our Lady of the Angels in downtown L.A. Lining the walls of the cathedral are colossal tapestries, perhaps ten to eleven feet tall, depicting dozens of saints in profile, facing the altar. In a clever theological twist, the artist, John Nava, used real-life Angelenos as models for those saints whose actual likenesses are unknown. So while Mother Teresa looks just like Mother Teresa, Saint Peter looks like someone you might run into on La Ciénega Boulevard. Poking around the cathedral's gift shop, I was delighted to come across note cards featuring images of the saints, and I took several back to the cast of *Judas*.

As it happened, during that same stay in L.A. I flipped on the television in my hotel room late one night just in time to catch *The Green Mile*, a film I had never seen, and was surprised to see not one but *two* actors from the play: Sam Rockwell and Jeffrey DeMunn. Jeffrey plays a kindhearted prison guard, while Sam plays an especially noxious character, a mean-spirited murderer called Wild Bill, sullenly passing time on death row.

When I asked Sam whether he enjoyed playing bad guys like Wild Bill and Judas, he nodded enthusiastically. "Oh yeah!" he said, grinning. "You get to do all sorts of crazy stuff. Hey, in *The Green Mile*, I had to pee on Tom Hanks!"

The Woman from Magdala

One of the note cards from the cathedral gift shop struck a chord with Yetta Gottesman, because it depicted her character, Mary Magdalene. The delicate tapestry presented a young woman with close-cropped black hair, her head bowed in prayer, her hands clasped to her chin.

Thanks in great part to Dan Brown's best-selling novel *The Da Vinci Code*, interest in the historical Mary Magdalene has risen stratospherically during the past few years. As with her fellow disciple, Judas, we know very little about her. Jesus cast seven demons out of her (we don't know how these demons had manifested themselves in her behavior); she remained at the cross with two other women when the other (male) disciples had all fled; she watched Jesus die; and she was the first one to whom Jesus appeared after the Resurrection. In a touching scene on Easter morning, a grieving Mary initially mistakes the risen Jesus for the local gardener.

Even with these distinguished credentials, Mary Magdalene (the name means "of Magdala," a town in Galilee) gradually became known as a prostitute, though there is no mention of this in the Gospels. (The word *maudlin* comes from her name, presumably the result of her grieving for a sinful past.) The most benign explanation for this confusion over Mary's identity is that there is a veritable crowd of Marys in the Gospel stories (besides Mary, the mother of Jesus, there is Mary of Bethany and Mary, the wife of Clopas). Mary Magdalene was also, oddly, conflated with a woman who had bathed Jesus' feet with her tears, dried them with her hair, and then anointed them with oil. In

AD 591, Pope Gregory I preached a sermon in which he proclaimed, "She whom Luke calls the sinful woman, whom John calls Mary, we believe to be the Mary from whom seven devils were ejected according to Mark."

This inaccurate identification became more or less church teaching for at least a millennium.

A less benign interpretation of this "confusion" is that the early church was threatened, even horrified, by the stunning example of a woman among the early disciples. Strictly based on the evidence in the Gospels, Mary Magdalene enjoyed an exalted standing. She was not only the first one to whom Jesus appeared after the Resurrection, but also the one who proclaimed the news of his resurrection to the other disciples, including those who would be the leaders of the early church communities: Peter, James, Andrew, and the rest.

Thus comes Mary's traditional title: Apostle to the Apostles. Her fidelity to Jesus during the Crucifixion, as well as Jesus' appearance to her, are marks of distinction that place her, at least in terms of her faith, *above* the men. Some of the "extracanonical," or "apocryphal," gospels (that is, those not included by the early church councils with the traditional four Gospels) picture her as the most favored of all the disciples. "[Christ loved] her more than all the disciples," says the text known as *The Gospel of Philip*.

Perhaps it was convenient for the early church fathers to dismiss Mary Magdalene and even insult her as a prostitute, fearful of what her role would mean for the place of women in the early church. As Jane Schaberg, a professor of religious studies at the University of Detroit Mercy, writes in *The Resurrection of Mary Magdalene*, "The pattern is a common one: the powerful woman disempowered, remembered as a whore or whorish."

As many historians have noted, the exaltation of a relatively few women in the early church—most notably the Virgin Mary—occurred at the same time that the contributions of almost every other woman in Jesus' circle were forgotten, ignored, or actively suppressed. Elisabeth Schüssler Fiorenza's influential book *In Memory of Her*, a reconstruction of the contributions of women among the disciples and in the early church, takes its title from the Gospel tale of the woman who anoints the feet of Jesus. In response to the woman's self-less action, Jesus announces that whenever the story is told, it will be told in memory of her.

Yet, as Schüssler Fiorenza notes, the Gospel writers don't bother to give us this woman's identity: "Even her name is lost to us." Despite Jesus' instruction to his disciples, the church preserved no memory of her. In a trenchant aside, Schüssler Fiorenza says, "The name of the betrayer is remembered, but the name of the faithful disciple is forgotten because she was a woman."

Given this milieu, it is not surprising that the role of someone like Mary Magdalene would be elided by the evangelists and the early church.

In many ways, Mary Magdalene is the star of *The Da Vinci Code*. In the novel, she fulfills one of the many long-lived rumors about her: she is the wife of Jesus, something that finds no credence anywhere in the New Testament. In the months after Dan Brown's novel was published, I found myself invited to give several presentations to church groups and called on by the media to comment on the historicity of the book. By far the most popular question was: Was Jesus married to Mary Magdalene? Or, as one young man in a Catholic audience put it, "Was Mary Magdalene really Mrs. Jesus?" (I was even asked that question when my talks had nothing to do with *The Da Vinci Code*.)

But by the simple criterion of "embarrassment," the theory fails. As John Meier points out in *A Marginal Jew*, being unmarried was seen as undesirable for most rabbis at the time, and it is unlikely that the Gospels would have concocted the story that he was celibate if he was in fact married. Also, the Gospels describe Jesus returning to his hometown and coming into contact with his mother, his brothers and sisters, and the townspeople of Nazareth. The silence about a wife (and children) in this context, writes Meier, probably indicates that Jesus did not have a wife and children in his past life in Nazareth. "The position that Jesus remained celibate on religious grounds [is] the more probable hypothesis," Meier concludes, after sifting through the evidence.

Dan Brown's presentation of Mary as "Mrs. Jesus" fails by another important criterion: Mary would have been referred to, like every other married woman identified in the Gospels, by her husband's name. She would almost certainly have been called not "Mary Magdalene" but "Mary, the wife of Jesus."

Unfortunately, many have read *The Da Vinci Code* as a reliable and factual account of the early church, despite all the evidence to the contrary. (When I told a group to remember that the book was fiction, one doubtful young man raised his hand and said, "Well, you *have* to say that, don't you, Father?") The most unfortunate part of the portrayal of Mary Magdalene in *The Da Vinci Code*, however, is that once again she is reduced to a subordinate role: she is the wife of Jesus. Rather than being honored as the most faithful of disciples, the first witness to the Resurrection, the remarkable leader in the early church, and a model for independent women, she is notable only for her husband. The marginalization of Mary Magdalene continues, albeit in a new form.

I was happy that Stephen took the time to set things right by Mary Magdalene in *The Last Days of Judas Iscariot*. His second act opens with Mary Magdalene standing beside the tough-talking Saint Monica, who describes Mary as the "only bitch I let hang with me up here."

Stephen Adly Guirgis's soft-spoken Magdalene quickly demolishes many of the myths about this astonishing woman as Saint Monica shouts out her approval:

> MARY MAGDALENE. My name is Mary of Magdala. I was a disciple of Jesus, I was present at the crucifixion, and I was the first person He appeared to after the resurrection.
>
> SAINT MONICA. Bitch got *clout*!

In a lively dialogue with Monica, Mary Magdalene sketches for the audience her background as one of the founders of the Christian religion, and she sets the record straight on other matters as well. "I was not a whore," she says. "I was an unmarried woman in a town of ill repute."

Finally, she offers a neat rejoinder to *The Da Vinci Code*:

> MARY MAGDALENE. And also, I was not the wife of Jesus either.
>
> SAINT MONICA. Still love ya!

When I presented the note card featuring Mary Magdalene to Yetta, her dark eyes filled with tears. After the show ended, she explained that the photo had given her more insight into the character. Yetta had done a great deal of research on Mary and had reached her own conclusions about her character. "It's easy for people to deal in stereotypes and prejudices, especially when it comes to women, so I wanted to read for myself about Mary Magdalene's life.

"I see her as a person who searched and finally found someone who understood and accepted her," said Yetta. "And in response to Jesus' acceptance, she led a life of passion, and she believed passionately in him."

Yetta had done some searching as well. Her father was Jewish and her mother a Catholic who had left the church; they had allowed Yetta to choose her own religion. But, as she said, "I haven't chosen yet." She is a delicately featured woman with dark hair and alabaster skin. In reference to her time at St. John's University, a Catholic college in New York City, she described herself as "probably the only Puerto Rican Jew in the whole place." Yetta tries to pray every day—in gratitude and for friends and family. "Even though there's a bit of the skeptic in me, I feel like I have a very close relationship with God. And when the lines of communication are open, my heart is, too." She has never felt completely alone in her life, always feeling that someone is looking out for her, and this she associates with God.

I asked what her image of God was like. Yetta thought for a moment before saying, "Well, he's not the guy with the white beard." Then she laughed. "And he doesn't have an English accent either!"

For her, the table readings were a way of learning something new. "I *loved* studying all that history!" Even after the play ended, she continued reading about Mary Magdalene. "It's a simple story," she said, "but I guess until now I always thought of it more as a fable, not history. Now I think of Jesus as a real man, someone far ahead of his time, a revolutionary. No one had done things the way he had done things, and no one had risked the way he risked things. And I thought of Mary Magdalene as a real woman, too. I never believed that stuff about her being a prostitute anyway. From what I've read, she was probably capable, straightforward, and passionate about what she believed in."

The image of Mary Magdalene remained taped to Yetta's dressing room mirror for the run of the show. As the biblical scholar Bruce

Chilton says in his biography *Mary Magdalene*, "Mary conveyed the truth of Spirit to those who followed her disciplines, whatever their backgrounds may have been, and she has not ceased to find disciples."

As the readings progressed, it seemed that each actor, like Sam, Liza, and Yetta, was developing a connection to the character he or she would play. At first, I wondered if the actors had time to read all the materials I was giving them; between rehearsals and auditions and all the rest, they were exceedingly busy people. But they were also intent on preparing for their roles. After I gave Elizabeth Rodriguez an abstruse essay on Saint Monica from Peter Brown's book *Augustine of Hippo*, she returned the next morning with a smile on her face. "Hey, Father Jim," she said. "Monica was tough!"

One day I walked into the dressing room and saw Stephen McKinley Henderson with his head down, reading intently. A stocky man with caramel-colored skin, freckles, and curly brown hair and possessed of a rich, deep voice, Stephen noticed me and held up a book on Pilate that I had given him and smiled. "Man, this is *fascinating!*" Stephen, who had been raised in the Baptist Church, came from a strongly Christian background. He had even considered a career as a minister, after a chaplain in college introduced him to contemporary theologians such as H. Richard Niebuhr, whose book *Christ and Culture*, addressing the various ways religion can engage society, made a lasting impression on Stephen. Even more influential was *Black Theology and Black Power*, by James Cone.

Stephen had spoken passionately about his work in the plays of his friend August Wilson, the American-born playwright who took as his subjects the black men and women in a poor neighborhood of Pittsburgh. Stephen had been in several of Wilson's works, including *Ma Rainey's Black Bottom* and *Jitney*. Contrary to those who believe that only the great European dramatists could capture important themes in their plays, Stephen believed that "there is no complexity of the human spirit that cannot be expressed in the African American culture."

With his heightened awareness of that culture, was he worried about portraying Pontius Pilate, the man who condemned Jesus, as a black man?

"Not at all!" he said. "There is something, well, *loftier*, I guess, about actors who are not as concerned about their egos and are willing to play a less savory character. That's the way that the good will be revealed more strongly in the other characters."

Poverty of Spirit

At table readings we explored not only the characters who would be featured in the production, but also theological concepts, some quite challenging, that were key to the play. After a lengthy conversation with the cast about the theological idea of "poverty of spirit," I gave Phil a copy of a short but notoriously dense book on the topic by the twentieth-century German theologian Johannes Baptist Metz.

"You gave him *that?*" said a friend when I told him of my gift of the Metz book. He rolled his eyes. "Well, that will kill any interest he has in the topic."

I hoped that it wouldn't. Poverty of spirit is an overlooked but crucial concept in Christian spirituality. "Blessed are the poor in spirit" is, after all, the first saying in Saint Matthew's account of the Sermon on the Mount. It would be important for the cast and crew to understand this spiritual concept as they worked on the play: spiritual poverty is the antidote to the kind of despair that kept Judas in hell.

Metz's book had been a great aid to me during a difficult period of my life. As part of my Jesuit training, I spent two years in Nairobi, Kenya, working with East African refugees. My job was to help the refugees who had settled in the slums of Nairobi start small businesses that would enable them to support themselves.

I was assigned to Nairobi after the novitiate period and two years of philosophy studies, when all Jesuits spend two or three years in full-time work before beginning their theology studies. Initially I was exhilarated by the prospect of working overseas. Once I arrived in Nairobi, however, I felt terribly homesick, cut off from my friends in the States, worried that I wouldn't be able to endure two years in East Africa, and concerned about contracting some horrible tropical illness. During this low ebb in my life, a Jesuit priest gave me a copy of *Poverty of Spirit*. I read it in a hammock strung between two tall trees behind the Jesuit community in Nairobi.

Metz speaks of poverty of spirit as the inherent poverty that every human being faces in daily life. This spiritual poverty comes with knowing our limitations and accepting that we are powerless to change certain aspects of our lives. It also requires an acceptance of the fact that we will face disappointments, pain, suffering, and, eventually, death.

"We are all members of a species that is not sufficient unto itself," writes Metz. "We are all creatures plagued by unending doubts and restless, unsatisfied hearts."

But unlike the material poverty that causes misery to so many people around the world and that I saw daily in my work with the refugees, spiritual poverty is something to be *sought*. We seek to develop this honest stance toward life because it leads us to understand how we must rely, ultimately, on God. In one of my favorite passages, Metz reflects on this connection: "If we leave our dreamy conceptions aside and focus on our naked poverty, when the mask falls and the core of our Being is revealed, it soon becomes obvious that we are religious 'by nature,' that religion is the secret dowry of our Being. In the midst of our existence there unfolds the bond . . . that ties us to the infinitely transcendent mystery of God, the insatiable interest in the Absolute that captivates us and underlines our poverty."

Suffering is an obvious part of human existence, no matter how much we would like to avoid it. "If I knew any way of escape," writes C. S. Lewis in *The Problem of Pain*, "I would crawl through sewers to find it." Poverty of spirit is a radical recognition of our humanity—our frail and limited humanity. Many of us cannot bear to confront it.

Poverty of spirit is inextricably linked with humility. Without spiritual poverty, says Metz, we resist admitting our reliance on God, we are tempted to try to make it on our own, and we are therefore more likely to despair when we find that things are not going the way we had planned. Because spiritual poverty allows us to recognize our fundamental reliance on God, it marks the beginning of the Christian spiritual journey. "Thus poverty of spirit is not just one virtue among many," writes Metz toward the end of his book. "It is the hidden component of every transcending act, the ground of every 'theological virtue.'"

Trevor Long believes that humility is required for an actor. "Humility comes in when you can make it clear what you're doing," he said. "And what I'm doing is not about me. That's how I look at it. At the beginning of every performance, I try to say to myself, *How can I best serve this production?* and *Where do I belong in the big picture?* I guess I could think, *I'm going to show them!* or *I'm going to be a big star!* But I try to find ways to make it less egotistical. Maybe that's why I'm not a little further along professionally, but it works for me."

I asked if it required even more humility to be an understudy, as he was for Judas and Jesus. Trevor was required to be at the Public Theater every night, at least until intermission, and during the run he never made it onstage.

"Sure," he said. "I would like to be more a part of things." Then he laughed. "But I'm just happy to be working!"

Poverty of spirit does not take away joy. Quite the contrary. It is the gateway to joy and happiness, because it enables us to surrender to ultimate reliance on God, which leads to a great freedom—the freedom to say, "It's not all up to me." It is at that point that we truly become human.

When I was working in Kenya, for example, it took me almost two years to realize that I couldn't solve everyone's problems. No matter how many hours I worked, no matter how many refugees I helped, no matter how many small businesses we funded, I knew that many of the refugees would still face lives of great suffering. This realization could have led to despair: the awful knowledge that even after completing my assignment, the lives of those with whom I worked, and with whom I became friends, would be the same, and might even worsen. But once I reached the point where I could embrace a certain measure of spiritual poverty, I was able to do my best and leave the rest up to God.

It was a hard path to travel. At one point, I said to my spiritual director in Nairobi, "Shouldn't I try to solve everyone's problems? Isn't that what Jesus did?"

He laughed and said, "I have news for you, Jim. You're not Jesus."

That approach may sound like a convenient excuse for avoiding the hard work required to make the world better, but it actually increases the effectiveness of one's work. It is less an excuse for hard work than an encouragement. A few expatriates I knew in Kenya working with social agencies burned out after growing frustrated by the seeming lack of results in their work. But those who strive for poverty of spirit begin to understand that while the work may be theirs, the ultimate results are in God's hands. This stance gives them the radical freedom to work hard without experiencing despair even if their efforts eventually come to naught. With this freedom comes a greater ability to serve, and with this ability comes a great deal of peace.

Poverty of spirit is also the gateway to gratitude. People facing despair often find themselves unable to focus on any part of their life for which they might feel grateful. And gratitude plays a central role in the Christian spiritual traditions. Saint Ignatius of Loyola's *Spiritual Exercises*, his famous manual on prayer, begins with a meditation on gratitude. When Jesuits direct spiritual retreats, as a matter of course they first ask retreatants to consider what they are most grateful for.

This need not be gratitude for something grand or unusual. Adrian Martinez, who played Saint Thomas, told me something that, with only slight alterations, could have come out of a devotional manual from the early church: "When I am in a place of gratitude, I feel that I can live in more abundance. Sure, there are big things to be grateful for, like when I get a role in a movie or a play. But it's just as important to see the little things. Like when my daughter, Paloma, first learned to smile! The days are better when I can learn to see everything as a gift." This stance, this ultimate reliance on God as the giver of all gifts, is an outgrowth of poverty of spirit, and of humility.

Though the ending of *The Last Days of Judas Iscariot* had yet to be written, it was clear that Judas would have to decide whether to embrace humility and seek reconciliation or reject it and continue his time in hell. It would be a choice for or against poverty of spirit.

Phil came up with an excellent metaphor to describe this choice. One afternoon he suggested to the cast: Imagine yourself in a room surrounded by walls of your own making. No matter what you do, you feel hemmed in. You have a choice: will you embrace or reject your powerlessness? The walls, Phil explained, are the bad decisions you have made. You feel trapped by where these decisions have led you. In such a situation, you can embrace humility and start afresh, or you can reject the possibility of any change in your life and therefore remain stuck.

Phil's metaphor succinctly pointed up the need to admit one's spiritual poverty, and it was an apt description of the state in which the character Judas found himself.

Phil's comments reminded me of Thomas Merton's observations about the value of hope in the face of despair. "How close God is to us when we come to recognize and to accept our abjection and to cast our care entirely upon Him!" Merton wrote in *No Man Is an Island*, a book of meditations he completed in 1955.

Merton's perceptive analysis of hope, despair, and poverty of spirit is strikingly similar to the observation that Jeffrey DeMunn made: God tells us that if we take a step forward, there will be "something underfoot." "Perfect hope," Merton said, "is achieved on the brink of despair, when instead of falling over the edge, we find ourselves walking on air. Hope is always ready to turn into despair but never does, for at the moment of supreme crisis, God's power is suddenly made perfect in our infirmity. So we learn to expect his mercy most calmly when all is most dangerous, to seek him quietly in the face of peril, certain that he cannot fail us."

Phil's image of being hemmed in also reminded me of a story from the book of Genesis in which Joseph's jealous brothers toss him into a deep well. "The pit was empty; there was no water in it," writes the author of Genesis. It is a fitting symbol for the utter hopelessness of the situation. But it's not the end of the story. "The Lord was with Joseph," reads a line later in the book. The more I thought about it, the more I liked Phil's description of despair as a room enclosed by walls of one's own making.

"Until recently," Phil said, "I hadn't thought much about Judas. He was just part of the story of Jesus, and I left it at that. Nor did I see his story as in any way pertaining to my own life. But now I think about him a lot, and his story is very enlightening to me. The truth about Judas is that although he is vilified by others, he is condemning himself. That is his sin: he's not able to let go of his resentment and self-loathing. And, like Judas, we often suffer because of our own actions and can create our own little hells. And only we have the key to get out of it."

I told him that I would certainly be borrowing those insights for a future homily. "You would have made a good Jesuit," I told him one afternoon. He laughed. "When I was young, my sister used to tell me I should become a preacher!"

Stephen McKinley Henderson admitted that the discussions on despair and hope held special meaning for him. "I'm realizing that I have to work to overcome a despair that I thought I had avoided." The actor had been raised in a poor neighborhood in Kansas City, Kansas, and still struggled with memories of the injustices he had witnessed there, as well as the suffering that the poor still face in this country. "It seemed—and it still seems—unfair," he said. "I realize that I am still carrying this heavy load of despair.

"But every day I come to those readings, I feel my load lighten a bit," he said. "Now, I have a little better understanding of the size and scope of God, how not to wallow in despair, and how not to deny that God can and does work in life. I'm finding my way through it all a little better."

Taking the Story Seriously

The cast's interest in theological questions continued well into the table readings. In late January, Sal Inzerillo ran into me in the lobby of the Public Theater. "Hey, Father Jim, I was wondering: Who are the Essenes? And what are the Dead Sea Scrolls?" Mums Grant asked me about the "apocryphal gospels," those not included in the Bible, such as *The Gospel of Thomas* and *The Gospel of Mary*.

Around the same time, Jeffrey DeMunn stopped me to talk about the idea of "anonymous Christians," that is, those who are "saved" by leading good lives even if they are unaware of the story of Jesus

Christ. It is a way of understanding salvation offered to those outside the Christian faith. I didn't even remember mentioning this somewhat controversial concept, which was popularized by the twentieth-century Jesuit theologian Karl Rahner. But Jeffrey did. "What can I read about the anonymous Christian?" I tracked down a few articles and gave them to him the next time we met. Even those who were not in the cast seemed interested in spiritual matters. During a rehearsal break one afternoon, I had a talk with assistant director Brian Roff about Eastern spiritualities and the Japanese Catholic writer Shusaku Endo.

Most days I found myself as engaged as I had ever been as a priest. For unlike my work among at least some Catholics at my parish and the magazine, here I interacted with people for whom the Bible seemed fresh and vital.

Though it was hard to tell how much of our discussions had affected the cast members' spiritual or religious lives, I could tell, from stray comments, that their views of Jesus might be changing gradually. "What I know about Jesus then and now," said Stephen Adly Guirgis, "is like the difference between seeing a great movie as a kid and seeing it as an adult. There's just so much more you can see when you're older, stuff that you miss when you're younger."

Occasional comments indicated that the play itself was having an effect on cast members' personal spiritual lives. This became more apparent after the play's run was over. A few months after the play closed, Stephen McKinley Henderson told me that he found himself more aware of the presence of God as a result of the table readings. Awareness is an important concept in both Western and Eastern spiritualities. In the Western sense, it relates to an awareness of God; in the Eastern sense, it is an awareness of reality and one's self.

But Stephen surprised me by saying that he could pinpoint exactly when this had happened for him. During rehearsals for *Judas*, the great

African American actor Ossie Davis died. That afternoon, Adrian Martinez found Stephen sitting in their common dressing room looking bereft.

"What's wrong?" asked Adrian. Stephen told him how much he wanted to go to Davis's wake. "But I can't go," he said. "And I really feel I should be there."

Just at that moment, the stage manager, Monica Moore, walked in and told Stephen that he probably wouldn't be needed that day. "Well, I went right up to Harlem and stood in line outside the Abyssinian Baptist Church and experienced this wonderful fellowship with all the mourners. And the next day the funeral was on television, and Adrian taped it for me on his VCR. Then Mums said he would put it on DVD. And, you know, I took that DVD to Los Angeles later on, and so many people who weren't able to go to the funeral watched that DVD."

Stephen paused as he recalled that day. "I really felt a kind of heightened awareness of God. It made me aware that there are all these little kindnesses and transcendent things going on. And, hey, you might think that they're little, but they meant all the world to me."

He let out a deep, rumbling laugh. "You know, Father Jim," he said, "God can bless better than you can pray. He can always *outbless* you!"

The actor and director Frank Vitolo is an old friend of Phil and Stephen and many other members of LAB. Frank has acted in the movies *Fame* and *Working Girl* and in the television series *L.A. Law, Mad about You,* and *Law & Order.* He considers Phil, whom he has known for twenty years, "as much a part of my family as my wife and daughters." Frank attended the early table readings and became a fixture at rehearsals, sometimes filling in for a cast member who was unable to be there. His candor and sense of humor make him a naturally likable person. After the show closed, Frank, who counts himself a devout Christian "who still screws things up," described his reaction to the cast's study of the Gospels.

"To see my friends confronting that material, to see all those Bibles lying around their dressing rooms, and to think of them maybe finding their way to God was so moving that I would sometimes have to leave the room and have a good cry. Because I knew it was God who was doing that work."

One morning in late January, we were moved to a rehearsal space in a building across the street from Martinson Hall while the set for *Judas* was being constructed. There we began talking about the inherent humanity of the disciples. Many Christians who are interested in the saints tend to overlook their natural failings.

Elizabeth Rodriquez told me, "I just never thought of the saints as human when I was growing up. They were, you know, *saintly*. And there was this huge distance between them and us, between what they did and what we did."

More often than not, sanctity is confused with perfection, which means that the saints are often seen as either inhuman or superhuman. Thus the revelation of any flaws is viewed as a threat to their "image." When Pope John Paul II died, a few weeks after the play's opening, criticisms of his papacy or admissions of his personal failings were seen by many Catholics as off-limits—embarrassing blots on his saintly record. But no saint was perfect. Holiness makes its home among human imperfections.

Some of the saints could even be unpleasant, particularly in their single-minded pursuit of their vision. Stories of their quirky behavior are sometimes related by their most devoted admirers as marks of their underlying humanity. When Mother Teresa once visited the United

States, she immediately instructed the American sisters in her religious order to get rid of their washing machines. The sisters should be living more simply, she declared, and should wash the clothes and bedsheets of the sick by hand, as her sisters in India did.

The lives of a few well-known saints feature episodes of outright nastiness. Saint Jerome, a brilliant polymath who translated the Bible into Latin, was a noted theologian, writer, and spiritual director. He was also surprisingly uncharitable when confronted with opposition. In the early fifth century he wrote a snide public letter to a theologian named Rufinus, addressing him "my most simple-minded friend." For good measure, he said that his opponent walked "like a tortoise." Jerome continued with his invective even after Rufinus's death, when a gentler appraisal of the man would have been expected.

Likewise, Saint Cyril of Alexandria, archbishop of the Egyptian city from 412 to 444, is described by *Butler's Lives of the Saints* as "brave but sometimes over vehement, indeed violent." During a church council in Ephesus in 431, Cyril led a group of his followers who deposed and sent into exile a bishop who had disagreed with some of Cyril's theological writings. Reconciliation and forgiveness were apparently not his strong suits. Edward A. Ryan, a Jesuit professor and church historian, said wryly, "We don't know anything about the last ten years of Cyril's life. Those must have been the years in which he became a saint."

Another misconception is that the saints are carbon copies of one another: all of them blandly pious men and women locked in constant prayer. But even the most cursory glance at their biographies reveals an extraordinary diversity in their personalities, their likes and dislikes, and the courses their lives took. They worked, prayed, and loved differently. They thought differently, too—and even quarreled. Perhaps the earliest example of this is the fierce debate that took place around AD 51 between Saint Paul and Saints Peter, James, and John over whether the Christian message should be extended to non-Jews. Paul won out, and the gospel was taken to the "Gentiles," with Peter and his friends no doubt nursing disappointment for a time.

A striking example of the variety among saintly men and women is the counterpoint between Dorothy Day and Mother Teresa, near contemporaries. Dorothy Day, the American-born cofounder of the Catholic Worker movement, spent much of her life caring for the poor in the United States, not simply by opening up a network of homeless shelters, but also by advocating publicly and often loudly for systemic political change. She was frequently jailed for her nonviolent protests. Hers was what the writer Robert Ellsberg has called a "political kind of holiness." Mother Teresa, on the other hand, famously cared for the poor but also pointedly refrained from commenting on the political factors underlying the causes of poverty, except in the most general of terms. The two women had different ways of responding to the demands of Christianity.

A more contemporary understanding of sanctity is that it means not perfection, which is unattainable, but being true to the person you are meant to be, the person created by God. Believers are called to follow as best they can their individual paths to personal holiness. This is part of what the Second Vatican Council termed the "universal call to holiness." The goal of every Christian is to grow in love and charity, but this common goal is lived out in different ways.

The lives of the saints show us, as Karl Rahner wrote, what it means to be holy in *this* particular way. Mother Teresa was not meant to be Dorothy Day. And Saint Peter was not meant to be Saint Paul. "If St. Aloysius had been as I am," wrote Pope John XXIII in an entry in his journals in 1903, "he would have become holy in a different way." Or, as Thomas Merton put it: "For me to be a saint means to be myself." But being oneself, or even being a saint, does not mean being perfect.

This concept—the essential humanity of the saints—was absolutely central to Stephen's presentation of the story of Jesus and his disciples, and I didn't think it was possible to stress it too much. After all, it's difficult to listen to Saint Thomas, as played by Adrian Martinez, a stocky man with frizzy black hair, stand before you holding a beer and admit that Judas was "a bit of a jerk-off" if you haven't accepted the fundamental humanity of the apostles.

So the cast began talking about the disparate crew of apostles that Jesus gathered around himself. Matthew worked as a tax collector; as an employee of Rome, he would have been despised by the Jews in Palestine. Peter, Andrew, James, and John were simple fishermen from the backwater of Galilee. The idea that a supposed prophet chose to continue to hang out with friends from Galilee was shocking for sophisticated people of the time. ("Can anything good come out of Nazareth?" asks Nathanael in the New Testament.)

I recalled an insight from a Jesuit priest many years ago. Think about Peter, this Jesuit had said. The Galilean fisherman was at once good and deeply flawed. A man who repeatedly didn't "get it." A man who doubted the miracles he saw, questioned the mission, refused to allow for the possibility that Jesus would ever have to suffer, and denied his best friend three times. Of the original twelve apostles, Peter perhaps best exemplified what Avery Cardinal Dulles, the dean of American Catholic theologians, called the "obtuseness of the disciples." Yet this was the person whom, according to the Gospels, Jesus chose to lead his church—perhaps because Peter was the one who understood his own human flaws well enough to recognize his need for divine assistance.

It was clear, I suggested to the cast one day, why Jesus selected Peter. Peter was a strong man, full of passion and energy and zeal for spreading the message of Jesus. He was strong enough to lead the church. But he was also *weak*, because he understood the need for both confidence in God and humility before God. Peter was weak enough to lead the church.

For a few seconds, there was silence around the table. Finally, Phil sat up and said, "*What?*" I was happy that the insight seemed to strike the cast as forcefully as it had struck me all those years ago in the Jesuit novitiate.

Talking with cast members after the play had ended its run, I learned of the effects that our talks about the humanity of the saints had made. "I realized," said Adrian Martinez, "that these were real people dealing with real events and that real sacrifices were made in their lives. Thinking about it like that makes all those Bible stories seem more visceral and more relevant to the present day." For Jeffrey DeMunn, it was something of a revelation. "The saints and apostles had always been semimythical to me. But during the table readings, I thought, *Wait a minute! They were real human beings.* That was revolutionary and just opened up the whole play."

If I had been in theology studies, I would have said that the cast and I were engaging in exegesis, the careful breaking open of the text. When I described how seriously the director and the cast took their work, an elderly priest said to me, "We should all take the New Testament so seriously."

Not everyone around the table at those readings was a Catholic like me, or a Christian, or even a believer. But even for the nonbeliever, the story of Jesus seemed to exert an undeniable pull. In a few weeks, we would offer "talk-back" sessions following the performances, during which the audience could ask questions of the "creative staff" and the cast. During those sessions, I was surprised at how many of the cast members described themselves as lapsed Catholics. I knew that each of them had thought more deeply about the Gospel stories than some professed "good Christians" I know.

It was gratifying to be invited into the creative process of the play and into the spiritual lives of cast members. And my friendships with them grew quickly. Still, there were occasional reminders that they saw me as a priest first. During one rehearsal, Elizabeth launched into Saint Monica's spectacularly foulmouthed monologue. Coming at the beginning of *Judas*, it not only explains how Judas was able to get a hearing in Purgatory but also reveals the playwright's desire to wake up audiences with his vibrant language.

Saint Monica's monologue was one of my favorites, though ironically it had marked the occasion for an early disagreement with Stephen. On first hearing it, I objected to what I felt was a tone of excessive anger. "Saint Monica's in heaven, isn't she?" I asked Stephen. "Why is she so angry?" It continued to bother me that someone in the company of God and the saints, supposedly free of worry and care, would be portrayed as wrathful.

"No, no," said Stephen each time I brought it up. "Monica's not angry! She's just strong!"

Over time, I began to understand that Monica's fire expresses not anger as much as passion for helping others. In real life, Monica had spent years praying fervently on behalf of her libertine son. This same passion would enable her to approach God on behalf of Judas.

Elizabeth's in-your-face performance perfectly communicated Monica's consuming desire. Elizabeth is herself a passionate and outspoken woman, and I enjoyed seeing how well the actress brought that particular facet of her personality to bear in her portrayal of a fourth-century woman whom biographers often reduced to a weepy, controlling mother. In the play, Saint Monica professes annoyance that anyone would "dis" her after all she had done for the church. Wearing a slinky blue pantsuit and silvery boots, she addressed the audience:

SAINT MONICA. I *am* a Nag, and if I wasn't a Nag, I wouldn't never
made it to be no Saint, and the church wouldn't
a had no Father of the Church named Saint
Augustine—'cuz I birthed the m—f—, raised him,
and when he started messin' up, like, all the time
and constantly, I nagged God's ass to save him! I
nagged and nagged and nagged and nagged till
God got so tired of my s—t that he did save my son,
and my son—Saint Augustine—he stopped bangin'
whores and sippin' on some wine and he became
learn-ed, so f—n' learn-ed that he's known as one of
the Fathers of the Church, and you could look that
s—t up! Go ahead, look it up right now, I'll wait!

Toward the end of the scene, Elizabeth fluffed a line in front of Phil
Hoffman, covered her face in embarrassment, and said, "S———t!"

Then she flushed red and said, "Sorry, Father Jim!"

I laughed. "After that monologue, you apologize for just saying
s———t?"

Elizabeth looked surprised. "The other stuff was just the character.
That *s———t* was *me!*"

As the table readings ended and we began to move into rehearsals,
I finally got to see them act more regularly. And they were terrific. The
normally soft-spoken Sam stunned me when, as Judas, he suddenly
started shouting obscenities at John Ortiz, as Jesus, a few feet away
from me. His strong voice filled the theater.

Yul Vázquez, another gentle soul, played El-Fayoumy, the bombastic prosecuting attorney given to flattery. In just a few weeks, Yul
had become one of my favorite people in the cast. Unfailingly friendly,
exceedingly polite, and always affectionate, Yul, a slender man with

dark hair, would greet me with a hearty "Father Jim!" and throw his arms around me and plant a kiss on my cheek. He was impossible not to like and reminded me of Jesus' description of the apostle Nathanael in the Gospel of John: a man "in whom there is no deceit."

Like many in the cast, Yul came to acting in a roundabout way. (Kohl Sudduth called this experience "falling backwards into acting.") Born in Cuba, Yul emigrated with his mother when he was two years old. He grew up in a family that freely mixed Catholicism with indigenous religions such as Santería, an African-derived religion that believes in the influence of *orishas*, or spirits that can bring success or healing into a follower's life. "I grew up in a mystical household," he said, "full of ghosts and spirits and forces, and I always had a curiosity about mysticism and spirituality."

He told me a story about his niece, who once noticed a woman sitting in a corner of a room in his house. "Who's that lady in the wheelchair wearing the glasses?" Yul's niece asked his mother. Though no one else saw anything, his mother replied calmly, "Well, that's my grandmother."

But for all his interest in mysticism, as a young man Yul was more interested in music. By high school, he had taken up the guitar. He spent the decade after he graduated from high school playing in various rock bands, first in Miami and then in New York. He enjoyed performing but admitted to moments of despair, when he wondered if his career would ever take off. One day, a fellow band member's girlfriend, who worked in a local talent agency, suggested that Yul try out for a part in the Oliver Stone movie *The Doors*, which was casting. "Why don't you come down?" she said.

Yul showed up "completely clueless," with shoulder-length hair and ripped jeans, to what turned out to be a prestigious agency. "There are no accidents, Father Jim," said Yul when he recounted the story. The agent told him that if he was serious about acting he would have to take lessons and recommended William Esper.

He loved acting school. "You're dealing with all the subtleties and nuances of being human." While studying with Esper, he met Sam Rockwell, with whom he found a friendship that was both immediate and lasting. After a few months of classes three times a week, Yul asked Esper whether he should continue. "I can't tell you what to do," said his teacher. "But if you're asking me if you have talent, the answer is yes."

He decided to quit his band and gave up his career in music. "Which was completely *crazy*! I basically gambled with my entire life."

Movie roles came quickly: he was cast in *The Mambo Kings* as a Latino musician, which led to roles in other films, Broadway shows, and television series. His turn as a recurring character on *Seinfeld* helped elevate his profile in the industry, and a few months before *Judas* began, Yul completed a role in Steven Spielberg's blockbuster *War of the Worlds*.

In 1992, Yul was accepted into the LAByrinth Theater Company. "LAB is a place where real work and real acting happen. It was really about the streets and the struggles of living." And he loves acting. "I've had these moments when you just step out of the way and you're grounded and attentive, and, well, it's about as close to enlightenment as I've ever experienced."

Yul said that he has felt protected by God throughout his life, but he had lived in fear of being punished by God should he do anything wrong. A few years ago, feeling a sort of emptiness, he commenced his own spiritual journey. "I knew there was something out there, but I wasn't sure how to *get* there. So I began reading as much as I could."

He started with a book called *In Search of the Miraculous*, by P. D. Ouspensky, a disciple of the mystic G. I. Gurdjieff, the twentieth-century Russian-born spiritual teacher known for his teaching that human beings are asleep and need to be awakened to the possibility that they can control their lives. "That book blew my wig off," said Yul.

His interest in the mystic's ideas prompted him to join the Gurdjieff Foundation, in order to probe Gurdjieff's teachings in greater depth. Recently, he had begun to practice Kundalini yoga, and he was trying to meditate daily. Yul had also started to investigate the Jewish mystical tradition of Kabbalah and even the interplay between quantum physics and the divine. "I'm like a starving child," he said. "I have a curious nature and I love learning about all these traditions."

As for his Christian roots, he explained that God the Father had loomed larger in his life than Jesus had. "But now, with this play, I feel like I'm in school again. The brilliant thing is that the saints and the apostles weren't just these spiritual beings; they were real people. I know it sounds crazy, but I never thought of Saint Peter as a fisherman. He was just a guy!"

The story of Saint Matthew as dramatized in *Judas* made a clear impression on Yul. In the Gospel of Matthew, Jesus approaches the tax collector and says, "Follow me." Matthew, as a Jewish tax collector, would have been a detested person in his town, unclean to his fellow Jews. And so Jesus' call to him was all the more remarkable. As was Matthew's immediate response.

"'Follow me'!" said Yul wonderingly. "That's so simple, and it's so hard, isn't it?" Jeffrey DeMunn, who played Saint Matthew, felt similarly. "Matthew I loved!" he said after the play ended. "He just said okay, dropped everything, and gave himself over to Jesus 100 percent. As a result, he needed *nothing*. That's something I aspire to. To be able to let go of those fears and needs and desires is a real goal for me. I would love to just lay it all down and respond to an invitation like that."

I asked Yul if he felt that God had ever offered him the same kind of invitation. "Well," he said after a pause, "I feel that it's more like there are signs and guideposts along the way, and God says, 'You're on the right road, dude!'"

Shortly after I met Yul, a Jesuit friend thought that he recognized Yul's name, looked him up on the Internet, and told me that "Bob, the intimidating gay guy" was his favorite *Seinfeld* character. (Yul described the role as a "militant Latino gay thug.") But until this point, I had never seen him act.

One morning during the readings, Yul suddenly rose from the table and began speaking his lines with a strange Levantine sibilance. To laughter from the rest of the cast, he complimented one witness, Satan, on his attire: "Ooh, Sss*atan*, your *trous*ersss, they have a lovely *sheen* to them! Gucci?"

The rehearsals marked the first time I experienced the full effect of the cast's acting abilities, and their talent for moving from friendly voices to tears or emotion was startling. It was as if they had been carrying a latent power within them, and it was now on display. I was looking forward to seeing what they would do with this play on stage.

Jesuit Theater, a Nearly Forgotten History

The more time I spent with the group, the more I enjoyed them. But I also felt slightly guilty about spending so much time at the theater. With the show about to go into previews, I told a Jesuit friend that perhaps I should curtail my nights at the theater to be better rested for my work at the magazine. But when I described the joy I felt in working with the cast, crew, and creative team, he rolled his eyes and told me what an important ministry I was doing. "You're getting all your work done at the magazine, aren't you?" he asked.

When I nodded, he said, "You're right where a Jesuit should be. Besides, don't you remember the history of Jesuit theater?"

I felt like an idiot. Until that moment, I had failed to connect the long tradition of "Jesuit theater" with the work I was doing at the Public Theater. When I mentioned this to a friend, Brother Rick Curry, a Jesuit who had founded the National Theatre Workshop of the Handicapped and an actor himself, he grimaced. Curry had done his doctoral dissertation on the topic.

"Father Martin needs to reread some of his Jesuit history," he said pointedly.

The long, but now largely forgotten, history of the Jesuits and theater began almost as soon as the Jesuits were founded by Saint Ignatius of Loyola in 1540. As John W. O'Malley, SJ, notes in *The First Jesuits*, many of the first members of the Society of Jesus had been students at the University of Paris, where plays and academic celebrations were a part of the curriculum and an integral part of student education. When the Jesuits began founding their own schools, they applied what they had learned in Paris. "From their experience," O'Malley writes, "they saw the enthusiasm thus engendered especially in younger students, and they set about exploiting it for appropriating skills learned in the classroom."

Besides having students give orations and recite poetry, Jesuits specifically began producing plays and stage pieces as a means of educating children. There were other, more practical reasons for the emphasis on theater. The first plays at the Jesuit schools in Rome, performed around 1551, were also intended as alternate entertainment for students at the time of carnival celebrations in the city. Eventually the plays took on a life of their own, enabling the Jesuits to develop in the students important skills (public speaking, memory, Latin) while bringing attention to the various themes of the plays. These early plays focused mainly on tales taken from classical literature and—like *Judas*—stories from the Bible.

In this way, drama became an integral part of Jesuit education. O'Malley notes, "[T]he significance of theater in all its aspects for Jesuit colleges can hardly be overestimated."

According to Rick Curry, the tradition of Jesuit theater flowed naturally from the spirituality of the Jesuits. In his *Spiritual Exercises*, Saint Ignatius of Loyola encouraged his men to use their imagination in prayer. Jesuits were asked to engage in a "composition of place," in which they would imagine themselves in a particular Bible scene during their prayer. "The move from that kind of prayer to theater was an obvious one," Curry told me. Joseph F. MacDonnell, SJ, makes that same point in his wonderful book, *Companions of Jesuits*, a boon to anyone interested in this unusual story.

Jesuit priests and brothers soon became known throughout Europe for their talent and expertise in theatrical productions. *The Catholic Encyclopedia* estimates (conservatively, it says) that between 1650 and 1700, there existed among the five hundred extant Jesuit schools a "vast international chain of the same number of playhouses, engaged in a coordinated production of plays." The same source estimates that an incredible one hundred thousand plays were produced during this period. That includes at least two plays a year in each of the schools, with several others staged for special occasions, such as royal visits. As a child, Louis XIV was often a member of the audience at the Jesuits' prestigious Clermont College, and in 1653, as sovereign, he attended a performance there accompanied by the exiled king of England.

What distinguished the Jesuit theatrical productions from those of their rivals was the often ingenious use of scenery and stage business, including intricately designed backdrops, realistic props, and complicated mechanical devices, such as trapdoors for ghostly apparitions, flying machines, and apparatuses to simulate clouds. Rick Curry notes that Jesuits either invented or perfected the screen known as the scrim, as well as the trapdoor. A Jesuit teaching mathematics in a Jesuit school might be enlisted to devise a series of pulleys to raise and lower backdrops. René Fülöp-Miller, in *The Power and Secret of the Jesuits*, writes: "On every conceivable occasion, the Jesuit producers made divinities appear in the clouds, ghosts rise up and eagles fly over the heavens, and the effect of these stage tricks was further enhanced by machines producing thunder and the noise of the winds. They even found ways and means of reproducing with a high degree of technical perfection the crossing of the Red Sea by the Israelites, storms at sea, and similar difficult scenes."

Indeed, while other school dramas at the time relied mainly on actors simply reading from scripts, the Jesuit instructors understood the impact of the visual. Costumes, for example, were considered highly important. In 1685, at the English Jesuit college of St. Omers, a report detailed the amount the school had allocated for "The Wardrobe for the Stage." One play at the school called for thirty costumes, with the headmaster requesting funds for materials that included "cloth of gold, brocades and silks, gems, silk stockings, and gloves." Notes from a later text from the school show that "acting suits" were as much a concern for the students as baseball or football uniforms were to later boys, as William H. McCabe, SJ, notes in *An Introduction to the Jesuit Theater*. St. Omers boys often wrote home to ask for additional money for their costumes. (In his dissertation, Curry describes other Jesuits at the time approaching the local nobility to borrow costumes.)

The scale of some of these plays beggars belief. In his magisterial work *A History of the Society of Jesus*, Jesuit historian William V. Bangert offers a description of what can only be called a big-budget production: a play staged in 1574 called *Constantine*, written by one of the teachers in the Jesuit school in Munich. "The town itself, beautifully decorated, was the stage," Bangert writes. "One thousand actors took part, and it lasted two days. The climactic point was the entry of Emperor Constantine into Rome driving four span of horses and surrounded by four hundred horsemen in glittering armor"—something even jaded New York theater crowds might consider impressive.

To say that these performances garnered "good reviews" would be a vast understatement, considering the public's nearly ecstatic reception. At one performance in seventeenth-century Vienna, the audience numbered three thousand. The Viennese court and nobility at the time were also in the habit of attending Jesuit performances. Police from neighboring towns had to be called upon to keep the surging crowds in check.

Besides the elaborate visual effects, music was used to the full. By the later 1700s, the musical and spoken portions of the Jesuit dramas had assumed equal importance. In an article in the *Oxford Companion to the Theatre*, one writer connects the growth of the Jesuit drama to later developments in opera. "The music dramas, cantatas, and oratorios of the Jesuits dating from the first half of the seventeenth century were the forerunners of the cult of opera which developed at the German Courts; opera in its turn suggested some of the more potent scenic and auditory effects of later Jesuit dramas."

Not surprisingly, these plays had a powerful effect on the students at the Jesuit schools. And it is here that the Jesuit tradition would most influence the development of modern drama. Some of the most prominent European playwrights of the time received their education at Jesuit colleges, where plays were a staple of the curriculum. Molière, Pierre Corneille, Jean Racine, and Voltaire were all students at Jesuit schools in France, and Lope de Vega and Pedro Calderón de la Barca were students in Spain. Molière, in fact, had written and acted in plays while a student at the Jesuit Clermont College. It was at Clermont that he also developed some of his strong opinions about the church hierarchy, which were reinforced by his drama teachers, who were then critical of some hierarchical abuses. Later, when Molière was forbidden to produce plays publicly, the Jesuits allowed him to use their theaters.

The curtain fell on the great era of Jesuit theater in 1773, when Pope Clement XIV suppressed the Society of Jesus. Long suspected of political intrigue, the Jesuits had run afoul of a variety of European monarchs and powerful political figures, and there was great rejoicing in many quarters when the pope disbanded the order. After its restoration in 1814, and facing a growing anticlericalism in Europe, a chastened Society of Jesus was less willing to draw attention to itself with public spectacles that drew thousands into town squares. Also, according to Rick Curry, the technical know-how that had been passed down from Jesuit to Jesuit was lost for a time after the suppression.

The legacy of Jesuit theater continues today in quieter ways— through Jesuit teachers who stage plays and musicals in high schools and universities around the world, and through the work of Jesuits who specialize in drama and theater, like Brother Rick Curry and his National Theatre Workshop of the Handicapped.

The more time I spent with LAB, the more I was reminded by my friends (a few of whom direct plays in Jesuit high schools) of Jesuit theater's long history. The work exemplified the Jesuit ideal of "finding God in all things," the distinctive spirituality that embraces some often surprising ways of communicating God's presence in the world. Johann Wolfgang von Goethe, the great German writer and poet, adverted to this in his book *Italian Journey* after seeing a Jesuit play. "This public performance has again convinced me of the cleverness of the Jesuits."

It has long been a practice of the Jesuits to go to places on the margins of the church, to be with those whom some might consider unlikely candidates to hear the gospel message. Jesuits have always worked in unusual settings: among my friends in the Society of Jesus are physicians, lawyers, writers, scientists, Web site designers, and actors. And in all these settings Jesuits try not only to communicate God's presence but also to experience God's presence, which, in all these situations, is already there. I felt I was doing some of that with the cast of *Judas*.

Being reminded of the history of Jesuit theater made me more grateful that I had been invited to work with the cast and crew of *Judas*. It seemed a continuation, if in a minuscule way, of the work done by the early Jesuits in theater. And I was happy to discover that in addition to producing classical works, the Jesuits themselves, as well as their students, were also in the habit of writing their own plays—a detail that reminded me of the early days of the LAByrinth Theater Company.

Gradually, the work of the play turned from theologizing to acting and directing. The actors started, as they said, to "get up" and "move around." The more they memorized their lines, the more they could be "off book." But when I protested that I shouldn't come any longer, since my work was finished, Phil demurred.

"Come whenever you can," he said. "You're always welcome."

Still, I realized that the time for freewheeling discussions with the cast was drawing to a close. Some days, in my enthusiasm, I interrupted Phil with largely extraneous theological reflections, when it seemed that he and the cast probably wanted to move on. After all, while I would have been happy to discuss the complicated social position of tax collectors in first-century Palestine yet again, Saint Matthew had to learn his "blocking" and rehearse his scene in time for previews, which were fast approaching.

"How many times did you interrupt Philip Seymour Hoffman today?" a Jesuit friend kept asking me. So I started to come to the theater less frequently and to pray for the cast more at home. But as the rehearsals continued, and the actors began to confess some of their worries and struggles, as well as their joys and excitements, I found that my role shifted from theological adviser to chaplain. That was a role I was happier to play.

ACT 3: FULLY HUMAN, FULLY DIVINE

February

On the days when I was too busy to visit the Public, I would often hear from company members, usually Sam or Stephen, who would update me on what funny things had occurred, who was sick, who was frustrated, who was struggling, and who had done especially well.

Toward the end of January, the cast gathered one afternoon around a small cardboard mock-up of Martinson Hall, with Phil and the set designer, Andromache Chalfant, describing the performance space they had planned. The seats would face the stage in a sort of U. Most of the seats would be placed on risers above the plain concrete floor. On the floor would be a desk for the judge, two chairs for the lawyers, and a single chair from which witnesses would give testimony. The jury members (who would include some people from the audience) would sit on the sides of the performance space. A catwalk would run above the stage. In the middle of the catwalk, over the judge's desk, would be a deep well, in which Judas would sit, silent and motionless. At stage right would be a sort of pulpit, on top of a column, that would hover above the audience: from there the saints would offer their monologues.

The Hope of Results

The construction of the set not only reminded everyone that opening night was approaching, but also highlighted some worries about the direction of the play. Just a few weeks before previews, the script still was in almost daily flux, and the ending seemed to change every week.

Around this time, Stephen admitted to me his difficulty in completing the play. His working pattern was hardly a secret. As detailed in a story that appeared in February in the Sunday *New York Times*, Stephen's approach combined hard work and procrastination, something that made him the object of good-natured teasing among LAB members (he often made light of it, too) but that could also be a source of considerable pain.

After spending a day at the readings, or reviewing the play with Phil, or undertaking additional historical research, or talking with me about one of the characters, Stephen would decide to finish or polish a scene that the actors were waiting for.

Then he would proceed to spend a few hours cleaning his messy apartment. Or he would watch television. Or smoke. Or take a nap. Or, with the best intentions, he would sit down at the computer and stare at the screen. The closer we got to previews, the more this began to plague him.

Though he trusted that God would somehow help him, he still felt stuck. For one thing, the subject matter could be overwhelming. "This is about some deep stuff," he said, "and sometimes I feel like I'm not smart enough to tackle it." There was something else: he was afraid of letting people down. "The biggest obstacle is the fear of failure and the fear of really embracing the task. I feel this huge responsibility to the company, to the cast, to Phil, and to God. And to my own expectations."

In general, he wanted to write but couldn't. His situation reminded me of Saint Paul's utterly human cry in his letter to the Romans: "I do not do the good I want, but the evil I do not want is what I do." Stephen's procrastination wasn't an evil, but Paul's lament got at the heart of the playwright's stuckness: his desire to do one thing and his tendency to do the opposite.

Phil Hoffman understood this part of Stephen's working life, having directed five of his plays. "I guess I know more about that than do those actors who are working with him for the first time. He has a way of pushing himself at the very last hour. But I know that it will all work out in the end." In Phil, Stephen had a confident and patient working partner.

Still, I felt sorry for Stephen and tried to encourage him as best I could. I knew he understood all the historical material that undergirded the play and that he could write terrific scenes for the actors. I knew he had a good, even great, play within him that would touch many people.

It was a delicate situation. For one thing, our working styles were completely at odds (I like to finish writing projects months ahead of time), and so it was hard for me to understand his "way of proceeding," as Jesuits say. For another, I hadn't the heart to lecture him about his working habits, since he seemed so physically worn out. When tired, Stephen had a habit of squeezing his eyes shut and then opening them wide, as if to dispel his fatigue. He did this more and more as the weeks went by.

A few months after the play closed, the *New Republic*'s theater critic, Robert Brustein, would list Stephen as one of the best people working in the theater today. So who was I to tell Stephen how to write? After all, I knew nothing about writing a play. Perhaps procrastination was even part of his creative process. (Some cast members believed this.) And I didn't want to overstep my role as his "theological adviser" and offer the playwright perhaps unwanted and unwelcome pastoral advice.

In the end, friendship simply took over. It was hard to see him struggle, and I couldn't resist giving him advice, especially when it seemed that his discouragement was giving way to a measure of despair. The playwright was feeling an increasing level of frustration from some of the actors. One of his closest friends in the company, Liza Colón-Zayas, told me after the play ended, "That play was hard for us not so much because of the material, but because for a long time it wasn't even written!" Others were tarter in expressing their frustration.

The irony that Stephen was writing a play about despair while experiencing it in his own life was not lost on him. Both of us wondered if his despairing of completing his ambitious project might give him some insight not only into ways in which Satan is traditionally seen as operating (in Christian theology, often subtly tempting humans to despair) but also into the plight of his lead character. Ultimately it would: Judas's last words in the final scene, when Jesus asks him to accept forgiveness, are "I can't."

Nevertheless, one thing that my life as a Jesuit and my study of Christian spirituality has taught me is that in one's personal life, despair is to be avoided at all costs. Writing in the sixteenth century, Saint Ignatius of Loyola spoke about despair in *The Spiritual Exercises*. A former soldier and courtier who became a priest, Ignatius faced significant periods of despair in his early life. His spiritual legacy, often called "Ignatian spirituality," focuses on, among other things, discernment—that is, understanding the various impulses of the human heart in order to make wise decisions and devote oneself to the service of God.

It is characteristic of what Ignatius calls the "enemy" of human nature to "cause gnawing anxiety, to sadden, and to set up obstacles."

Ignatius, an insightful spiritual master with a clear-eyed grasp of human psychology, concluded, "In this way he unsettles these persons by false reasons aimed at preventing their progress." In Stephen's case, despair would only lead to an unfinished play, unsettled actors, and a bereft playwright.

I shared an insight with Stephen that came, once again, from Thomas Merton. A few months before, I had been asked by Jesuit superiors to refrain from writing on a topic concerning the Catholic Church that had been deemed "too controversial." In any event, I had turned for guidance to Daniel Berrigan, the Jesuit social activist who had been jailed in the 1960s for his nonviolent resistance to the Vietnam War. Berrigan had been a great friend of Thomas Merton, who himself had been silenced (from writing about nonviolence during the cold war). I thought Berrigan might be able to give me some perspective on the frustration I was experiencing.

In response to a brief letter, Father Berrigan counseled patience, asking me to remember that I was in this "for the long haul," and mailed me a quote from Thomas Merton. It was taken from Merton's "Letter to a Young Activist," written in 1966. I had posted it above my desk a few months before I met Stephen.

One night I read it to him over the phone. Stephen's worries were partly centered on the expectations of other actors, his friends, and his professional colleagues, and also on what the reviewers would think of his play. I hoped that Merton's thoughts might help him gain some distance from all of this. When I had first encountered these lines, I felt that Merton was speaking directly to me. Now the Trappist monk could have been writing to Stephen.

> Do not depend on the hope of results. When you are doing
> the sort of work you have taken on . . . you may have to
> face the fact that your work will be apparently worthless

and even achieve no result at all, if not perhaps results opposite to what you expect. As you get used to this idea you start more and more to concentrate not on the results but on the value, the rightness, the truth of the work itself. And there, too, a great deal has to be gone through, as gradually you struggle less and less for an idea and more and more for specific people. The range tends to narrow down, but it gets much more real. In the end, it is the reality of personal relationships that saves everything.

My relationship with Stephen became more complex as I continued to offer him a bit of spiritual counseling about his personal situation, but I was grateful that he took me into his confidence. I hoped I was being of some help and started to pray for him more.

At the same time, Sam was facing some rocky times and had begun sharing some of his difficulties with me. Over the past few months, I had grown increasingly friendly with Sam, and my initial impression of the actor had been proven correct. Sam was a kind and openhearted man who was willing to listen to advice. From the time of our first meeting, I had never heard him say a cross word about anyone in the cast or crew (or anyone else, for that matter). Difficulties with the production were framed as frustrations, not complaints. I felt that I could learn a lot from him about humility, as well as charity.

The evening that Sam and I stopped by the Jesuit church after our visit to the Metropolitan Museum, we ended up having a long conversation in the empty pews. Not long afterward, following a long day of readings, Sam, who had told me that he was not religious, asked if we could go to a church to talk. I wondered if I could find a church that was open in the early evening. We walked a few blocks north to St. Francis Xavier, the Jesuit parish on Sixteenth Street, and found a side door that was open, casting a warm light onto the dark stone steps.

As the parish choir practiced in the background, we found two empty chairs placed before a small side altar that was incised with the motto of the Jesuit order: *Ad majorem Dei gloriam,* "for the greater glory of God." It was moving to listen to Sam's honest recounting of his struggles, a window into the life of a person I had, after all, met just recently. Being a priest often means that I am invited into people's personal lives—some I know well, some I barely know at all, and some I will soon know well. Near the end of our discussion, to my surprise, Sam asked if I could help him pray.

Afterward, Sam began to wonder if perhaps some of his personal life might not be mirroring that of Judas: Sam, too, was dealing with the human temptation to give in to despair and anger and fear. "Despair is pretty self-indulgent, isn't it?" he said, summing up Thomas Merton. "But it's a fascinating emotion for an actor to play."

He paused. "I guess I recommend it for an actor, but I don't recommend it for a person."

We left the church and shared a cab ride uptown: Sam was going to see a friend in a Broadway show; I was hurrying back for a book club meeting at a Jesuit parish.

My prayer for Sam was that, whether or not it helped him understand his character, he would soon be led out of his dark night. It was the same prayer I was praying for Stephen.

For many in the cast, it was a tense time, and even in the midst of the bonhomie, one could sense growing concern over the slow progress of the script. Phil later confided to me that he was in a tough position, being a kind of moderator between the actors, who wanted more pages, and Stephen, who was still working on the play. "And I know it's hard for the actors if they don't see the entire play," said Phil. But the supportive environment of LAB seemed to help the actors feel less stress than they might have in another setting.

So did occasional flashes of humor. During one particularly tense rehearsal, Phil, sitting quietly in the risers, asked John Ortiz to try out his entrance as Jesus. The back wall of the stage consisted of a long hallway punctuated by a series of semiopaque windows. Many in the cast would make their entrances through a doorway at the end of the hallway, which opened directly onto the stage. For his entrance, John was to walk slowly down the dramatically lit hallway, open the door, and emerge onto the stage, bathed in a bright light.

As John slowly walked past the windows, his outline illuminated by a yellow light, the previously taciturn Phil suddenly leaped out of his chair. He ran across the stage, knelt on the floor, and shouted deliriously, "Jesus! Jesus! Oh my God, it's *Jesus*! It's really you!"

Laughter followed, and the tension in the room lessened significantly.

Over time, Stephen wrote a handful of superb monologues that successfully described some of Judas's motivation for betraying Jesus. These last-minute additions would be some of the most effective parts of the play. My favorite was Saint Peter's tale of meeting Jesus, partly because of the quiet delivery of Mums Grant, who stood over the audience in the pulpit fingering a fishing net. Saint Peter was clad as a current-day fisherman, wearing overalls, boots, and a khaki-colored hat festooned with brightly colored fishing lures.

"My name is Peter," he says as he carefully mends his net. "They got a Basilica named after me in Rome, which is ironic, 'cuz, back in the day, if you even said the word 'Rome' in my presence—more than likely I'd a beat you with my stick."

Peter tells the story, loosely based on the Gospel of Luke, of meeting Jesus of Nazareth by the Sea of Galilee in the early morning. After

right? Jesus made it even simpler. He had just one commandment: Love your neighbor as yourself!"

I asked Mums how he viewed organized religion now. "I'm tossed," he said. On the one hand, he felt that Christianity offers an ideology that's been so affected by social norms and cultural prejudices that "there's no way it could be pure." On the other hand, "I know the Gospels fairly well, and I think if Jesus were around today, he'd be turning over the tables and asking us what we were *doing* with our lives!"

His stance toward religion, however, has changed as he's grown older. His next comment reminded me of Saint Paul's first letter to the Corinthians, where he tells the Christian community in Corinth that upon becoming a man, he "put an end to childish ways."

"When I was younger," said Mums, "I remember yawning in the pews. Those stories just went in one ear and out the other. When you're young, you're just sort of *responding* to things. But now that I'm thirty-five, I'm thinking about how to make things work in life, and how to attain happiness. And *at base*, in the Gospels there is still this teaching of love that I need. I mean, people still f--k things up, and it's hard to get to church, but this is opening things up for me. Saint Peter is helping me wrap my arms around all this. So right now I'm feeling that it's no coincidence that I'm doing a play on the Gospels."

Who Is Jesus, Anyway?

The day before the first night of previews, John and Sam rehearsed the final scene in front of Phil, Stephen, and me. Stephen came into the rehearsal space bleary-eyed and carrying a cup of coffee. Phil also looked wan, and when he pulled off his knit cap his hair was plastered to his skull; he had just come from a photo shoot for the poster of

Capote. When I saw the photo months later outside a movie theater, I remembered Phil remarking how strange it was trying to be in character while being photographed.

John and Sam ran through the intense scene, in which Jesus confronts Judas, offering him forgiveness in the face of Judas's increasing anger and despair. Each time, they shouted their lines back and forth with such intensity that I wondered if they could ever do it as passionately again, and each time they did.

At one point, John, wearing a long-sleeved T-shirt and faded jeans, sat on the dusty floor and said, "I'm not sure how I'm supposed to be relating to Judas. Am I a man and know him as a man? Or am I God and know everything about him?" Phil had encouraged John to make Jesus as human as possible, while never losing sight of the deep spiritual strength of the man. It would be a difficult balance.

John's artistic dilemma reflected what he would describe as his personal struggles with faith. John was raised a desultory Catholic and had quickly drifted from the church, finding other religious traditions, such as Buddhism, more nourishing. But after his marriage to a Catholic woman, he found himself drawn back to the Catholic Church, specifically to his childhood parish in Bedford-Stuyvesant.

"When I was young," he said, "I was something of a free spirit and went to places that weren't very rooted or grounded at all. I guess coming back to my faith is about finding my roots, finding a foundation." Onstage he frequently felt a sense of connection with the larger world. He now sought that same feeling in his daily life.

God had been a strong, if distant, presence during his childhood and adolescence, "someone I would meet when I had died," he said. "But in the last several years, things have changed. Now he's more someone I meet while I'm alive. Someone I am aware of more in the here and now."

But while God now felt close, Jesus of Nazareth remained distant, a "mythical, almost magical, superstitious figure," he said. "I was really turned off when people talked about Jesus like this superstar. Their relationship with him seemed totally blown out of proportion. It was *ridiculous* to me!"

His acceptance of the role of Jesus did not simply reflect a desire to participate in Stephen's new play; it was also part of his quest to understand Jesus. "One of the main reasons I took what was originally a small part was to help me along my spiritual quest. I wanted to learn all that I could about Jesus."

He mentioned that he had also recently quit drinking. "I figured I needed all the help I could get, and maybe playing the part of Jesus would help me get some answers." He laughed when he recalled this. "I guess it was kind of selfish of me!"

John's struggle to understand how to play Jesus was not just a personal creative dilemma; it also reflected the ancient theological struggle to understand the two "natures" of Jesus Christ. Was he divine or human?

The traditional answer in Christian theology is that Jesus is "fully human and fully divine." But had you questioned a Christian in the second century, you might not have gotten that exact response. During the first few centuries of the church's existence, questions about the identity of Jesus bedeviled bishops, theologians, and laypersons, prompting excommunications, declarations of anathema, and charges of heresy.

It was inevitable that the early Christian communities would take up the matter. The Reverend Richard McBrien, a Catholic priest and professor of theology at Notre Dame, offers in *Catholicism*, his widely used textbook, three reasons why the early Christians would have explored the issue in great depth. First, like anyone else, the early Christians were naturally inquisitive people. Second, the challenge of dissenting opinions would have made a clear enunciation of the faith critical for the unity of the fledgling community. And third, the need to communicate Christian beliefs to the larger world required a clear theological message.

Questions about Jesus' nature would have been natural for anyone with even a passing familiarity with Jewish belief and Greek philosophy. The early Christians would have found support for the idea of a *purely* divine Jesus in the biblical texts; many Gospel passages—such as those describing the miracles and the Resurrection—portray a superhuman Jesus. And, as difficult as this may be for the agnostic who wants to follow a Jesus who is simply human, John Meier points out that the four Gospels find the most common ground in their claims about the miraculous deeds of Jesus. "The statement that Jesus acted as and was viewed as an exorcist and healer during his public ministry has as much historical corroboration as almost any other statement we can make about the Jesus of history. Indeed, as a global affirmation about Jesus and his ministry it has much better attestation than many other assertions made about Jesus, assertions that people often take for granted."

Meier concludes that anyone seeking to portray the historical Jesus "without giving due weight to his fame as a miracle-worker is not delineating this strange and complex Jew, but rather a domesticated Jesus reminiscent of the bland moralist created by Thomas Jefferson."

Even Jesus' *detractors* alluded to the miracles. For instance, the Gospels report the Pharisees complaining that Jesus has healed someone on the Sabbath. (Some argue, however, that this is merely a clever ploy by the Gospel writers.) Jesus' detractors were not bothered by the *fact* that he performed miracles. They were more interested in the origin of his power: was it from God or from Satan?

And while belief in the miracles performed by Jesus of Nazareth is ultimately a question of faith, there are independent, or extrabiblical, sources that attest to his prowess as a miracle worker. The Jewish historian Flavius Josephus, writing in AD 93, described Jesus in his *Antiquities of the Jews* as a *paradoxon ergon poietes*: a "worker of wondrous deeds."

But for the devout Jew interested in the Christian movement, there was one big problem: if there was only one God, how could Jesus be divine? Saint Irenaeus of Lyons, in his influential second-century tract *Against Heresies*, wrote: "The Father is God, and the Son is God." Wasn't this an affront to monotheism? The Hebrew Scriptures have God saying, "I am the Lord your God . . . you shall have no other gods before me." This alone would have been a stumbling block for Jews who wanted to accept Christianity.

Moreover, if Jesus was divine, would that mean that he *wasn't* human? And if he wasn't human, would that mean that he didn't suffer during the Crucifixion? But that notion was contradicted by the Gospel narratives of the last few hours of his life. And it denied the value of his suffering in the lives of many believers.

Much of what is known about what historians term the "Christological controversies" of the early church was preserved in the writings of those who *won* the debates. The losing arguments were eventually labeled heresies and therefore had fewer disciples to preserve them. The available evidence, though, indicates two heretical positions.

The first was that Jesus only *appeared* to be human. The groups who maintained this position were gathered under the umbrella term *Docetists* (from the Greek word *dokein*, meaning "to appear"). The Docetists believed that Jesus was simply God appearing to be a human being, almost pretending.

Not surprisingly, many early church leaders argued forcefully against this position, which effectively denied the humanity of Jesus, making his sufferings nothing more than good acting. "There is only one physician," wrote Saint Ignatius of Antioch, "both carnal and spiritual, born and unborn, God become man."

The second position was held by the Adoptionists, who believed that Jesus was simply a human being and not divine at all. Jesus of Nazareth was merely the "adopted" son of God. The Ebionites, for example, held that Jesus was a human being born naturally of Joseph and Mary.

Some attempts at a middle ground held that Jesus was something greater than just a human being but not exactly God. The most popular of these middle grounds was put forth by the doctrine known as Arianism, named after Arius, the fourth-century priest who was its main proponent. Arius stated that for God to have imparted his "substance" to another being, God would have to be divisible or changeable, something that the Greek mind-set would have definitively rejected. Therefore, Arius concluded, the Word of God, or the divine Son who the Gospel of John says took flesh in Jesus, must have been a *created* being, a creature who was dependent on God. Or, in Arius's famous formulation, "there was once when he [Jesus] was not." For Arius, Jesus was in some sense more divine than other human beings, but he was not equal to God.

What might seem now to be abstruse questions about the nature of Jesus were actually followed carefully by many everyday Christians. During my theology studies, I read with amazement how Arius, living in Alexandria, enjoyed what the historian Henry Chadwick calls in *The Early Church* "an immense following both among the young women and among the dockers for whom he wrote theological sea-shanties." (It would be the only time during my studies that I came across the phrase *theological sea-shanties*.)

In the early fourth century, the emperor Constantine, recently converted to Christianity, grew increasingly intolerant of disunity in the church, which had begun to threaten the unity of his empire. To settle these questions of the nature of Jesus, Constantine convened the Council of Nicaea in 325. There the assembled bishops ultimately settled on a theological middle ground: Jesus was not created and was not less than God. This statement definitively rejected Arianism. Jesus was not "made" by God; he was God, and he was of the same "substance" or "being" of God the Father. The Nicene Creed, written during that council, is still familiar to Catholics today, who pronounce it during their Sunday Masses: "We believe in one Lord, Jesus Christ . . . begotten, not made, one in Being with the Father."

In a few centuries, then, Christianity had moved from a religion animated by personal experience with Jesus to one based primarily on common Scriptures to one that included strict doctrinal formulations and decrees. This last variation represented quite a distance from the unwieldy Jesus who caused havoc and who infuriated the religious authorities of his time by setting aside some of their legalisms.

Something else was happening as well. As Roger Haight, SJ, told us in theology studies, "Jesus moved from being a prophet to an object of worship."

But the Council of Nicaea was hardly the final word on the matter. The next several decades saw a dizzying array of interpretations of Nicaea, each accenting Jesus' divinity or humanity in a different way. In graduate studies, it took my church history class weeks to slog its way through the writings of the various schools of the time. (One of my professors bluntly called it a "morass.") The Alexandrians, for example, suggested that Jesus need have no human soul at all. On the other side were the Antiochenes, who emphasized the humanity of Christ. Other schools would imply that Jesus had two distinct "minds" and "wills," one divine and one human.

One of the Antiochenes, a bishop of Constantinople named Nestorius, suggested that Mary could not be said to be the "mother of God," a title familiar to most Catholics today, but only the "mother of Jesus."

When I read about Nestorius in graduate school, I thought, *That doesn't sound so crazy.* But had I been living in the fifth century, I would have found myself on the wrong side of the Council of Ephesus, which in 431 took aim at Nestorius, condemning his writings and deposed him as bishop. After the Council of Ephesus, Nestorius was forced into exile.

I've always felt sorry for the poor bishop, and when we were asked in one church history class to pick our "favorite heresy," I chose Nestorianism. Interestingly, a few Nestorian churches still endure, some in Iraq, Iran, and Syria, the direct descendants of this early "heretical" belief.

Ultimately, the Christian community would accept the conclusion of the Council of Chalcedon, which, in 451, reaffirmed that Jesus was both fully human and fully divine: God incarnate. But while Chalcedon formulated this important idea in Christian theology, it made it no less difficult for Christians to understand it. It's an almost impossible idea to grasp—still a "mystery," to use a hackneyed term.

Today, if you asked random Christians about their understanding of Jesus, some would likely paint a picture of a sort of heavenly know-it-all, blissfully removed from the plane of ordinary human beings. Others would say that while they certainly see him as a great preacher, they have a hard time accepting all those miracle stories. In other words, at least a few contemporary Christians are closet Docetists, and a good deal more are closet Adoptionists.

During the readings for *Judas*, Stephen McKinley Henderson shared with me his way of approaching the question of Jesus' nature: "My faith is bound to the belief that he is the Messiah. But what's most meaningful to me is his humanity, because it means that Jesus understands what it means to be human."

John Ortiz found himself emphasizing Jesus' human side and was drawn to his quiet strength. "One of the big differences between this and all the other characters I've done is his inner peace," said John. "In other roles, there is all this conflict and chaos and even violence. With Jesus, there is a similar passion, but not as much conflict. It's all about clarity and peace." It sounded to me like a fine balance between the human and the divine.

Still, I knew that—as was the case in the early church—no matter how one portrayed Jesus of Nazareth, someone's idea about Jesus would be challenged. If he was shown as only human, it scandalize devout Christians who considered his miraculous deeds central to their faith. But if he was portrayed as only divine, it would upset those who were drawn to his humanity. John's original question turned on what theologians call the "self-knowledge" of Jesus. How did Jesus understand *himself*? Did he know he was the Son of God? Did he know the fate that would befall him?

The answers to those questions depend on one's approach to Jesus' divinity, which argues for his omniscience, and his humanity, which argues for his possessing a more limited knowledge of things.

How did Jesus see himself? In her book *Consider Jesus*, Sister Elizabeth Johnson, a professor of theology at Fordham University, describes how the early church struggled to understand who Jesus was. Johnson is an expert on Christology, the theological discipline that focuses on questions surrounding the person of Jesus Christ. In a chapter entitled "Jesus' Self-Knowledge," she lays out a peculiar conundrum: If Jesus knew he was God, then he could hardly be said to have lived a human life. But if he was God, then how could he *not* know this, since God knows everything? Johnson pointedly reminds readers that however he understood himself, Jesus would not have used the language of the early church fathers. And, as the Protestant theologian Krister Stendahl has written, the ancient world did not have the same idea of "self-consciousness" that we do today.

"We cannot know for sure what he thought about himself," writes Johnson in *Consider Jesus*. "Obviously Jesus did not wake up in the morning and look in the mirror and say, *I am the Son of God with a truly human nature and a truly divine nature.*"

Nor is it likely that he arrived at an understanding of his identity and mission in one moment. Rather, Johnson argues that, like other men and women, Jesus gradually grew in his knowledge of who he was. "It takes his whole life for him to understand himself in concrete terms."

This is the approach that seems most sensible to me. (Although with any of these theories, the best theological answer may be "Who knows?") It is difficult, if not impossible, to imagine that as a young adolescent working in his father's carpentry shop in Nazareth, Jesus arrived at the notion that he was the Messiah all at once. It may be more likely that such an understanding dawned on him gradually. As an adolescent, he probably read the Hebrew Scriptures, studying the traditional history of his people and the oppression they suffered in Egypt—and continued to suffer at the hands of the Romans. Later, as Jesus took up his carpentry work and probably traveled around Galilee and the surrounding areas, he might have encountered firsthand the suffering of the Jewish people and felt his heart, as the New Testament says of him later in life, "moved with pity."

Perhaps the carpenter from Nazareth, while feeling a growing sense of compassion for those who suffered, also noticed within himself the desire to help in some yet undefined way.

Yet about this critical period in the life of Jesus of Nazareth, the time between the ages of twelve and thirty—when he began what is called his public ministry—there is absolutely nothing known. Surprisingly, none of the four Gospels mentions anything about his young adulthood, a time when even today men and women are focused on questions of identity. Scripture scholars often call this period of Jesus' life the "hidden life."

But even when he reached the age of thirty and began his public ministry, Jesus of Nazareth may *still* have been unclear about who he was. At the beginning of his public ministry, Jesus seems surprisingly unsure about what he is supposed to do. One could argue that when Jesus went to the Jordan River to be baptized by his cousin John the Baptist, it was because he was attracted, like many Jews at the time, to John's fiery preaching. That is, Jesus may have gone to hear what John had to say and to see if it would help him understand what he was meant to do.

The Scripture scholar John Dominic Crossan suggests that Jesus also would have learned from John's approach and ultimate execution what would and would not work. Crossan suggests that John the Baptist was hoping for God to come as a warrior who would act violently against Israel's enemies, and that John's aim was to swell the ranks of repentant Jews through baptism until those ranks prompted the coming of the messianic age. Others add that Jesus also would have had a deep appreciation for John's way of doing things: a number of scholars posit that Jesus was for a time John's follower.

Like John, Jesus would emphasize the radical nature of the kingdom of God, but he would do so through more poetic and nonviolent means, and through the signs and symbols about his message that were spoken most powerfully by his miracles. As one of my New Testament professors used to say, Jesus' words give meaning to his miracles, and his miracles give meaning to his words.

Whatever drew Jesus to the banks of the Jordan River, something happened at his baptism that was so profound for him (the Gospels describe it as the heavens opening and a voice speaking) that it convinced him of a his divine mission. Afterward, Jesus journeyed into the desert to continue his process of discernment. In the Gospels, he is described as fasting for "forty days and forty nights," another way of saying "a long time." (Ellis Winward and Michael Soule write in *The Limits of Mortality* that a human being could survive at most thirty days without food and water and be conscious for no more than twenty-five.)

Clearly, Jesus was tested in some way during his time in the desert, though interpretations of what happened vary widely. Traditional artistic representations (including those in Martin Scorsese's *Last Temptation of Christ*) have Satan appearing in some physical way. Others surmise that Jesus experienced these tests, or temptations, within himself. Traditionally, Jesus is tempted to take up a life of power, security, and status, in contrast to the hard life of service that he eventually follows. While there are varying understandings of what Jesus' temptations in the desert involved, it is not an episode that one can dismiss as irrelevant to the Gospels. William Barclay suggests that this episode was most likely passed along to the disciples by Jesus himself, and so should be considered seriously.

Biblical narratives of the testing in the desert are complicated and obscured for the modern person by centuries of paintings that depict small demons and animals tempting Jesus. (In *The Last Temptation of Christ*, Jesus is tempted by, in order, a snake, a lion, and a flame.) Yet this may actually be the easiest part of Jesus' life to understand for the contemporary man and woman. Jesus, thinking intently about his mission, was subject to some very human temptations: for power, for security, and for easy answers. In the end, though, he rejected these temptations and returned to Galilee to begin his ministry. For Johannes Baptist Metz, writing in *Poverty of Spirit*, this is a critical point in the life of Jesus of Nazareth, as it reveals his fundamental acceptance of his own humanity.

"Jesus subjected himself to our plight," writes Metz. "He immersed himself in our misery and followed our road to the end. He did not escape from the torment of our life. . . . He was not spared from the dark mystery of our poverty as human beings."

But even after his sojourn in the Judean wilderness, Jesus may have experienced a lingering reticence. What is considered his first miracle seems a reluctant one. We find this story, called the wedding feast at Cana, in the Gospel of John. In that famous passage, Jesus has gone to a small town called Cana to attend a wedding, and the wine runs out. (In Stephen's play, Judas disses the host as "too cheap to buy enough wine for his own . . . wedding.")

When Jesus' mother points this out to him, suggesting that he *do* something, Jesus says, "Woman, what concern is that to you and to me?"

In other words, what does this have to do with me? I'm not the person you think I am. Here is Jesus still grappling with his mission, with his vocation, with his identity, and with what Thomas Merton called the "true self."

In response, his mother gives him the freedom to do what he wants. "Do whatever he tells you," she says to the hosts' servants. (Interestingly, the Gospel portrays Mary as somehow understanding her son's mission earlier than Jesus does.)

As John's Gospel tells the story, Jesus finally grasps what is required of him. He tells the servants to fill large earthen jars with water and serve the guests. But it is not water that comes out of the jars; it is wine. Jesus' career as a miracle worker has begun.

I have always wondered if Jesus himself wasn't surprised by his first miracle. If there was ever a time when he might have been surprised in his journey toward self-knowledge, it is in Cana.

At the same time, the miracle at Cana seems to strengthen Jesus' understanding of his mission, to inspire him to trust in his own discernment and in his ability to do miraculous things in the name of the God of the Jewish people.

As the Gospel stories continue, Jesus is shown as growing in confidence in his mission, which flows from his relationship with his Father, and in his identity. His miracles are a sign of this. In other passages, his assurance virtually leaps off the page, as in a story that is told in Matthew, Mark, and Luke.

"If you choose," says a leper, "you can make me clean."

"I do choose," says Jesus. "Be made clean!"

Jesus continues to grow in his awareness of his mission and his true self. And near the end of his earthly ministry, at least as portrayed in Matthew, Mark, and Luke, he emerges as one able to see what needs to be done. He has by this point more fully embraced his identity and his ministry.

There is a final test: his time in the Garden of Gethsemane immediately before the beginning of his passion. At the end of his life, Jesus struggles to completely embrace his mission. "If it is possible, let this cup pass from me," he says, hoping that perhaps that kind of suffering is not what God intends.

But somehow he comes to believe, through prayer and reflection, that his impending suffering, whatever it might be, is what God is asking of him at this moment in his life. He grasps that it is part of the reality of his life. It is here, it seems to me, in accepting the cup of suffering, that Jesus most fully accepts his identity. His vocation includes suffering, as does every vocation of every person. In the garden, Jesus accepts this essential human truth. Johannes Baptist Metz would say that he embraces his underlying "poverty of spirit."

Interestingly, Metz suggests that Judas's betrayal of Jesus is an outright rejection of the poverty of spirit that Jesus embraced. "Judas' betrayal," writes Metz, "may have been the result of frenzied impatience with Jesus' poverty, or a futile attempt to pressure Jesus into using his divine resources instead of accepting human impotence. In any case, it is not an isolated instance. Poverty of spirit is always betrayed most by those who are closest to it. It is the disciples of Christ in the Church who criticize and subvert it most savagely."

The Gospels paint a picture of a Jesus who is now completely free. He is not disturbed when he is arrested in the garden after his betrayal by Judas. In response to Peter's striking one of the high priest's slaves, Jesus calmly heals the man and points the disciples to an acceptance of his path. When faced with Pilate's questioning, he refuses even to defend himself. He is, according to the Gospel narratives, largely silent during the Passion. As he moves toward death, carrying his cross, he is firm in his acceptance of his true self, whose life includes suffering and death. His crucifixion becomes a deeply human act, not only because dying is one of the most human acts, but also because it is an outgrowth of his acceptance of his identity.

But Jesus' death is not the final act in the drama of his life. The resurrection of Jesus is at the heart of the Christian faith. Yet I've always believed that Jesus did not know for certain that he would be raised from the dead. I may be entirely incorrect, but I think that while he suspected that something astonishing would come from his acceptance of his mission and his obedience to his Father—as it always had in the past—he did not know precisely what it would be. There are several indications of this in the Gospels. Even as he hung on the cross, freely giving himself to his mission, he cried out in pain and confusion: "My God, my God, why have you forsaken me?"

For me, Jesus' possible ignorance of his own future makes his ultimate acceptance of his reality more meaningful. He trusted God completely enough that he could become his true self, and he knew that by following his mission, even in the midst of unimaginable suffering, he would somehow bring new life to others. Perhaps he didn't know what this new life would be, until the morning of that first Easter, when his true self was finally revealed in all its splendor and glory. Perhaps even he was surprised at the new life given him by God.

Perhaps it was only then that, in Elizabeth Johnson's words, "his ultimate identity burst upon him with all clarity."

This understanding of Jesus, that he came gradually to know his true self, is most persuasive to me. And this is the way that John Ortiz—a man who had grown in his own self-understanding—seemed finally to understand Jesus. John's performance embraced this: his Jesus was not so much human and divine as personal and confident.

Sal Inzerillo had a good way of describing the confidence evinced by the Jesus of Stephen's play. "Jesus had a real *tenacity* about him," said Sal. "He embodied a tenacity toward his work and a sense of loyalty toward his relationships."

After the play ended, John explained how the role had affected his understanding of Jesus. "You know, I used to see those T-shirts that say *Jesus Is My Homeboy*, which I thought was totally ridiculous. But now I can understand the feeling. I feel like he is someone I might call a friend. He's confident and compassionate: sort of a peaceful warrior for what he believes. I think I've moved from seeing Jesus as others see him, which can be massive and distorted and out of proportion, to seeing him in a more personal and intimate way. And that means so much to me now."

He paused and laughed. "But I still don't think I'd wear one of those T-shirts!"

Satan Appears

Jesus wasn't the only character the cast and creative team of *Judas* struggled to grasp. Depicting Satan, who would appear a few times in the play, also required much thought and careful interpretation, on the part of both Stephen and Eric Bogosian, who would play the character.

In one of Sam's favorite scenes, Judas encounters Satan in a seedy bar, shortly after Judas has handed Jesus over to the Roman soldiers. The scene had been a difficult one for Stephen to write, perhaps because he was standing on notoriously difficult theological ground. On the one hand, Stephen was adamant in wanting to avoid a portrayal of Judas as so obviously manipulated by Satan that his free will would be in doubt. The playwright put absolutely no stock in any theological approach that regarded Satan as an actual person who intervenes in human affairs. On the other hand, I encouraged Stephen to consider Satan as something less than a person but more than just an outmoded theological construct. Though I also don't think of Satan as an individual, I made the point to Stephen that there are some evils—genocide, murder, torture—that are difficult to ascribe to simple defects in human nature.

I quoted Charles Baudelaire, who said, "The devil's greatest trick would be to convince us that he doesn't exist." Even the greatest of saints, I told Stephen one night, regularly spoke of recognizing within themselves the ineluctable tendency to choose not the good but the bad. And I encouraged Stephen to meditate on the ways in which Satan has been depicted throughout the history of Christian spirituality—tempting human beings in subtle ways.

For example, in Saint Ignatius's *Spiritual Exercises*, he posits three ways in which the "enemy of human nature" works. First, Satan acts as the "army commander," who well understands the weakness of his enemy and attacks in precisely that spot. Namely, Satan locates the weak point in one's character—pride, envy, a need for security—and directs his energies there.

Second, Satan acts as the "false lover," who wishes not to be revealed to anyone else. In other words, Satan can act most effectively when one's desires to do evil are not revealed. If shared with another person, those sinful actions are more clearly seen as damaging to others or to oneself. Left concealed, those selfish or sinful actions seem more reasonable. Finally, says Ignatius, Satan acts as the "spoiled child." Here Satan relentlessly, even obsessively, demands that one follow his ways, until he gets his way.

In the final version of the encounter between Judas and Satan in the play, Stephen drew on the image of the army commander, who hones in on his prey's weakness. Judas enters the bar already drunk and seethes with an almost uncontrollable rage—at himself, at Jesus, and at the world. Phil told Sam that he wanted the audience to see Judas as a distinct danger to himself and to others. The audience should feel uncomfortable with such anger at close range. "'How am I this evening?'" he snaps after Satan greets him. "What are you, a f——n' maître d', man?" Sam all but spat on Eric during the beginning of the scene.

The relaxed and confident Satan takes no offense at the man's imprecations. He slowly befriends Judas and eventually, slyly, tempts him to suicide. But in Stephen's world, Satan does not have to convince; he need only suggest.

We have no choice in life, he says blandly, playing on Judas's despair. What's more, hell's not such a bad place after all. "Vastly underrated," says Satan.

Gradually Judas confides some of his fears. "What if someone were to betray, for example . . . the Messiah—"

"I'd say," says Satan, "that if this clown we're talking about betrayed the Messiah, that, probably, '*it would've been better for that man if he had never been born.*'" Judas is stunned. "That's a f——g heavy trip, man," he says.

Eric Bogosian had spent a good deal of time researching his role as Satan. Not only was he widely read in religious matters, but he had also been brought up in a family of faithful members of the Armenian Apostolic Church, which had fostered in him an early appreciation for religion. "On Sundays," he said, recalling his childhood, "we would go early to my grandmother's house, and, along with the rest of my family, we would be in church from seven in the morning until noon. The kids were in Sunday school until ten, and then we would march into the church and join everyone for the rest of the service."

As a young man, Eric drifted away from the church, but as an adult he became interested in Eastern mysticism. Gradually, he started to reexamine Christianity and to identify what he called "the profundity and spirituality of the message of Jesus that I had first experienced when I was a child."

"Today I still accept the idea that there was a Jesus and that he was holy," he said, "but I also believe that the Buddha was holy, and I even see them, in a way, as affiliated." Some traits of organized religion he finds repellent: for example, the internecine battles among the various Christian denominations and the fundamentalist readings of Scripture. His wide reading helped him see the inconsistencies in the various Hebrew and Christian Scriptures, which led him to downplay the importance in his own life of questions about the historicity of the events in the life of Jesus.

Eric began his acting career when he won the role of Capulet in a high school production of *Romeo and Juliet* in Watertown, Massachusetts. "I loved it so much that it *hurt*," he said. "After that, I did as much acting as I could in high school." Doubtful that he could make a living as an actor, he studied English at the University of Chicago but kept gravitating toward the theater department. He dropped out and attended Oberlin College, a school well known for its emphasis on the arts.

When he moved to New York City in the 1970s, he landed in the middle of the performance art scene that was flowering in Soho and the East Village. In 1977, he found work running the dance program at The Kitchen, at the time one of the centers for performance artists in the city. "The people I interfaced with were not really theater people but encouraged me to start writing these little pieces for the stage."

Almost as soon as he arrived in New York, he began performing the monologues that became his trademark, with the shows becoming larger and more complex. In 1981, Joseph Papp, the founder of the Public Theater, invited Eric to write a solo play to be staged in Martinson Hall, where *Judas* would be performed many years later. It was called *Men Inside*. "I wanted to write a piece about all the various voices inside me, which moved from character to character to character," he said. "But unlike some of the other actors who have used this method, like Whoopi Goldberg and Richard Pryor, I never played myself."

Acting roles in more than a dozen films and television shows followed, as did appearances in other plays of his own creation, including *Talk Radio*, *subUrbia*, *Drinking in America*, and the wonderfully named *Pounding Nails in the Floor with My Forehead*. His performances have won him Obie Awards and a Drama Desk Award, and he has toured with his plays throughout the United States and Europe. *Talk Radio* was adapted into a movie in 1988, directed by Oliver Stone, and a film adaptation of *subUrbia* was directed by Richard Linklater in 1996.

During the run of *Judas*, Eric gave me a copy of his first novel, *Mall*, which limns the lives of a group of lonely, isolated, and troubled individuals who come together at a suburban shopping mall. The novel's greatest strength lies in its ability to convincingly portray a wide variety of entirely believable characters. It indicated an author with great reserves of empathy and compassion.

Eric's participation in *Judas* marked a continuation of his spiritual path. "The play has led me further to a sense of discovery, and a sense of seeking God, like seeing a little trickle of water that eventually leads you to the river." His basic belief in God from childhood has remained. "All of this has grown within me over the last twenty years. I've always felt that there is meaning lying behind everything, and this appeals to me more than the move toward meaninglessness."

Eric pointed to an experience with his son, which encapsulated his feelings about the divine. When he related the tale, I was struck both by his natural gifts as a storyteller and his capacity to express something notoriously difficult to put into words.

"I once went camping with my son," he said, "and we were out in the woods, at the peak of a small mountain, on top of a huge rock, and under the stars. He told me that he was shaking, and I saw that he was almost vibrating, which was probably because he was so far away from everything that he knew: he's a city kid, after all. And I said, 'You don't have to be scared,' and I reached around and embraced him. At the same time, I myself felt embraced, and at that moment felt entirely safe. I felt that if anything happens, God will be enough. It's very much like the Gospel story of the loaves and the fishes. Most people think of that passage as a sort of magic trick, but for me it's a sense that what is already here will always be enough."

He contrasted this stance with that of Judas. "For me, I try to remain open to that connection. Judas, though, eventually rejected it."

Taking on the role of Satan prompted Eric not only to read about the history of thought on Satan, specifically in Goethe's *Faust*, but also to ponder the qualities of his character. "His physical qualities were important to me," he said. Eric grew a goatee and, unlike the rest of the cast, wore makeup, to emphasize his character's vanity. He worked closely with Mimi O'Donnell, the costume designer, on finding the right clothes. "And I also wore some small things that would help me, even if they were unseen by the audience. I bought a little ring on Eighth Street with a pentagram on it. And I wore a silver serpentine bracelet I had found in India a few years ago, and I even wore a medallion that I had bought at the Vatican with an image of Pope John Paul II. That seemed an especially *insolent* thing to do.

"But basically," he said, "it was Stephen's idea of Satan." As an actor, he said, he relies mostly on what is on the page. "Initially, it was difficult: Satan sometimes had a sense of humor and was confident and sometimes seemed petty a few moments later. It verged on a mystery for me." In time, Eric began to understand Satan as letting Judas make up his own mind but never standing in the way of Judas's despair. "He was giving Judas just enough rope to hang himself, if you'll pardon the expression."

The scene with Judas and Satan was, in Sam Rockwell's words, "gold." Judas's abrupt shift from anger to sadness was a tough one for Sam to nail. "It's an incredible challenge as an actor to come onstage in one state and change emotionally," he said. But the scene was meaningful for another reason. "It gave me permission to feel angry in the way everyone feels when they don't take the high road. We're interested in Judas because we're human and we don't fulfill our lives to their highest potential. Judas is much closer to who we are than we think."

Ready for Previews?

As previews approached, the cast and creative team expressed growing fears about the length of the play. Having only rehearsed scenes individually, they had little way of knowing how long the entire play would be. Two hours? Three? More? By the beginning of February, it was clear that there would be no time for dress rehearsals before previews started, an unusual situation: the first time the cast would perform the complete play, it would be in front of a paying audience. Stephen started to. worry more. And smoke more. Our conversations about despair started to take on greater import.

On the morning of February 8, the day the previews would begin, Stephen and I were interviewed together for an article in *Time Out New York*. The friendly interviewer was particularly interested in our relationship, and I knew we made an unlikely looking pair: Stephen in his faded jeans and sweatshirt and three day's growth of beard, with a cigarette dangling from his mouth, and me in my black clerical shirt, which I rarely wore to the theater but had donned in case a photographer would be present. (When I am photographed not in clerical attire, it typically prompts angry letters and phone calls to the offices of our magazine asking if I'm ashamed to be a priest.)

"You're quite the odd couple," said the interviewer.

Stephen said to me later, "You *know* that line'll be in his piece!" Sure enough, in an article called "Hell to Pay," Jason Zinoman wrote, "Seated in a tiny rehearsal room at the Public Theater, the playwright with the hair-trigger temper and the calm priest are an odd couple."

At the end of the interview, Stephen invited Zinoman to the performance that evening and said, "Tonight's going to be a train wreck."

"Don't be ridiculous," I said. "It'll be terrific."

But I had my worries.

By now I felt that I, too, had a stake in the play's success. For the past few months, I had talked about little else with my Jesuit friends, and as soon as the dates for previews were announced, they had started asking when they could see the show with me. Early on, I wasn't sure if it was proper for me to request complimentary tickets. When I mentioned this to Yul and Sam one afternoon, they laughed. "Are you *insane*, man?" said Sam. "Of *course* you'll get comps!" The company manager of LAB, a preternaturally efficient young woman named Abby, subsequently explained that each cast member (including me) was allowed one free ticket per week, plus three tickets at a staff discount, plus any more one might need at the last minute, depending on the availability of seats.

"Just let me know, Father Jim!" said Abby cheerfully.

Poor Abby! I think I spoke with her more than I spoke with my mother over the next few weeks. Every Jesuit priest and brother in New York, it seemed, had heard that I was working with *Judas* and was hoping for (free) tickets. Besides the *Time Out* piece, a Sunday *New York Times* article the previous week had also identified me as the play's theological adviser.

When I told Yul how much time I spent arranging tickets for friends, he rolled his eyes theatrically. "Father Jim," he said, "take it from me. That'll turn into a full-time job. Just tell them to call the box office!"

Nonetheless, I was gratified to have so many friends taking an active interest in the play, and more often than not I ended up accompanying them to the performances. "Oh *man*," said an amazed Sam. "You don't have to *go* with them!" I just hoped that my Jesuit friends and acquaintances would like the play—and not find any egregious theological mistakes. My biggest nightmare was sitting next to a Jesuit who would turn to me and say something like, "You idiot! Caiaphas wasn't the high priest!"

To guard against this, and to protect Stephen from any errors, I pored over new versions of his script, which were handed out with increasing frequency as previews approached. (Stephen's final version read: "Last Full Script Ever.") Though the playwright had taken pains to present the historical material accurately, each new script would usually contain one minuscule flaw.

One version of the script, for example, had Judas mockingly refer to Jesus' changing water into wine as "Miller time in ol' Jericho!"

"Actually," I said to Stephen, "it was in *Cana*, not Jericho."

"Are you *sure*?" he said. Earlier I had told him, incorrectly, that there was only one Simon the apostle: Simon Peter. He looked it up and pointedly reminded me that Simon the Zealot was an apostle, too.

Yes, I'm sure, I said. It's definitely the wedding feast at Cana.

The next day at rehearsals, Sam read out the new line. Seated on the catwalk high above the stage, he taunted Jesus about the miracle. "No problem, you just 'presto change-o'—" he shouted to John Ortiz, "and it was f——n' Miller time in ol' Canaan!"

"No!" I said, interrupting him. "It's *Cana*!"

"That's what I said," Sam said from above. "Wasn't it?"

"You just told me that last *night*!" shouted Stephen, obviously tired and stressed out.

"It's *Cana*, not Canaan," I said. "Cana is a little town in Galilee. Canaan is the land that the Hebrews entered after leaving Egypt."

Stephen buried his face in his hands. "Ohhhhh . . . fff——k," he said, to general laughter. Ultimately, the line was corrected, with Sam nailing it at every performance. But a few months later, when the book version of the play was published, I noted with some chagrin that in the Gospel according to Stephen Adly Guirgis, Jesus' first miracle occurred in Canaan.

∽⃝∽

Arriving early for the first preview in my clerical collar and black suit, and with a few friends in tow, I met a tired Stephen outside the theater nervously having a smoke. "How are you?" I asked. "Not too good, Jim," he said. "Not too good."

Gamely, I tried to encourage him, but he was anxiety-ridden about the audience's reaction, the length of the play, and—the central concern of everyone in the cast—the reviewers. (Over the next few weeks, I would hear the name of the *New York Times*'s chief theater critic, Ben Brantley, almost as often as I would hear the name of Jesus.) I started to make my way to Martinson Hall but was stopped in the lobby by a young usher.

"Sorry," she said. "The house isn't open yet. You can't go upstairs"

"Um . . ." I certainly wasn't going to identify myself as the theological advisor. I said instead, "I'm with the cast."

"Oh!" She laughed. "For a minute I thought you were a real priest!"

"I am, actually."

"Oh my *God*! Sorry . . . I mean . . . well . . . um . . . you can just go upstairs . . . Father."

It was discomfiting to see the risers filling up with people; it was as if they were somehow intruding on our personal space. I missed the plastic tables and chairs that had provided a place for our long conversations. But I was also excited to finally see onstage what we had been working on for so many months.

As my friends and I seated ourselves, I described to them how the play would begin, where the actors would sit, when Saint Monica would appear, where—

"You're not going to tell me all the lines, are you?" one asked darkly.

The play began in a darkened theater, which gradually filled with the sound of thunder and gently falling rain. A single spotlight shone on Deborah Rush, playing the mother of Judas Iscariot. When I first met Deborah, a blond actress with delicate features, I had a hard time imagining her as Mrs. Iscariot. Adding to the incongruity was her costume. Mimi O'Donnell had dressed her in a pink cashmere sweater and a long skirt: Judas's mother looked as if she had just stepped out of a Talbots catalog.

But as soon as she opened her mouth that first night of previews, I understood Stephen's casting decision and Mimi's intention. Judas's mother was Everywoman—or, rather, Everymother—and the type of person this New York audience would need to introduce the play. "No parent should have to bury a child," she said, her hands clasped in front of her. "No mother should have to bury a son. Mothers are not meant to bury sons. It is not in the natural order of things . . ." And then, finally, after all those weeks, the play began.

I was pleasantly surprised at how much I enjoyed it all: I laughed at things I had read dozens of times in the script and had heard dozens of times at the readings, but that were made more vital by the actors onstage. The set worked well, especially the overhead pulpit, from which the saints delivered their speeches. (One reviewer later disagreed; he called the device "hackneyed.") At the same time, I spotted some errors I had failed to correct in the script. In his monologue, Saint Peter spoke of his younger brother "Jimmy" introducing him to Jesus. How did I miss that? Peter's brother was named Andrew. I pulled out a pen and wrote a note on the palm of my hand.

The audience members were appreciative (many were family and friends of the cast), and the play ended to loud applause. Unfortunately, the play also ended three hours and forty-five minutes after it had begun.

"Boy," whispered my friend during the ovations. "That was a little . . . long."

A Christological Crisis

The next morning, I got a call from Sam. He sounded worried.

"Hey, Jim," he said, "you have to come and see this new Jesus scene. It's a lot different." Stephen had changed the ending again.

That night, I wandered into the theater and took my seat in the back row, the "house seats," where the cast and crew sat. In the final scene, in place of a placid Jesus, a confused Jesus confronted an even angrier Judas and said: "Look, I, um . . . I don't always . . . know . . . what to say, okay? How to say. Words . . . they don't . . . come easy always. You probably think they should, but they don't. I'm not a talk guy. I don't always know the way to . . . reach you. I try, I really try . . . Will you please look at me, Judas?"

For the first time, I was unnerved by the play. When I returned home, I telephoned Sam and told him that I found the final scene unsettling. Why was Jesus so confused? And then so angry? What happened to the original Jesus? Sam gently—and then not-so-gently—encouraged me to telephone Stephen.

"You have to call him," he said. "He'll listen to you."

Stephen immediately wanted to know what I thought about the new dialogue. Back in preaching class, years ago, I had been trained to begin with what I liked when critiquing other classmates' homilies. What do you commend, my professor would say, and then what do you recommend? So I told Stephen what I thought had been successful.

"Yeah, I know all that," he said. "What *didn't* you like?" I confided that I found Jesus too uncentered, too scattered, to be even remotely recognizable. At the risk of hurting Stephen's feelings during such a stressful time, I decided to be honest.

"I have no idea who that Jesus was," I said. "I wouldn't follow that Jesus around the corner, let alone to the ends of the earth."

As soon as I said it, I was horrified by my bluntness.

Stephen was silent. This was unusual. Normally, our lively telephone conversations had us speaking over and interrupting each other. I hoped that I hadn't offended him: this was an important scene, and I instantly regretted my honesty, worried that I had overstepped my boundaries. After all, I was the theological adviser, not the playwright.

But Stephen listened attentively and then asked more questions about Jesus. "Okay, Jim," he said finally. "That helps. Thanks."

That night I didn't sleep well, concerned that I had offended or demoralized Stephen, and also worried that he would keep the angry Jesus.

Early the next morning, I got a call from Stephen. "Could you come to a reading this afternoon?"

A few hours later, at the theater, he explained that he had changed Jesus because he felt that he was too "divine." Stephen wanted to make him more human. But human doesn't mean angry, does it? I asked. He gave me a look that said, It does to me.

"But I changed it again," he said, rubbing sleep out of his eyes. "You'll see."

Now Jesus' character fell somewhere between placid and angry. He met Judas with sympathy but also expressed frustration at Judas's despair. His opening monologue was also cut considerably. But he still told the audience that he was everywhere and with everyone. "And make no mistake," he said, "'Who I Love' is every last one. I *am* every last one." That was how it stayed for the remainder of the run.

The essentials of the scene remained: a faithful Jesus tries to help Judas see the futility of despair; Judas rejects the invitation to be forgiven and, finally, retreats into despair, with Jesus washing his feet at the end. Theologically, the playwright had found his own balance between divinity and humanity, a Christology that best expressed who Jesus was for him, and who Jesus would be for his play. And Stephen kept one of Judas's most effective lines, which Sam shouted tenderly: "Why . . . didn't you make me good enough . . . so that you could've loved me?"

ACT 4: THE MESSIAH HAS A COLD

March

During the two weeks of previews, I attended as many evening performances as I could. Since the Public continued to offer me complimentary tickets, I brought plenty of friends—Jesuits, Catholics, Christians, Jews, agnostics, and atheists—along with me. To a person, they enjoyed the show even in its earliest incarnation, although "Too long" would be a common refrain until closing night of the entire run. Perhaps not surprisingly, those who knew something about the Gospels appreciated it the most. Still, when I turned to see a Jesuit friend wiping away tears after the confrontation between Judas and Jesus, I was surprised. My familiarity with the play often blinded me to the powerful emotional effect it could have on people.

As I had during the readings, I was spending a lot of my free time at the Public Theater. The evenings could be long, with the talk-backs after the show lasting sometimes half an hour. By the time I had chatted with the cast afterward, it would be close to midnight. I was lucky if I made it to bed by one. In general, the actors were night owls, which made sense given their professional schedules.

Yul Vázquez explained in more detail why late nights are built into the acting life. Most plays run until around ten or eleven at night, and even actors who eschew a post-show meal may be so wired from their performances that it's difficult for them to fall sleep until a few hours later. Consequently, cast and crew sleep later into the day, and many rehearsals do not start until midmorning. Not only that, but actors also like to support their friends in the theater, and so even when they're not in a show themselves, they're attending other performances.

Still, I continued to be amazed whenever I was invited to lunches that began at two in the afternoon or dinners that began at nine. A few weeks after the play ended, Sam and Yul and Yul's wife, Linda, came to a Mass I celebrated at St. Ignatius Loyola Church one Sunday evening. After a long dinner in a downtown restaurant, I stood up to leave. "Hey, man, where are you *going*?" said Sam. "It's only eleven o'clock!"

After a particularly good night at the Public, I would occasionally phone one of the actors (who I knew was still up) to compliment his or her performance. I was surprised at how seriously they listened to a novice's commentary. ("Oh yeah?" Sam would often say after I told him he had done well. "You think so?") Just as often, one of the actors would phone me after a tough performance and say tentatively, "What'd you think about tonight?"

By this point, I was no longer needed as a theological adviser, except when a stray question needed to be answered. ("Do you think Thomas was surprised to see Jesus after the Resurrection?" asked Adrian Martinez a few days into previews.) Instead, I was working as a kind of chaplain, an especially gratifying job with this group. Despite the stress of a show whose final script was available only a few days after previews, the actors and the crew were always welcoming and affectionate. Upon my arrival in the dressing room, they always offered me hugs and kisses. It was easy to feel comfortable with them, and I was happy they felt comfortable with me. Over the run of the play, one actor's good friend would die (a few hours before curtain); another would struggle with professional decisions surrounding a new film; another would experience problems with a new girlfriend; and so on.

One day, during the rehearsals that continued during previews, a cell phone rang. Oddly, it sounded like it came from the stage. Kohl Sudduth stammered an apology and answered his phone, and in the bright stage lights, we could see a wave of sadness wash over his face. "It's my dad," he said. He bolted offstage, leaving the other actors speechless.

Knowing that Kohl was a Buddhist made me briefly hesitant to follow him, but I saw how foolish that was. "Why don't you check on him," suggested Phil. I caught up with Kohl in the dressing room, still clutching his cell phone. His father, who lived in Ohio, had suffered a heart attack. His stepmother had called from the hospital. "I don't know what to do," he said, telegraphing his conflicting desires to be with his father and to not abandon the play.

When I asked Kohl if he wanted to talk, he said yes, and we found a dressing room that was empty—a rarity during a busy day. Surrounded by costumes hanging from hooks on the wall, Kohl wept and spoke of his worries for his father, his frustrations at being far from home, and his fears of letting down the cast. After he finished, I asked if he'd like to ask God for what he needed. Kohl's was the best kind of prayer: simple and sincere. Just as we stood to leave, a woman bearing costumes burst into the room and said, "Oh, good, I need this room."

Months after the play, I thanked Kohl for his openness. He smiled, thanked me, and said that for a disaffected-Methodist-turned-Buddhist, praying with a Catholic priest had been a new experience. "But I figure that the Buddha doesn't care much about the details, and neither does God. It's all connected." What's more, spending time with the Gospels during the preceding weeks had reawakened his childhood interest in Jesus. "I always dug Jesus. He was always unflinching, doing what needed to be done," he said. "But now I see him even more as a great teacher, a great bodhisattva, who has been grossly misrepresented. It makes me want to learn more about him."

Chastity and Friendship

I was moved that Kohl and the other actors seemed to trust me so much after having known me for just a few months. The satisfaction this gave me was a reminder of how valuable the vow of chastity is in the life of a priest. Chastity is always a difficult proposition, but it is made easier when you can feel love so readily from so many people.

Chastity is often depicted in the popular culture and mainstream media purely as a negative construct: the prohibition of sex. And that's true. But for those in religious communities and in the priesthood, chastity is also a way to love—one that is slightly different from how people who are in sexual relationships love. The goal of chastity is love. Unfortunately, in the public mind, the stereotype of the cold, repressed priest or the frustrated, cruel sister is inextricably tied to chastity. (It's now also tied to the newer stereotype of the pedophile priest.) Yet among the celibate men and women I know are the most loving people I could ever meet: A German sister who has spent years in dedicated work with Sudanese refugees, for whom she is a sort of mother. A patient elderly priest who has been a spiritual counselor to dozens of men and women who feel that he understands them the best. A young and energetic Jesuit priest who for many years has worked with Native Americans on reservations in South Dakota; a man of short stature with a great sense of humor, he is called by the Lakota "Small Man with Big Laugh." All these people are true celibates.

Celibacy can be lonely, of course. Beyond the sacrifice of not having a sexual partner, there is the deeper sacrifice of not having an emotional partner, someone you can rely on consistently. But there are also some practical benefits to celibacy. During the long hours I spent at the Public Theater, I never had to worry that someone at home was wondering whether or not I was being faithful, or if someone was feeling ignored or jealous. Likewise, there was no one at the Public Theater who wondered if my interest in them was motivated by a desire to develop a sexual relationship with them. Celibacy in human relationships can be very freeing, and when practiced well, it can allow intimate relationships to develop swiftly.

Ironically, even those who dismiss celibacy as unhealthy or sick or twisted usually grudgingly admit that some of the world's most loving people have followed the celibate path: Saint Francis of Assisi, Mother Teresa, Pope John XXIII, Jesus of Nazareth. Each of these people chose celibacy not as a way of escaping from relationships but as an alternative way of expressing love.

For me, the experience of being with the cast members of *Judas* was one example of what happens when chastity works well. I grew in love for these men and women, and I was able to feel, and freely receive, their affection for me.

Traditions and Superstitions

During the February previews, I was also introduced to some of the traditions of the theater. I thought about the French Jesuits in the New World patiently learning about the culture of seventeenth-century Hurons and Iroquois, as my education in the theater was part of my own "inculturation" into a new world. I learned, for example, to leave the dressing room a few minutes before curtain, when the actors seemed to need time for themselves—whether for reviewing the script, meditating, or doing their vocal warm-ups. Usually I wouldn't need a watch to know when curtain was close; as if on cue, the actors would start to vocalize: "Mmmmmmmaaaaaah!"

Stephen McKinley Henderson, who not only acted but also taught theater at the State University of New York at Buffalo, was my guide to some other theatrical traditions. From time to time, I would look to him for explanations about practices and terms that were still unfamiliar to me. The "techs," for example, were the technical rehearsals—during which the technical aspects of the performance were tested—that took place shortly before opening night. Yul Vázquez had warned me off tech rehearsals, saying that they were notoriously tedious. "Don't come, Father Jim," he said. "I'm warning you!" I came anyway, thinking that Yul might be jaded about a process that would probably interest a newcomer. When I left after an hour of listening to the lighting crew asking Phil where he wanted a particular spotlight, I passed Yul on the way out. "I told you so!" he whispered with a grin.

One day, Stephen explained the origin of the term *greenroom*, the sort of anteroom around which most dressing rooms in theaters are arranged. (The term is also used for the rooms in which guests on television talk shows cool their heels until airtime.) In the era of Greek theater, when actors wore heavy costumes that included masks and elaborate wigs that needed to be changed frequently, the air backstage grew almost noxious with body odor. To combat this, sweet-smelling eucalyptus branches were strewn on the backstage floor. When the actors stepped upon the green branches, the fragrance was released into the air. Hence, the greenroom.

Superstitions were also on display during the run of *Judas*. Though I had little background in the theater, I knew enough not to say, "Good luck," considered both bad luck and bad form. One night before

The Public Theater,
New York City,
Winter 2005.

The cast and creative team of the original production of *The Last Days of Judas Iscariot*. Front row (from left to right): Philip Seymour Hoffman, Elizabeth Canavan, Yetta Gottesman, Liza Colón-Zayas, Elizabeth Rodriguez, Maggie Burke, John Ortiz. Back row: Craig "Mums" Grant, Stephen Adly Guirgis, Eric Bogosian, Salvatore Inzerillo, Stephen McKinley Henderson, Kohl Sudduth, Adrian Martinez, Sam Rockwell, Yul Vázquez.

© Carol Rosegg

Saint Monica (Elizabeth Rodriguez, left) and Mary Magdalene (Yetta Gottesman) share their memories of Jesus at the beginning of act 2.

© Carol Rosegg

In a flashback, following the Crucifixion, Satan (Eric Bogosian, right) tells an anxious Judas (Sam Rockwell) that hell is "vastly underrated."

The defense attorney, Fabiana Aziza Cunningham (Callie Thorne), derides Pontius Pilate (Stephen McKinley Henderson) with the words, "You didn't wash your hands, Pontius Pilate—History did it for you," as Judge Littlefield (Jeffrey DeMunn) listens.

The prosecuting attorney, Yusef El-Fayoumy (Yul Vázquez, center), assails the credibility of Dr. Sigmund Freud (Adrian Martinez) before an impatient Judge Littlefield (Jeffrey DeMunn).

In the play's final scene, Jesus (John Ortiz, right) begins to speak with Judas (Sam Rockwell) about forgiveness.

Stephen Adly Guirgis (left), author of *The Last Days of Judas Iscariot*, with James Martin, SJ (center), and Sam Rockwell (right), New York City, May 2007.

curtain, I asked Jeffrey DeMunn, who was one of the most experienced actors in the cast, to explain the phrase "Break a leg." Jeffrey offered several possible explanations, one having to do with Sarah Bernhardt's having one leg, another with a Yiddish expression that made its way into the American theater, but the most likely having to do with a certain kind of bow taken by actors.

"It's been said that, in the past, when actors did especially well, they would take a particularly low form of a bow, twisting their legs behind them," said Jeffrey. "So saying 'Break a leg' meant that you would give a performance that would lead to the kind of audience reception requiring that special kind of bow."

In another bow to superstition, many theaters still use a "ghost light," typically a bare bulb on a stand that remains lit after the evening's performance is over and the other lights have been extinguished. Eric Bogosian said that while this has obvious practical benefits (such as preventing people from injuring themselves in the dark), it may also be a superstitious attempt to keep away evil spirits.

"Actors are superstitious," said Eric. "They look to organizing their reality around signs and symbols." I asked him why this might be.

"Well," he said, "it's not what you would call a *coherent* profession. No one in their right mind would decide to do this: the unknowns are many and the rewards are so few. Other professions can rely simply on hard work. But our successes have to do with whether we are embraced by the audience, which is always an unknown, and our auditions are always fraught with unknowns. So I suppose that actors will believe in anything that will give them luck and that organizes these very non-rational things in their lives."

I was wholly ignorant of most of these superstitious practices. One evening, I began telling Yul how well Eric had done as Satan the night before. As I was speaking, Eric entered the dressing room area, and I told him how electric his performance had been.

His face froze. "I can't hear that right now!" he said, and ducked into his dressing room and closed the door. Yul raised his eyebrows and shrugged.

After a minute, Eric opened the door and said, "I'm sorry, Father Jim. You can tell me that stuff on closing night, but not right before a performance." I told him I understood.

"I'm sort of a diva about that," he said. "Do you have divas in the Jesuits?" I pointed to myself, and he laughed.

A Theatrical Vocation

Though I had read about the quality of stage performances changing from one night to the next, I had never seen any play more than once (unless you count *Bye Bye Birdie* in high school). As previews of *Judas* continued, though, I could see that the show was gradually improving: the funny lines were funnier, the sad parts sadder, and the overall timing tighter. The play was still long, but the presence of so many friends and family of the cast seemed to spur them on. Often seated at the side of the stage as part of the "jury," I was able to watch the cast and the audience at the same time. At one point, I saw Yul Vázquez silhouetted against the audience, and I realized I was seeing someone fully living out his vocation.

Especially in Catholic circles, the word *vocation* was at one point almost exclusively reserved for priests, sisters, and brothers. One prayed that a young man might "have" or "get" a vocation to the priesthood, for example. The word itself, derived from the Latin *vocare*, "to call," indicated that the vocation came from outside: one was "called" by God to the priesthood or to become a nun. And in the popular imagination, once you had a vocation, there was nothing you could do to escape it. "It's no good trying to deny it," people would say. "You have a vocation." It was almost like a disease.

More recently, the notion of vocation has been understood in broader terms, applicable not simply to those who are ordained or who take religious vows, but to everyone. Some are called to be priests and sisters and brothers, to be sure, but others are called to be husbands and wives, fathers and mothers, as well as lawyers, doctors, scientists, artists—and actors, directors, playwrights, set designers, lighting designers, and costume designers. At the heart of the modern understanding of vocation is discovering our individual spiritual path and becoming the person we are meant to be.

Contemporary spiritual writers suggest that the seeds of one's vocation are found most easily in one's desires. Understanding our desires and hopes, in this construct, is a way to discover what we are meant to do and who we are meant to be. In his book *Letting God Come Close*, Jesuit priest William A. Barry, a popular writer on spirituality, spends an entire chapter on the role of desire in the spiritual life. He advises spiritual directors, pastoral counselors, and retreat directors to pay attention to this key aspect of the heart. Retreat directors, Barry says, "do their most important work when they help [others] to discover what they really want."

At first blush, this may appear to be an encouragement of selfishness or greed—as in, "I want a new car!" or "I want to be famous!" But it is not about mere surface wants or transient wishes; it is about one's deepest desires. The idea has a distinguished pedigree: in the Gospel accounts, Jesus of Nazareth frequently asks those he encounters to express their desire. This is particularly true in the famous healing narratives. In the Gospel of Mark, for example, when Jesus meets the blind beggar Bartimaeus, Jesus' first question is simple: "What do you want me to do for you?" He is asking the man to name his desire.

So it is not the case that one needs to "get" a vocation as much as one needs to discover it within oneself. Understanding one's desires and hopes is a touchstone of spiritual growth. In this light, our deepest desires manifest God's desires for us and for the world. This is true for both the saints and the rest of humanity. Certainly the saints—and I use the term broadly—embraced a particular way of life because they felt it was the best way to follow God.

But their vocations were rooted in their human hopes and aspirations. Saint Francis of Assisi pursued a life of poverty because he desired a life that would conform to that of Jesus of Nazareth. Mother Teresa worked with the sick and dying in Calcutta because she felt the desire to serve the poorest of the poor. Thomas Merton ended up in a Trappist monastery in Kentucky because he felt an overwhelming desire for a contemplative life. The Reverend Dr. Martin Luther King Jr. worked for justice because he desired a just world.

On another level, a husband and wife are drawn together through desire and, one could say, discover their vocation as a married couple in this way. Likewise, a good doctor is initially attracted to medicine through a kind of desire. Writers begin their careers because they enjoy writing. All vocations—including acting—stem from a kind of longing.

After jokingly suggesting that he had no skills for anything else, Adrian Martinez said that he considered acting as much of a vocation as any other profession, even the priesthood. "I feel that God created me to do this kind of work, and the feedback I get indicates this, too." Sal, who played Simon the Zealot, also viewed his career as a vocation. "It's an all-encompassing way of spending your life. And when you're doing it right, it's like being *alive!*" Elizabeth Rodriguez said something strikingly similar: "When I'm working hard and even exhausted and afraid, that's when I feel most fully alive. That's when I feel closest to enlightenment." Eric Bogosian's description of his path to his profession included as succinct a description of a vocation as I've ever heard: "I loved it so much that it *hurt*. And if you told me that I could never act again, I wouldn't know what I'd do."

And when Stephen Adly Guirgis spoke about writing, he did so in the explicit language of vocation. "The strongest relationship I have with God is when I'm writing," he told me, "when I'm aware of the collaboration between myself and God. It's like this unconscious feeling of being able to create."

The twentieth-century Protestant theologian Karl Barth agreed with the application of vocation extended into any legitimate profession—especially acting. At the end of a discussion of vocation in his great work *Church Dogmatics*, Barth wrote of seeing a "variety show" on Saturday night in which the actors "executed a real righteousness of works." The next morning he listened to a dreadful Sunday sermon, which he termed "a real piece of theological bungling." This story comes in the middle of a meditation on the way that "right work"—that is, work done to the best of one's abilities and talents—is also "righteous work."

Barth concludes with this pungent observation that could serve as a salutary reminder to many in the clergy: "Could I resist the impression that, formally at least, the right thing had been done at the place of very secular amusement and not at the place where the Gospel is preached and worship offered?"

Reviewing Detachment

On opening night, March 2, I arrived early. The dressing room, actually a large lounge surrounded by small rooms, was crammed with flowers and baskets of fruit and food. At a religious convention a few weeks before, I had told a friend who works at a Catholic publishing house about my work at the Public. Intrigued by the project, he sent a carton of two new books on the saints, which I wrapped up and gave to Stephen, Phil, and the cast.

I was glad I had brought gifts, because the cast had gifts for me as well. I received a pack of "Heavenly Mints" from Callie, and a coaster embroidered with a picture of a nun holding a cocktail glass, "Sister Mary Mimosa," from Stephen McKinley Henderson. And from George C. Wolfe, the then producer of the Public Theater, each of us received a lemon yellow long-sleeved shirt featuring Stephen's description of heaven. During the first act, the presiding judge threatens his lazy bailiff, who is still trapped in Purgatory. "Wanna get to Heaven someday?" he asks. "Eat fried chicken and mashed potatoes, feel the sun on your face." When the bailiff says he does, the judge thunders, *"Then call the next damn case!!!"*

So our shirts read: *Eat Fried Chicken and Mashed Potatoes and Feel the Sun on Your Face*—all in all, not a bad eschatological hope.

After the performance, there was a crush of visitors in the dressing room: mainly friends and family, but with a few surprises. I could see people eddying around Deborah; one of her friends was causing a stir. As I drew closer, I saw the reason for the commotion.

"Father Jim," she said. "This is my friend, Meryl Streep." Even some of the other actors seemed nervous around her, so I didn't feel embarrassed at being tongue-tied. It was all I could do not to blurt out, "I loved *Out of Africa!*" (During my time in Kenya, I must have seen it a dozen times on the Jesuit community's ancient VCR.) She was gracious and generous with her praise of *Judas*. "Wasn't it wonderful?" she said. I agreed that it was, and stepped aside to let the actors have their time with her.

Presently, we all made our way to a dark and crowded bar on the Lower East Side. I met girlfriends and boyfriends and husbands and wives and agents and publicists and more members of LAB. Amid the noisy crowd, photographers took photos of Phil and Sam and Stephen that would show up in newspapers and magazines over the next few days. (The photo of me in my clerical collar with a drink in my hand was one that fortunately did not make it into the papers.) The bar had special drinks made for us: the Judastini, Purgatory Punch, and so on. "Father Jim," said Sam, "you *have* to have a drink!" I had two, which was above my limit. The next day was a full day for me at the magazine, and by midnight I was ready to leave. I told Elizabeth and her boyfriend, Brett, that I was worried about the reviews.

"Oh no!" said Brett. "You're becoming an actor!"

Everyone seemed to care about one particular reviewer: Ben Brantley, the chief theater critic for the *New York Times*. The next morning, nursing a slight hangover, I ducked into our community reading room at seven to read his review, which appeared on the inside of the Arts section, accompanied by a color photograph of Sam and Eric as Judas and Satan.

The *Times* review, largely disappointing, would be analyzed by the cast and crew almost as much as the Gospel stories had been. While I was pleased to read that the paper's critic found in the show "a stirring sense of Christian existential pain" and a script that presented "dilemmas of ancient Galilee in terms winningly accessible to the 21st century," I winced when I read Stephen's play described as a "heavily footnoted position paper on a big, big subject."

As if to underline his point, Brantley said that two people in the audience had fallen asleep in the second act, a markedly unfair accusation, since many theatergoers snooze for a variety of reasons unrelated to the play, and because while the show was many things, dull was not one of them. Particularly irksome for me was Brantley's dismissive description of the show as an "unusually lively senior class project" by the "class cutup" who recruited some "really cool friends" to be in his production.

On the heels of Brantley's review came another negative review in the *New Yorker* by John Lahr, who called the play "woeful" (and not in a good way). As had some of my friends, a few reviewers took aim at the play's length. "God's Justice May Be Eternal, but in Guirgis's *Judas*, It's Interminable Too," read the headline from the *Village Voice*.

The harsh reviews were countered by positive ones, some adulatory. The theater critic from the *Guardian* of London (I was impressed that a British critic was even reviewing the play) called it "extraordinary" and made a flattering comparison: "Not since Tony Kushner's *Angels in America* have I seen a play so unafraid to acknowledge the power of the spirit." A few weeks after the play closed, Robert Brustein, the theater critic for the *New Republic*, said that the play "confirms Guirgis's place as one of our most electric young dramatists" and compared Stephen favorably to Eugene O'Neill. Brustein quoted liberally from Stephen's script and was also impressed with the difficulty of the subject material. "Merely to undertake it is an act of considerable courage and audacity—and slapstick skill."

The Manichaean dichotomy of the reviewers' positions was striking: they either loved *Judas* or hated it. There was little middle ground. In stark contrast to several negative reviews, the Associated Press deemed the show "fascinating," *Time Out New York* labeled it one of its must-sees for the week, and the Catholic magazine *Commonweal* termed it a "landmark event in contemporary American theater." And in their year-end roundups, both *Time* and *Entertainment Weekly* included the production in their top-ten lists for the theater. It took third place in both magazines, with *Entertainment Weekly* calling it "unjustly overlooked."

The actors had varying responses to the reviews. Yul read them assiduously, while Sam said he never read any reviews until a run had ended. Elizabeth's boyfriend, Brett, himself a playwright, read the reviews but tried to keep them secret from Elizabeth. "Yeah," she said, "but then I can hear him telling everyone else anyway!" Deborah told me that during a low point in her life, she confessed to her friend Kevin Kline that she was upset about a review that had failed even to mention her performance. "You read *reviewwwws*?" shouted Kline. Since then, Deborah not only avoids them, but also counsels other actors to do so.

The *Times* review, though, came in for harsh criticism from everyone. "I saw Brantley," said one crew member, "and he was laughing his ass off the whole time!"

Though I was obviously biased, it seemed to me that some of the reviewers had failed to grasp the underlying themes of the play and were put off by the overtly religious outlook of the script. One even said that the scene with Mother Teresa was extraneous, though it helped explain despair, a key concept in the play. I wondered if perhaps I was responsible for some of the bad reviews; maybe I hadn't done my job well enough. Maybe I hadn't explained some of these theological concepts sufficiently.

While I offered some of the actors the insights from Thomas Merton on the importance of trusting in one's own efforts rather than relying on results, I started to realize why actors get so upset about reviews. When I told a friend how bothered I was by some of the reviews, he laughed. "What about your famous Jesuit detachment?" At the time, I felt that it was a virtue I sorely lacked.

༺༝༻

Nearly every major spiritual writer—in nearly all the major religions—argues for a measure of detachment in pursuit of the spiritual life. Detachment marks an intersection of Eastern and Western spiritualities. It is a central element in the Christian spiritual tradition, and it lies at the heart of Buddhist practice. The second of the Four Noble Truths of Buddhism (concerned with attaining enlightenment) teaches that suffering is caused by craving, or unnecessary attachments. The more that the unenlightened attach themselves to impermanent things in this world, the more they will continue to suffer. Desire (*tanha*) leads to attachment (*upadana*), which leads inevitably to suffering. Detachment, therefore, is a necessary precondition for achieving Nirvana.

The Christian emphasis on detachment, which has its roots in Jewish practice, began early: Jesus of Nazareth consistently pointed his disciples to a road that was free of encumbrances. Over and over in the Gospels, Jesus reminds people, through strikingly direct parables and sayings, that nothing should come between God and his followers. Perhaps the most famous story illustrating Jesus' thoughts on the matter is that of the rich young man. The story is included in all the synoptic Gospels, underscoring its importance for the early church. In Matthew, Mark, and Luke, a rich young man approaches Jesus and asks the rabbi a simple question: "What must I do to inherit eternal life?"

In the Gospel of Mark, Jesus answers, "You know the commandments" and lists several of them.

"Teacher," says the young man, "I have kept all these since my youth." The man is not a bad or evil person. Quite the contrary, he's a devout Jew, someone whom Jesus and his circle of disciples would have held in admiration.

"You lack one thing," says Jesus; "go, sell what you own, and give the money to the poor, and you will have treasure in heaven; then come, follow me."

Saint Mark gives a poignant description of the man's reaction. "When he heard this, he was shocked and went away grieving, for he had many possessions." In the Gospel of Matthew, the man also walks away grieving.

Jesus then turns to his disciples and says, "How hard it will be for those who have wealth to enter the kingdom of God!" Later, he adds, "It is easier for a camel to go through the eye of a needle than for someone who is rich to enter the kingdom of God."

Stephen and I discussed this parable frequently. He was disturbed by the stern warning against wealth, but he was even more bothered by the fact that Jesus' request seemed unfair and even unjust. The man was being asked to do something that seemed impossible—who could give up all their possessions in an instant?

I responded that Jesus wasn't so much asking him to do something simply because it was impossible as putting his finger on the one thing that was getting between the young man and God. Jesus knew what was preventing him from fully committing himself to discipleship. It was the same thing that kept many from the kingdom of God: attachment to wealth.

For another person, Jesus might say, "Give up your occupation," as he did to Saint Peter when he called him from his trade as a fisherman. "Look," says Peter in the Gospel of Matthew, after the rich young man has walked away, "we have left everything and followed you." To another, Jesus might say, "Give up your sense of unworthiness," as he did to Saint Matthew, calling him away from the ignominy of being a Jewish tax collector. Anything that got in the way of the freedom to follow God had to be set aside, and what needed to be set aside differed for every person.

Underneath all this, Jesus was really asking for a conversion, a true change of heart. And he knew that what he counseled was not impossible. After the rich young man leaves, the disciples must have been thunderstruck by what they have heard: If a devout and wealthy Jew cannot enter the kingdom of God, then who can be saved? So they ask Jesus, "Then who can be saved?"

"For mortals it is impossible," says Jesus, "but for God all things are possible."

The early Christian community strove to put Jesus' counsel into practice, taking as their examples the lives of the apostles, who had indeed left behind life as they knew it to follow Jesus of Nazareth and had been richly rewarded. The life of detachment and freedom was a realistic possibility, as Jesus suggested, and would lead to a life of lasting wealth. There is no one, Jesus said, who has left anything behind who will not "receive a hundredfold."

Kohl Sudduth, the Zen practitioner among the cast, said that over the years, he had grown in his appreciation of the place of this spiritual practice in Buddhism. "I thought at first that detachment meant that you didn't feel anything, but it has nothing to do with that," he told me over dinner at a vegetarian restaurant. "Instead it means that you feel everything deeply and directly. You're just not attached to it."

As part of Trevor Long's circuitous spiritual journey—from Hermann Hesse to Norman Vincent Peale to Thomas Merton to the New Testament to the writings of Buddha—the understudy to Jesus and Judas found that detachment had a direct application to his work. "I'm someone who holds on a lot, and sometimes I feel stuck," he said. "It comes from a fear of not being in control and fearing change. That's really what drew me to spirituality. But that's why acting is so appealing. It gets you out of yourself—almost literally—and into another person's life."

For his part, Kohl felt he needed to practice detachment from some of the pitfalls of his profession. "Detachment from pride is a challenge for actors. Acting can be so ego-inflating, which isn't good for living a spiritual life." The practice was helpful in practical ways, too. "When it comes to rehearsals," Kohl said, "I walk in, do my thing, walk out, and leave it all in the room." But he admitted that it's hard to do. "It's an ideal," he said. "Sometimes I end up beating myself up anyway. But I'm getting there!"

According to the spiritual masters from almost any tradition, complete detachment is the way to true conversion. In the Christian tradition, conversion (from a Latin word meaning "to turn back") is a change in life that requires a drastic reordering of priorities—what the rich young man was called to do in the Gospels. Pedro Arrupe, the former superior general of the Jesuits and himself a spiritual writer, once wrote: "Conversion is not a giving away of something that we can well afford to lose. It goes much deeper than that. It is a putting away of something that we are: our old self with its all-too-human, all-too-worldly prejudices, convictions, attitudes, values, ways of thinking and acting, habits that have become so much a part of us that it is agony even to think of parting with them, and yet which are precisely what prevent us from rightly interpreting the signs of the times, from seeing life steadily and seeing it whole."

Those negative reviews of *The Last Days of Judas Iscariot* were therefore a small test of my detachment. Could I accept that the work I had been doing with the cast and crew was valuable in itself, no matter what the *New York Times* or the *New Yorker* said about the play? (Was I detached from the need for public acclaim?) How well could I accept the fact that I would not be lauded as the "theological adviser" of the biggest Off-Broadway hit that season? (Was I detached from a sense of pride?) Some of the cast members and I talked about these challenges both before and after the reviews appeared.

But I discovered that my own detachment had its limits. One day Stephen read to me over the phone a review in the *Village Voice*, and I tried to help him put it into perspective.

"Listen to this part," he said, quoting the review: "'In addition to making less theological sense than any dramatist who ever tackled the Christ myth—'"

"*What?*" I said, stung. "How can he say that?"

"Oh yeah!" Stephen laughed. "*Now* the reviews bother you, huh?"

⊙

As early as the first week of previews in February, the Public Theater began offering "talk-backs" for *Judas*, where the audience could ask questions of the cast and the creative team following the show. The Public called this offering "Beyond the Stage." And though anyone who didn't like the show would doubtless have left before the talk-backs, the response was enthusiastic.

Talk-backs were held once a week and ran through March until the show's closing night, April 3. I enjoyed them immensely. (The cast enjoyed them less: after the performance, many of them just wanted to grab a bite to eat or just unwind.) Once the house lights went up, a few chairs would be placed on the bare stage in front of the audience. Roughly half the audience would stay. Since I didn't have to get out of costume, I would be the first person onstage.

I was asked one question consistently: "Does the bad language bother you?" I would say, first, that the Gospel story was being "inculturated" for a new audience. Second, the language was a reminder that the saints were real people; and third, if Jesus hung around fishermen and prostitutes, he probably heard the same kind of language we heard on the stage. I also liked the fact that, on the most basic level, the language was shocking; as Jesus knew from his dramatic parables, shock was one way of getting people's attention.

But there was another reason for the profane language. During one talk-back, Stephen admitted that he wrote for, and from, the world in which he lived. "When I live in a world of financial security and retirement planning, maybe I'll start to write that way, too."

For me, the play's streetwise and sometimes vulgar language was not only a theological asset but also a theatrical one. Saint Monica's foulmouthed speech made the people in the audience laugh, which allowed them to more easily hear her essential message: God does not give up on us. As Saint Ignatius of Loyola said, to communicate with those who see the world differently, you must sometimes go in their door and lead them out your door. To make his points, Stephen went in the door of humor and came out the door of spirituality.

Saint Monica was possibly the most successful example of this. Ironically, Elizabeth Rodriguez had had her doubts about playing the saint, even though Stephen had written the character with Elizabeth in mind. "When I first read it and saw all that crassness in her language, I thought: *Is that* all *I am to Stephen?* From the minute Saint Monica opens her mouth, she's talking like a truck driver!"

In time, she grew to appreciate her character. Her readings from books such as Peter Brown's *Augustine of Hippo* helped her understand this fourth-century Roman matron. "The key to Saint Monica is finding her heart," said Elizabeth. "And Monica's heart is her underlying passion to find the truth. There aren't many people who have a purpose in the world, but she's found hers, and she'll do anything to accomplish it. The fact that she sees just the slightest flicker of hope in Judas is all she needs."

During talk-backs, the cast said things I hadn't heard them say before, at least not explicitly. One night, Stephen spoke about how working on *Judas* had influenced his relationship with religion. "It's prompted me to be more *vocal* about questions about God. I'll say things, for example, in interviews and to the media about religion. Like, I think there's a real need right now not to let religion be somehow taken over by the right wing in this country. Actually, I think that if Jesus were around today, both the right *and* the left would be horrified. But the fact that I'm even thinking about things in this way is new for me."

Another night someone asked what Stephen's "goal" was for the play. "I never write with a result in mind," he said. "But I hoped the play would cause nonreligious people to reconsider things, religious people to think about how strong their faith is, and those in between to be stimulated to embrace spirituality a bit. And that seems to have happened, and that's meant a lot to me." He noted that he had received more mail about this show than any other.

I was amazed at how blunt the audiences could be, especially with Stephen. This was New York, after all, where everyone is not only a critic but also, apparently, a budding playwright or an aspiring actor. Very occasionally, people were downright nasty, or at least thoughtless. Callie Thorne was astonished that a few theatergoers were "insanely rude." But Stephen gave as good as he got, and for me the highlight of the talk-backs was Stephen's tart responses to some of the more direct questions:

> Q: You know, that one scene stopped the action dead in its tracks. What were you thinking when you wrote it?
>
> A: Well, I wasn't thinking, *Gee, how can I write a scene that will stop the action of the play?*
>
> Q: The language in your play was really offensive. Couldn't you have made the same points without all the foul language?
>
> A: [*long pause*] Maybe.

One night, an audience member asked me and Stephen if we were surprised that the show had generated little controversy.

I was. Early on, I told Phil and Stephen to prepare for protesters brandishing rosaries. Other shows that dealt with the subject matter, such as Terrence McNally's *Corpus Christi*, which featured Jesus and Judas as lovers, had drawn the rage of several Christian groups. I was also convinced that the foul language of the saints in the play would offend some Christians. But, in the end, I said to the audience, the respectful and deep consideration of Christianity in *Judas* seemed to have trumped any problems people might have had with the language or the contemporary portrayal of the saints.

Stephen had another viewpoint. "Well, it's not like Jesus and Judas were lovers."

"Thank God, too," I said.

"That was in the first draft," said Kohl, to laughter.

My Jesuit friends seemed particularly to enjoy the show. One night, I invited three Catholic theologians to the play. One, Elizabeth Johnson, a Catholic sister and distinguished professor of theology at Fordham University, was the author of *Consider Jesus*, the short book about the historical Jesus that Stephen had found useful for his work. Another, Roger Haight, a Jesuit priest and one of my professors in theology studies, was the author of a more controversial work, *Jesus, Symbol of God*, which had recently run afoul of some Vatican authorities. The third, a Jesuit named Drew Christiansen, was a well-respected moral theologian who had a wealth of experience with Jewish-Christian relations and a vast reservoir of knowledge about Judaism.

On the subway ride to the theater, I suddenly wondered what I was getting myself into. The presence of these three scholars would be a sort of final test of the script's accuracy.

That night, I sat in my usual place in the house seats, watching my guests more than the show, trying to determine whether they were enjoying it. Halfway through act 1, I remembered that Sister Johnson had also written books about the saints, so the show would be especially vulnerable to her criticism. I wondered how she would take Saint Monica's foul mouth.

But I relaxed when I saw them laughing loudly at the funny parts and paying especial attention to the more serious parts. Afterward, they were effusive in their praise. Sister Elizabeth called it "operatic," and Roger said it was "very dense" (high praise from a theologian). These were among the reviews that meant the most to me.

When we met up with the cast in the lobby, Stephen praised Sister Elizabeth's book, while Roger and Drew praised the performances of the actors. "I'm glad you liked it," said Sam, laughing, "because it's too late for me to change it anyway!"

Walking Mookie at Night

Over the four-week run of *Judas*, the cast astonished me with their resilience, their hard work, and their sheer dogged persistence, turning up every day (twice a day on weekends) despite a variety of challenges in their offstage lives. They had family illnesses to deal with, financial woes to attend to, and professional responsibilities to fulfill. Eric Bogosian, for example, was juggling a busy schedule of auditions in New York. Likewise for Elizabeth Rodriguez, for whom one audition required a quick flight to Los Angeles. Adrian Martinez, for example, starred in a movie that opened during the run. Stephen McKinley Henderson was preparing to teach an acting seminar. Sam had some photo shoots and a movie opening scheduled just a few weeks after the play's closing. Nearly all of the actors were auditioning for one thing or another, a process that even the most experienced of them described with varying degrees of annoyance.

"Auditioning can be brutal," said Yul Vázquez. "You're nervous, you go into a cold room with everyone staring at you, and you have one crack to get them to invite you to their party."

Toward the end of the run, Callie, who played the defense attorney, was shooting the television series *Rescue Me* in the morning and afternoons and appearing onstage in *Judas* at night. Her schedule was brutal. "I get up at five a.m.," she said. "Then I get dressed and walk my dog, Mookie. I'm picked up by a driver at six. We drive over to the set and I put in a full twelve-hour day. Then I have to race home, walk Mookie, and run over to the Public Theater for the eight o'clock show, and I work until eleven. And then we have talk-backs."

A few months after the show ended, I would see Callie in *Rescue Me,* the critically acclaimed series that centered around life in a New York firehouse; she was in one of the main roles that season. Callie portrayed the lead character's foulmouthed and slightly unhinged girlfriend, a juicy but physically demanding role that required frequent screaming, copious weeping, and hurling plates of food at her sullen firefighter boyfriend, played by Denis Leary. The intensity of Callie's performance in *Rescue Me* increased my appreciation of the consistency that she demonstrated during the run of *Judas.* Her ability to do both jobs at once, and do both well, seemed little short of amazing.

The next year would find Callie juggling roles on three shows: *Rescue Me, The Wire,* and *ER.* When I asked how she balanced the demands on her time, she laughed. "Well, I don't have a social life!" She described the party scene as something that was more or less expected of actors, but said that she was uncomfortable with the social part of the profession. "I'm much more comfortable working like a crazy person and just going home, taking care of Mookie, and relaxing."

Callie's role in *Judas* required her to memorize reams of dialogue. Like Yul Vázquez, the prosecuting attorney, she was also onstage for almost the entire two-and-one-half-hour show. And as it did with the rest of the cast, *Judas* took a toll on her. "It's certainly the most demanding play I've ever done—in terms of the readings, the memorization, and the intensity of the rehearsals, and the run itself. Usually there's just one part that's hard, but they were all difficult. And given the subject material, it seemed that there was more at stake—as if it was do-or-die every night. It was just exhausting."

Adrian had to tackle two roles in the same production that couldn't have been more different: the boastful and hyperactive Sigmund Freud, brought in to discuss the mental state of those who commit suicide, and the plainspoken Saint Thomas, who admits he was "the first one to say that I would die for Jesus" and also "the first to head for the hills doing ninety when the Romans came." As amusing as he was as the zany Dr. Freud, it was Adrian's sensitive portrayal of Saint Thomas, as a regretful disciple, that most touched me.

As recounted in the Gospel of John, the apostle Thomas is not present with the disciples when Christ first appears after his resurrection. In response to their reports of seeing Christ, Thomas famously doubts, asserting that only when he is able to put his fingers into the wounds of Jesus will he believe. A few days later, Jesus appears again and says to Thomas, "Put your finger here and see my hands. Reach out your hand and put it in my side. Do not doubt but believe." Thomas does so and says, "My Lord and my God!" (I have always wondered if his belief was based not simply on what he was shown, but on Christ's understanding what his old friend *needed* to be shown.)

In the play, Thomas wonders ruefully why he got the "benefit of his doubt" and Judas did not. In Adrian's hands, Thomas was probably the most human of the saints onstage. "He was a real person," said Adrian, "and he represents the doubts that all of us have. So playing Thomas was just about being honest."

Adrian juggled these two roles in the middle of several auditions and a publicity campaign for the indie film *Mail Order Wife*, all while he and his wife were expecting a baby. One evening, suited up as the Viennese doctor, he looked wan. "I have the worst stomach flu," he said weakly.

Having spent two years in Nairobi, I had some experience with gastrointestinal problems. I advised him to buy some Imodium, an over-the-counter remedy that had been a kind of salvation for me in East Africa. The next night, I asked if the Imodium had worked. He put his arm around me. "Father Jim," he said, "you know about the New Testament *and* you know about diarrhea. I thank you."

Adrian wasn't the only one who soldiered on in the face of illness. Thanks to the cold weather and the long hours, almost everyone in the cast and crew fell sick during the run. John Ortiz, besides going on auditions for a big-budget film in Miami, endured a nasty flu that landed him red-eyed and runny-nosed in the dressing room one night, nursing a cup of hot soup. "The Messiah has a cold," said one of the crew members.

Of all the roles in the play, Sam's seemed among the most demanding. Some of this was undoubtedly a result of how it mirrored the turmoil going on in his personal life. But much of it was the role itself. "I feel like a zombie," he told me one night as we left the theater. "It's a curious thing. But I guess it's not surprising. If you play a role like Adolf Hitler or Judas, I mean, if you really go there, it will take a toll on you."

Yet I heard no complaining. Frank Vitolo, the actor who was a longtime friend of Phil, Stephen, and many in the cast, said that this was not simply because a priest was around. A native New Yorker who, at age forty-seven, had worked in the world of theater, film, and television for many years, Frank had a disarmingly direct way of speaking and told me in no uncertain terms how fortunate I was to be working with these men and women.

"During the readings and the rehearsals and the run, these guys never stopped," he said after the show had ended. "They were working twelve, thirteen, fourteen hours a day! And even with all the changes and rewrites—rewrites even after previews—they never said a *peep*! And, look, I was in and out of that dressing room every day, hanging out, lying on the couch. In any other play, there would have been bitching and squawking and calling agents and all that crap, but there was *none* of that here!"

I asked him why this was. Certainly, he said, it had to do with the material of the play, and also the respect the cast and crew had for the playwright and the director. But Frank pointed to something else, something I had recognized but had not expected would influence the production: the humility of the members of *Judas*.

"Look," said Frank, "this is not coming from some dumb-ass perspective. I've been in this business for a long time. What these people are doing is what the Group Theatre did in the 1930s. They're making history. It's hard to see that when you're in the middle of it, but that's the truth. And Philip Seymour Hoffman and Stephen Adly Guirgis? Both of them could walk around and say, 'Look at me! Look at me!' but they don't. They're the most humble people I know. I don't know *anyone* else like that!"

Frank was on a roll. "Look at Yul Vázquez! You talk about humility! He was onstage almost the whole time and had pages and pages of dialogue to memorize. And I never once remember that guy asking for a line! He came into the *readings* able to do things off book. Man, that's humility. That's *art*!"

Another part of the cast's art was their willingness to continue to improve things during the run. Each time I sat in the audience, I

re wouldn't be no . . . story, okay? My name is MONICA—better
own to you mere mortals as SAINT Monica . . ." I was surprised to
d that I knew it word for word. They howled.

A few months later, John Ortiz asked me to repeat my perfor-
nce on the final night of the company's summer intensive workshop
Bennington College. Elizabeth was busy filming *Miami Vice* in
rida, but when her boyfriend, Brett, told her earlier in the day about
y upcoming performance, she said, "You tell Father Jim to *work* it!"
is I did, to hoots and hollers from the audience.

Having seen the show perhaps twenty times, I knew a number
passages cold. One night in the dressing room, I did Saint Peter's
onologue for Mums Grant, who was dog-tired from the long run.
Father Jim," he said sleepily, "you best not get too good at that! I might
st call in sick."

During intermission one night, Sam stormed into the dressing
oom. "Man, there's some guy out there coughing and coughing and
oughing. It's driving me f-----g *crazy*!" It was in the middle of the run,
when everyone was fighting either fatigue or a cold or both. The other
members in the cast agreed: the man's cough was amazingly loud and
remarkably disturbing to both the audience and the actors.

An hour or so later, during the evening's talk-backs, I heard it: a
oud hacking cough, almost a bark. I spotted who was doing it—an
elderly man in the first row.

Afterward, the coughing man approached me and cheerfully said
that he was a parishioner at a Jesuit parish in the Midwest. For a few
minutes, we talked about the theology that underpinned the play: how
despair worked in the spiritual life and the place of forgiveness in the
Christian tradition. Then he began to speak more personally, about his
own struggle with despair in his life after some difficult recent events.
He lowered his voice (but kept coughing loudly).

noticed something new in the actors' performances, another nuance
to Stephen's script, and previously unseen facets of Phil's direction.
One evening, I sat level with the stage and watched with amazement as
Pontius Pilate, played by Stephen McKinley Henderson, responded to
the defense attorney's charge of perjury.

In the scene, the defense attorney took Pilate to task for twisting the evidence about his involvement in the death of Jesus. As Pilate
stood to leave the courtroom, she taunted him: "If you were a man,
Pilate—you'd own up to the truth!"

Pilate narrowed his eyes, spun around, and exploded, much as I
imagine the original Pilate might have done. His scorching rage was
almost frightening at such close range:

> PILATE.   Whatchu know about what's a lie and what's the
> truth?! Whatchu know about my history?! Alls you
> got to go on is some book written four different
> ways by four different Jews wasn't even there in the
> first place! And whatchu know about my life *after*
> Palestine? Whatchu know about what I mighta did or
> didn't do when I got back home to the Motherland?
> Dass right—you don't know jack—do you? They
> didn't write down that part of the story, did they?

Stephen's immersion in his role had obviously paid off. "You know,"
he told me, "I realized that everybody lives according to a sort of *code* in
their lives. I live according to a code and have tried to do my best, and
I still feel guilty about certain things in life. So I can feel Pilate's sense
of remorse. And of course the words of Pilate are written in an African
American rhythm, too." His searing performance made the audience
sit up straight in their seats every night.

It was gratifying to know that I had played a small part in the development of these characters who made such an impact on the people in the audience. When I saw the faces of people listening to Mother Teresa speak about despair, or Saint Peter tell his story, or Simon the Zealot explain some of the theories about why Judas had betrayed his teacher, it always consoled me, as did the knowledge that some of my efforts were helping people think, even if in a small way, more critically about issues that are not often raised in the theater—or in any form of entertainment, for that matter. Frankly, they are questions that often go unattended even in religious settings. So every performance made me grateful.

∞

As much as the cast had prepared for the performances, there were some things that couldn't be controlled. One night, as Mother Teresa was about to take the witness stand, I heard sounds of a disturbance and the shuffling of chairs a few rows behind me. I wondered who was being so rude as to make that much noise. When I turned around, I saw that an elderly woman had fainted. Monica Moore, the stage manager, stopped the show. "Ladies and gentleman," she said, "we are going to take a short break while a sick audience member is cared for."

A few minutes later, an EMT team assisted the woman out of the theater, and the cast quietly left the stage. Afterward, when we found out that the woman was fine, the incident prompted some backstage teasing of John: "What kind of Jesus are you if you can't even help a woman who *fainted*?"

On the evening of Easter Sunday, Callie Thorne's Fabiana Aziza Cunningham shouted out the beginning of a theological challenge to God: "Either God's not All-Powerful and therefore useless—" at which

point all the lights in the theater went out. This v[...]
After some nervous shifting among the audience, [...]

In response, Eric Bogosian's Satan ad-libbed dr[...]
get for doing a play like this on Easter."

As the run continued, I spent more time in the [...]
in the audience and started to see how much the ca[...]
miss their time with one another once the play had er[...]
theater is the best part of my day," said Sal Inzerillo. Eri[...]
is a little like sports. It gives you an excuse to hang ou[...]

During the shows, a television monitor in the dre[...]
show what was going on onstage, while the cast hung[...]
gammon, reading books and magazines, snacking, ch[...]
cially on two-performance days, sleeping. If I hadn't be[...]
a few days, cast members would fill me in on the lates[...]
gotten a part in a film, who was sick, who had done s[...]
onstage the night before ("Father Jim," said Elizabeth [...]
Monica slipped on her high heels and almost broke her n[...]

My time backstage with the actors also gave me ad[...]
tunities to meet with those who were still struggling[...]
problems. So in time I felt that I could let down some of[...]
the cast as well. One night, I joked with Elizabeth and[...]
cast that I had heard her Saint Monica monologue so m[...]
I could easily sub for her if she ever took ill.

"Okay, Father Jim," she said, crossing her arms o[...]
"Let's hear it!"

I stood up and commenced the now-familiar mono[...]
had become one of my favorite parts of the show, not jus[...]
guage but for Elizabeth's vivid performance. "Hey, y'all.[...]
my world . . . So this is the part of the story, where, if it w[...]

For a few minutes I felt as if I were in the confessional rather than standing on the stage of the Public Theater. It was a strange, almost vertiginous, experience. And I thought: Am I the theological adviser, the pastoral counselor, the confessor, or some other hybrid? And what was my role with the cast and crew now: dramaturge, priest, counselor, or friend?

Then it dawned on me that I was trying to do what Jesuits are supposed to do: encounter people in all sorts of settings, especially unusual ones. There are a number of ways of expressing this goal: helping souls, being on the margins. My favorite definition of our work comes from the theologian John Courtney Murray who said that Jesuits should explain the church to the world, and the world to the church. And maybe standing on an Off-Broadway stage after midnight talking about forgiveness wasn't such a bad way of aiming for that goal.

At the end of our chat, we shook hands and the man said, "Thanks for listening to me. By the way, I had a bit of a cough tonight. You don't think it disturbed anyone, do you?"

ACT 5: HEARTS ON FIRE

April

The day before closing night, Pope John Paul II, who had led the Catholic Church for twenty-six years, died after an extended illness. As a result, the offices of *America* magazine, where I work, were deluged with requests for interviews from the media. I spent the next two days on the telephone with journalists and shuttling between television studios, answering questions about John Paul II, the papacy, the upcoming conclave, and the leading candidates to succeed him. ("Hey, celebrity priest!" said Sam that night on the phone.)

By the time I got to the theater on April 3, I was tired and overwhelmed—by the death of the pope, and by something else. One television anchor said as I walked onto the set of his news program, "Father, I can see how upset you are about the death of the pope." I hadn't the heart to tell him that though the pope's death was undeniably poignant, I was just as sad about the play coming to an end.

After two months of readings and rehearsals, two weeks of previews, and a four-week run, the cast, crew, and creative team were even more tired. And sadder, too. On closing night, the dressing room was filled with frenzied activity: people giving long hugs, exchanging gifts and cards, filming one another on video cameras, carefully taking down the photos and holy cards they had tacked up on their mirrors, and packing up their personal belongings—including, I was happy to see, some books on the saints that I had given them many weeks before.

The performance was the best one I had seen. Phil told me later that the play had "come into its own" as the run progressed. On closing night, it seemed as if the cast members weren't holding any emotions in check. And the play, after all the planning and tinkering and changing and editing, finally seemed complete.

Last Full Script Ever

The show opened with the familiar sound of rain in a darkened theater. By now, there were two changes in the cast. Deborah Rush's contract had ended; she was scheduled to move on to another play. She was replaced by Maggie Burke, a diminutive, dark-haired woman, as the mother of Judas, who spoke of her pain at having to bury her son. Deborah had played the scene quietly, without tears, though she told me that the writing was so powerful that she could easily have cried through the entire speech. Maggie appeared onstage as an angry mother who could barely control her fury over her son's fate.

The next scene opened on a harshly lit stage, with a single chair placed in the center of the floor. Liza Colón-Zayas, as the angel Gloria, strolled onto the narrow catwalk above the stage to explain where we were: a place called Hope, "right over here in downtown Purgatory." To the side of the stage, behind a wooden desk, a tired judge with frizzy white hair, played by Jeffrey DeMunn, banged his gavel and shouted, "Next case!"

Gloria continued to describe the differences between Purgatory and Hope. "Purgatory . . . has plumbing, and bodegas, and they even got a movie theater," she said as she took off her wings and hung them on a hook. "Hope—well it ain't got none a that." Her monologue always drew laughs during the run, but I never stopped wondering why Stephen had used this device. To me, it would have been easier to set the play in

Purgatory, and might have made the action clearer, but the playwright wanted us to live in Hope, at least for those two and a half hours.

Judas's attorney, Fabiana Aziza Cunningham—now played by Elizabeth Canavan, after Callie's run had ended—rose to request that the court hear the case of Judas Iscariot. As the judge and the bailiff argued over whether Cunningham's case should be heard, the prosecuting attorney, Yusef El-Fayoumy, ran onto the stage—literally ran. Yul Vázquez, sporting a three-day beard and slicked-back hair and wearing a ratty suit, skidded to a stop so fast that he often slipped. The bombastic prosecutor declared himself to be "willing and able to prosecute this sham of a case and defend the Gates of Heaven and the Kingdom of God!" He also flirted with his attractive courtroom opponent, who was dressed in a skintight skirt. "You have great legs, Fabiana. Free for dinner, perhaps?"

In the face of the judge's intransigence, and over the objections of the prosecution, the defense attorney cited the need for mercy and forgiveness in the divine economy. The judge remained unconvinced. "Your client sold out the son of God, for Chrissakes!"

To trump the judge's refusal to hear the case, Cunningham appealed to Saint Monica. With that, the lights dimmed, and a fanfare announced the saint's appearance—in the highest rafters of the theater, where she was illuminated by a single spotlight. "Hey, y'all," shouted Monica as she waved to the audience from her lofty perch.

After Monica described her intercessory skills, she climbed down a long ladder wearing silvery high-heeled boots, a feat of physical daring that never failed to impress me. She crossed the catwalk to meet Judas, who was seated cross-legged in a well, nearly motionless. Sam Rockwell, now with a full beard, wore a tattered white shirt and loose drawstring pants. In an attempt to shock him out of his stupor, Monica let loose a stream of invective. "Yo, Judas, you got change for thirty pieces of silver . . . ?!" But it was to no avail.

Gradually, though, Saint Monica began to see Judas as a pitiable person, "the leastest" of all God's creatures, as she said. She decided to take up his case and intercede for him. Saint Monica secured a writ signed by God, which Cunningham presented to the judge, who was now more annoyed than ever. The trial could begin.

But before the proceedings started, a few of the jury members were introduced. Gloria, the angel, shared jury duties with Butch Honeywell (played by Kohl Sudduth), an Everyman who was blithely unaware that he was dead; and Loretta (played by Yetta Gottesman), a woman on life support in a hospital back on earth. They sat in the jury seats on the sides of the stage. Gloria reminded the audience that not a lot is known about Judas "except that he was chosen to be an Apostle, he betrayed Jesus, and then he hung his-self. Not a lot to go on—especially when we're meant to rely on facts."

The first witness called was Henrietta Iscariot, who provided a brief defense of her son, recalling a kind deed that he had done as a boy. As she retold the story, Judas rushed onto the stage, slid to a halt, and began silently playing with a top. (Sam would have more than a few problems getting that top to spin from time to time.) Another Galilean boy, played by Mums Grant, ambled onstage wearing shorts and sandals to tell how difficult life was under the Roman occupiers. Judas had suffered, too; he confided that the Romans had killed his father. After the two shared their stories, Judas offered the boy his top, which his mother pointed to as a sign of his humanity.

Mother Teresa entered as the next witness. Liza hobbled slowly onstage with a cane, dressed in the familiar blue and white habit, and sat in the chair, her feet barely touching the floor. The prosecuting attorney was so enamored of Mother Teresa that he wept in her presence, which some audience members found amusing, others touching. "Mother! . . . You are the Oasis!" he said tearfully as he buried his face in the sleeve of her habit. His copious weeping forced him to leave the stage, which allowed for the appearance of two saints: Peter and Matthew.

From the catwalk, picked out by two spotlights, the saints spoke of their close relationships with Jesus of Nazareth. Mums Grant, as Saint Peter, mended his fishing net and told of Jesus' call to him beside the Sea of Galilee. Jeffrey DeMunn, who had changed out of his judicial robes and into the costume of Matthew, the tax collector called by Jesus, reminded the audience that tax collectors such as himself were seen as unclean, but having been called by Jesus, "I was clean again . . . I was *clean*." In the dark, Jeffrey climbed a ladder down to the stage, re-robed, and banged his gavel, restarting the proceedings.

In the courtroom, Mother Teresa returned to her testimony, speaking in a heavy Puerto Rican accent about the corrosive effect of despair, and accused Judas of falling into that sin. "The music of God's love and Grace kept playing, but he, he made himself hard of hearing," she said. The defense attorney didn't let Mother Teresa off easy, admonishing her for her shortcomings—accepting benefactions from dictators and despots—and saying that she knew little of the spiritual life.

"Defense calls Simon the Zealot to the stand," shouted the defense attorney after Mother Teresa had finished. A scruffy Sal Inzerillo strode onstage wearing a sweatshirt and too-short pants, accentuating his height and size, and holding a staff. Simon's testimony underscored the violence of the occupying Romans and linked Judas with the Zealots. "Well, he didn't go to the meetings or nuthin', but, yeah, he was pretty much a zealot if you ax me." He offered his explanation that Judas had been trying to force Jesus' hand. "Personally, I think Judas was trying to throw Jesus into the deep end of the pool—make him swim." It always made me smile to recall the provenance of the insight: from William Barclay to me to Sam and Stephen to Sal to the audience.

Next came the prosecution's star witness. "Most reverent señor," said El-Fayoumy, "with your magisterial permission, Prosecution now conjures Satan—Prince of Darkness—to the stand!"

Eric Bogosian was a superb Satan: oily, seductive, sly. He ambled onstage in an expensive charcoal-gray suit, often to applause. (During the few nights when Eric was unable to appear, Stephen Adly Guirgis took over the role: his Satan was more offhand and friendly.) When Satan was "conjured," he played to his conjurer. To the flattering prosecutor, he was a flatterer; they complimented each other on their attire, and their honesty. "I must say, Claimer of the Damned, your candor is quite refreshing," said El-Fayoumy.

In a flashback, Satan showed how he didn't have to tempt Judas at all. The lights dimmed, and we were in a seedy bar. Judas staggered onstage roaring drunk and spewing invective at Satan. Sam was a terrific drunk, and was also able to tap into a well of anger that surprised me, given his usual placid demeanor. Toward the end of the scene he calmed down and spoke to Satan about hell, which Satan described as "vastly underrated." Judas asked Satan what would happen if someone had betrayed Jesus of Nazareth. When Satan, quoting the Bible, suggested that it would have been better for that man "*if he had never been born*," Judas crumpled in despair. "Never been born???!!! That's heavy, man."

The flashback ended with Judas angrily denouncing Jesus. The prosecutor was triumphant. The gavel banged, and act 1 came to an end.

Stephen had tinkered a bit with the beginning of act 2. In its final incarnation, Saint Monica stood on the catwalk and pointed to Mary Magdalene, played by Yetta Gottesman, her long dark hair spilling over a flowing mauve dress. "This is Mary Mags—she the only bitch I let hang with me up here. Tell 'em whatchu gotta say." Mary Magdalene swiftly dispensed with two traditional images of her—whore and wife of Jesus—and spoke of her love for Jesus and the love that her teacher had for Judas, his "alter ego," as she said.

The next scene was the one that consistently drew the most laughter: the testimony of Sigmund Freud, called upon to discuss suicide. Adrian Martinez wore owlish glasses, and his frizzy black hair was parted down the middle and plastered to his head. Though Adrian looked nothing at all like Freud, he perfectly conveyed Herr Doktor's insouciant attitude toward the proceedings. The defense encouraged him to absolve Judas of his responsibility for killing himself. The prosecution, on the other hand, baited him mercilessly, reminding the jury of Dr. Freud's historic (and prodigious) use of cocaine. "Is that your real nose?" El-Fayoumy asked.

The ability to move quickly from farce to tragedy was one of Stephen's skills, and with the appearance of Caiaphas the Elder—played by Jeffrey DeMunn, wearing a dark suit and a yarmulke—the proceedings ventured into darker territory. Here began the in-depth examination of the "responsibility" for the death of Jesus. After the prosecution established the contempt that Caiaphas had for Pilate, the defense rose to accuse Caiaphas of handing over Jesus to the Roman authorities. After a quiet recitation of the facts, Caiaphas recounted the blasphemous actions of Jesus, his voice rising in anger: "*Who was he to forgive sin?!* Only God can do that! If that's not crossing the line, then I don't know what is!!" When Caiaphas argued that he was following the Jewish law, the defense attorney taunted him by saying that he had been appointed with Rome's blessing, and so was really serving Rome. In the rebuttal, the prosecution reminded the jury that it was Judas who approached Caiaphas, not the other way around.

As Caiaphas began to leave the stage, the prosecution told the high priest that he understood how difficult things were for him.

At this point, Caiaphas spun around to confront him. Here the whole tenor of the play changed. Caiaphas spat out his contempt for the lawyer's banal sentiments, after centuries of Christian persecution of the Jews. "I'm not interested in your forgiveness," he said. "Why? Because you have no idea. The people who need forgiving? The people who perpetrated the lies and exaggerations that became sacrosanct fact and led to hatred and violence for the past two thousand years? They are the ones who need forgiving—and not by you—but by me—me—and my people." During the exchange, El-Fayoumy seemed to shrink visibly, deflating under the weight of Caiaphas's rage.

A break from the heaviness came with Adrian's appearance on the catwalk, holding a beer can. "My name is Thomas," he said cheerfully. "At the Last Supper, I was the first one to say that I would die for Jesus, and I was also the first one to head for the hills doing ninety when the Romans came and arrested him." Thomas described Judas as "a bit of a jerk-off" but a loyal man and wondered why he hadn't been given the benefit of the doubt. When Thomas doubted, Jesus appeared to him after the Resurrection. When Judas doubted, he was led into despair and killed himself. "Judas was a d——k, but he deserved better," said Thomas. "Just one Saint's opinion."

As soon as Thomas left the catwalk, the defense introduced "ancient surveillance footage" showing what happened after Jesus' arrest. The lights dimmed, and a huge white screen was brought onstage. A grainy black-and-white film unspooled, revealing a repentant Judas desperately trying to recant before Pontius Pilate. Pilate disdained the man. "Whatchu need to do is relax, brother," he said. The short film ended with Judas collapsed on the ground in misery.

Pilate was already seated onstage when the lights came up again. Stephen McKinley Henderson wore golfing attire and glared at the lawyers. After the defense had him state his credentials, Pilate spoke about his need to "put his foot down" on the Jews. "Orders from Rome," he explained "—what's a brothah to do?" But the defense reminded the jury that only Pilate had the authority to crucify—not the high priest, not King Herod, and not the Jewish people. "Am I on trial here?" he exploded. The defense condemned the Roman procurator of Judea for his actions: there is nothing to suggest, she said, that he would have given a second thought to killing Jesus of Nazareth. "You didn't wash your hands, Pontius Pilate—History did it for you," she concluded.

In response, Pilate testily explained his decision to kill Jesus. He wanted to spare him, he said, but was compelled by fear of a Jewish insurrection. "I did what I had to do to preserve the damn peace! Why?! 'Cuz that was my damn job!"

There was a final witness. Now called by the defense, Satan mirrored Cunningham's worst fears. He baited her with her missteps in life, with her failures. And when she asked him whether he tempted human beings, Satan airily denied it. Their dialogue became a complicated theological disquisition on free will, with the defense growing more confused by the minute. In frustration, she shouted, "You're a . . . liar!!" Satan looked at her with a saturnine expression and said, "I'm truly sorry you feel that way."

In the final scene, Judas and Jesus had their confrontation. Though I had read it and seen it dozens of times, on closing night it brought me to tears.

In its final incarnation, the scene started with John Ortiz, dressed in a white shirt, khaki pants, and sandals, walking onto a dark stage. "Right now, I am in Fallujah. I am in Darfur," he said, and began a long monologue on his omnipresence and compassion. He walked over to a ladder and climbed up to the catwalk to confront Judas, who sat motionless. A bucket sat beside Judas.

Jesus gently laid a hand on Judas. *"DON'T F——N' TOUCH ME!"* shouted Judas.

Jesus withdrew. "I'm sorry."

"JUST BACK OFF MY GRILL, MAN!" Judas screamed. *"BACK OFF!"*

Jesus reminded Judas that he was always beside him, always with him. "Where's your *heart* in all this, Judas?" asked Jesus. "You were *all heart*. You were my heart! Don't you know that?!"

JUDAS. I'll tell you what I know: I watched you trip over your own dusty feet to heal the sick, the blind, the lame, the unclean—*any two-bit stranger stubbed their f—n' toe!* When some lowly distant relative— too cheap to buy enough wine for his own f—n' wedding—suddenly runs out of booze—no problem, you just "presto change-o"—*and it was f—n' Miller time in ol' Cana again, wasn't it, bro?! But when I f—n' needed you—where the f—k were you, huh?!*

JESUS. Judas—

JUDAS. You forgave Peter and bullshit Thomas—you knocked Paul of Tarsus off a horse—you raised Lazarus from the *f—n' dead*—but me? Me? Your "heart"? . . . *What about me??!! What about me, Jesus?! Huh?!* You just, you just—I made a mistake! And if that was wrong, then you should have told me! And if a broken heart wasn't sufficient reason to hang, *THEN YOU SHOULD HAVE TOLD ME THAT, TOO!*

When Judas spat in Jesus' face, Jesus offered him forgiveness, asking, "Will you feed my lambs?"—the same request he made to Saint Peter in the Gospel of John.

But Judas could not. Or would not. As he uttered his final words of despair, "I can't," Judas slowly slipped back into silence. The stage directions read, "JUDAS is frozen again."

Onto the catwalk came Butch Honeywell, the plainspoken foreman of the jury, who until this point in the play had had only a few lines. In a long monologue, Butch, standing before the silent Jesus and Judas, spun the story of his own personal betrayal: he had once cheated on his young wife, and ruined his life. When Butch reached the end of his intimate story of human failure, he dropped his head and wept. The lights dimmed, with a spotlight on Jesus and Judas.

In the final directions of the script:

> JESUS *sighs, takes off his shirt, plunges it in the bucket, rinses it, and begins to wash* JUDAS's *feet.* JESUS *washes meticulously and with care. He washes. And washes. Perhaps the water is mixed with tears.*
> *Lights fade.*
> *The end.*

For me, it was a stunning scene, and it encapsulated not only the despair of Judas, but also the compassion and persistence of Jesus. I was reminded of Phil's comment that he saw Jesus as essentially a person who would cause "havoc," in public as well as in people's inner lives.

For Callie, the scene was almost impossible to watch from backstage, because of its dead-on description of the workings of despair. "Some nights I would cry so hard I would have to leave the room," she said.

"Here were these two individuals—one couldn't hear and one couldn't be heard. That scene would just break my heart, because it reminded me that even though I deny it, God is with me all the time."

After the play ended, John Ortiz told me that this scene had helped him understand compassion. "My experience of trying to love Judas—loving him unconditionally and loving him as he *was*—helped me to see how Jesus loves me."

Dramatic Faith

When the lights went down on the closing night performance, the audience stood up to cheer and stamp their feet on the risers. The cast assembled for the last time to accept the audience's praise. Stephen was called onstage, took a well-deserved bow, and exited the stage with the cast. In my seat in the front row, I found myself tearful, hoping that no one would see. This was it, I thought. *The Last Days of Judas Iscariot* would never again exist in this form, with this cast, on this stage. What everyone had worked for all these months was now finished.

Now I better understood how the show had influenced my faith. *The Last Days of Judas Iscariot* began its first readings in January, just a few weeks before Lent began that year. The play opened for previews the day before Ash Wednesday. The run continued throughout the season of Lent, and the play closed shortly after Easter Sunday. This timetable meant that during the run, the stories of the final days of Jesus' ministry—his entry into Jerusalem, his last meal with his friends, his betrayal at the hands of Judas, and his capture, trial, and crucifixion—were being read during daily Masses. At the same time I was thinking about Jesus and Judas onstage, I was thinking about them while I was in church.

And I was thinking about the story in my prayer.

The most common type of prayer used by Jesuits comes from *The Spiritual Exercises* of Saint Ignatius. It goes by many names: "imaginative prayer," "composition of place," and "Ignatian contemplation." In this spiritual practice, one attempts to place oneself imaginatively in a scene from the Bible. For example, a person might imagine himself by the Sea of Galilee at the moment Jesus called Peter to push his boat out to sea, cast out his nets, and draw in the miraculous catch of fish that marked the beginning of his new life. Or a person might imagine herself present at the site of Jesus' first miracle, the wedding feast in Cana, when the water was changed into wine in front of the startled guests and (perhaps) the startled Jesus.

In each meditation, one tries to notice what feelings are evoked: perhaps gratitude for times of conversion in one's life, or longing to follow God more closely, or even sorrow for the times that one has felt separated from God. Underlying all of this is the trust that God works even through the imagination.

On closing night, it dawned on me that for the past six months, I had engaged in precisely the kind of extended meditation that Saint Ignatius had recommended. I had placed myself in scenes from the Gospels, heard the saints and the apostles speak boldly about their astounding experiences, and observed the consequences of good and bad decisions in a life. The play had helped me to pray.

In the process, I discovered something surprising: I believed the story I saw onstage. Six months earlier, during my first meeting with Sam, I had suggested that Judas probably was a devout follower of Jesus and probably betrayed Jesus because he wanted to force his teacher's hand, and that Jesus probably pitied Judas more than he condemned him. These insights were based on my years of reading about the "historical Jesus." Those academic speculations about Judas, a man about whom we know almost nothing, seemed to make the most sense to me, at least intellectually.

I had long believed in the Gospel narrative: the story of the life, death, and resurrection of Jesus. But now I believed in another part of the story. It seemed clearer that Judas had been a friend to Jesus and had initially wanted him to succeed. Of course Jesus and Judas loved each other, and still loved each other, but in the way that two friends do who find themselves no longer able to connect. And of course Jesus would have pitied Judas for his actions and wanted to offer him forgiveness. Maybe he already had. What I had surmised with Sam months ago I now felt sure of.

Stephen McKinley Henderson put it eloquently: "The only thing Jesus despairs of is the despair of others."

The play affected me on another, perhaps deeper, level as well. Each night at the Public Theater, the cast of *Judas* told, to a new audience, the tale of Jesus of Nazareth and his circle of friends. Watching the actors reminded me of the original tellers of the tale, who were also the original participants in the drama: people such as Peter and Mary Magdalene and Matthew and Thomas and Simon the Zealot. After witnessing Jesus' life over a three-year period—seeing his amazing miracles and hearing his parables and stories and being witnesses to his passion, death, and resurrection—the first disciples would have found it impossible to be silent, to refrain from telling their own versions of the tale. They, like many people in the arts, would have been compelled to express what they had witnessed.

This first generation of storytellers would have passed their stories on to members of the early church, who huddled behind closed doors and gathered in back rooms to tell the stories to one another and to new members of their group. Perhaps these people heard the stories directly from one of the apostles. And perhaps these earliest Christians, now one degree removed from the action, needed to dramatize things, to "get up," as actors say, to communicate their tales more effectively. Who knows if, in those hidden rooms, first in Judea, then in Asia Minor, the early Christians might not have acted out some of these scenes for one another?

Finally, we come to the evangelists, the writers of the Gospels, who would set down the stories on the page. Like any good playwright, Matthew, Mark, Luke, and John needed an eye for narrative structure—an understanding of where to place a miracle story and where to place a saying of Jesus, for example—as well as a good ear for dialogue and clever turns of phrase. If you study the texts carefully, you can see how the later Gospels used the earlier ones and subtly altered the structure of the story to meet the needs of their communities. Sometimes they even explained things that were not clear in the earlier telling.

The four evangelists would have understood how a well-told story can convey truth. Some of the storytellers were Jews writing for a Jewish audience steeped in the stories of the Hebrew Scriptures. The listeners would have heard echoes from the ancient Scriptures as they listened to what had happened to Jesus. They might have asked themselves, Didn't the story of Jesus sound like the story in Genesis of Joseph, who was also betrayed, by his twelve brothers, but who in the end redeemed them? Didn't the story of Jesus remind them of the prophecies of Isaiah, who spoke of someone who would bring sight to the blind, heal the lame, and set captives free?

The evangelists also spoke Greek, as did many of their listeners, and so they likely knew the tradition of the Homeric bards and were familiar with the Greek plays that told of the doings of earlier gods.

Many of the Gospel stories, in fact, seem like little dramas, with vivid characters and surprising endings and memorable dialogue.

Sometimes it almost seems that the evangelists were writing specifically for the stage. When Saint Mark tells about the paralytic man being healed, he sets a marvelous scene. The event is related in all three synoptic Gospels. A great crowd gathers outside a man's home to see the great prophet Jesus of Nazareth. When four men bring along their friend, a paralytic man lying on a mat, they cannot get through the crowd to Jesus. So they clamber onto the roof and begin to tear it apart. We can imagine a first-century audience saying, "Unbelievable! That man must have really wanted to meet Jesus! And his friends must have really loved him to do that!"

The man, still lying on his mat, is gently lowered to the ground and deposited before Jesus. Seeing the men's faith, Jesus is filled with compassion and tells the paralytic man that his sins are forgiven. But the religious authorities in the crowd are shocked. They ask, as does Caiaphas in Stephen's play, "Who can forgive sins but God alone?" In response, Jesus says, "'But so that you may know that the Son of Man has authority on earth to forgive sins'—he said to the paralytic—'I say to you, stand up, take your mat and go to your home.'"

With that little aside, Mark is giving some stage directions. And then comes the dramatic ending: the man is healed, picks up his mat, and walks away. The crowds are amazed. "We have never seen anything like this!" they say.

It is not difficult to imagine people in antiquity applauding after hearing the miraculous ending to the story—an ending everyone wants, because it presents a just and compassionate response from God. The evangelists told their stories so well that we are reading their tales two thousand years later.

Phil Hoffman found the experience of telling that story a moving one. As a boy, he had been powerfully drawn to the Christian faith when he began accompanying his sister to meetings of her evangelical group. Now he was, in essence, responsible for an entire group of people reenacting the Gospel, or at least parts of it, every night.

"I wanted people to see Christ the way I saw him," he told me after the play ended. "I wanted them to see a Christ who fought for people with desperate conviction. And I wanted him to be tough and real and exciting!"

Then he said, bluntly, "I hoped the play would make people feel closer to God, and make it easier for them to see things about God, and maybe not be so skeptical."

Faithful Drama

Seeing the story of Jesus and Judas told every night reminded me of the importance of narrative in the spiritual life. Each night, the actors were presenting the same story over and over, the way the evangelists had done, in the hope that something personal might be sparked within the lives of the audience.

When I was on retreat some years ago, a spiritual director told me, "We're all stories." When pressed for an explanation, he said, "When you ask someone who they are, they will tell you a story. They will say: I was born here, I went to school here, I moved here." People see their lives as stories, he said. That's one reason people connect with stories so easily.

The dramatic arts that my friends had mastered—writing, directing, acting—were essential tools for telling a good story. Along with writing and preaching and painting and sculpting, acting has long been an important means of conveying religious truth. As Sister Martha Kirk writes in *A New Dictionary of Sacramental Worship*, our contemporary and Western distinctions between drama and religious ritual did not exist for much of the history of civilization. Ancient Greek and Roman dramas found their origins in religious ritual and in cultic activities that were highly dramatic. Likewise, the Hebrew Scriptures contain numerous examples of the dramatization of God's message: Jeremiah breaks a pot to give force to the image of God's wrath. Ezekiel lies on the ground to illustrate the destruction of Jerusalem.

Even the story of the Last Supper contains overtly dramatic actions. Not only did Jesus reenact the Passover during the seder, as all Jewish men and women did and still do, but he also enacted for the disciples his ideal of service: the washing of feet. Rather than telling his disciples that they should be servants, he stripped off his tunic and washed the feet of Peter. Jesus literally acted out his message.

The whole of the liturgical year—the annual cycle of church feast days and commemorations—can be seen as a kind of extended drama. While the secular calendar moves from January to December, the liturgical calendar follows another timetable: beginning with the birth of Jesus, continuing through his young adulthood, baptism, and ministry of preaching and healing, and ending with his passion, death, and resurrection. During the liturgical year, believers participate in this drama, finding themselves alternately uplifted and saddened, much as one would be in a richly imagined performance onstage.

And clearly, the central act of worship in the Catholic Church, the celebration of the Mass, is a drama. It is a dramatic retelling of the passion, death, and resurrection that includes dialogue between the presider and the congregation, who act as a kind of Greek chorus. The gestures, symbols, and ritual of the Mass are a means of telling a story and pointing to another, deeper reality. The Masses for the holy

Stories are important for believers. In a way, Jesus of Nazareth was himself a story told by God. If Jesus believed that the best way to communicate spiritual truths was through parables, one might assume the same of God. God needed to tell something to humanity, so he came up with a parable, too: Jesus. Someone asked Jesus, "What is the kingdom of God like?" In response, he told parables of wheat and weeds, fish and nets, mustard seeds and birds, and wayward sons and forgiving fathers. We ask God, "What are you like?" and God gives us the story of Jesus. Jesus is the parable of God.

When the cast returned for a final curtain call on the last night, Elizabeth Rodriguez grabbed my hand and pulled me onstage to take a bow with them. As I stood with the cast of *Judas*, I was overwhelmed with emotion: gratitude, sadness, appreciation, wonder. The tears that filled my eyes shouldn't have been embarrassing but were—I generally don't cry in front of two hundred people. And I thought that I had finally begun to understand the draw of the theater for the men and women with whom I had worked during the past few months. Afterward, I had to excuse myself to duck into the bathroom and let the emotions spill out. It was a bit of a physical relief as well; though I was terribly sad to see it end, the tiring pace of working full-time at the magazine and helping out at the theater was something I couldn't have kept up for much longer.

The closing night party was held in an upstairs room at another dimly lit bar, where the cast drank and danced and retold funny stories of the past few weeks. When I bumped into Phil, I apologized for continually interrupting him at rehearsals, but he just laughed. "No, no, you were always welcome!" Upstairs, I danced with Saint Monica and Mary Magdalene and Mother Teresa into the wee hours.

Leaving the bar was difficult. I knew it would mark the official end of the play and a wonderful period in my life. I loved this group of artists and felt loved by them. I had experienced a bond with an unusual kind of community and now felt a sense of loss as my time with them was ending. But the ministry of a Jesuit and a priest necessitates moving on to the next task. We love those with whom we work, but we also seek that famous detachment that allows us to love freely.

My time with the group was a great gift—or, to quote Scripture, a "full measure." The first was obvious: getting to know some generous men and women who welcomed me into both their professional and their personal lives. The second was the opportunity to help, if in a small way, create something new. Third was the opportunity to see how the theater works from an insider's vantage point. And the fourth gift was being able to sit around and talk with these extraordinary people about some of the most human of questions: What is faith? Who is God? What do I believe?

It was all a surprise, too. I hadn't sought out the opportunity to work on a play. I hadn't looked for a chance to work with actors. I hadn't expected to use, in this sort of way, all the reading I had done about the historical Jesus. Like many of the great blessings in life, it was unexpected and unmerited. I had encountered what one spiritual writer called the God of surprises.

And sometimes, during those early readings, as we sat around those big folding tables in the theater talking about Jesus of Nazareth, I felt as if I were hearing the story, which I thought I had known so well, for the first time.

Just a Little More Faith

The play had moved the actors along their individual spiritual paths, but in different ways. After the run ended, I asked some of them whether they thought about faith any differently. In doing so, I had to adjust my expectations. For secretly I'd harbored the hope that spending time with the Gospel stories would help all the actors become more spiritual, more religious, and, in some cases, more Christian.

But the play's effect was infinitely subtler than that, and I was reminded (once again) that people's spiritual lives are far too complex to be measured as if they were fuel gauges set to either full or empty.

I was curious how playing a contemporary icon of holiness had affected Liza Colón-Zayas. "You know, I went into the role of Mother Teresa thinking that she was like this pure spirit or something," she said over dinner at an Ethiopian restaurant a few weeks after the play had closed. "But I learned from my reading and our discussions that she was human, and that she had these opinions that I strongly disagreed with, but I still felt that I could really respect her for her work with the poor.

"Stephen's play was really about not being so sure about what's been drilled into your head about religion," she said. "It helped me to see that it's okay to question things. During those table readings, we were able to look at the other side of the coin. I mean, everything used to seem conditional when it came to religion, but I think that with God things are unconditional. Like, when I was in that cult, I used to think of Jesus as a parole officer!"

I laughed when I heard her analogy. I had never heard it put quite that way. "No, *really*!" she said, laughing. "Now I know that you can be a f--kup, and Jesus will still be there for you. And I don't really fear death anymore, like I used to. Now I think it'll all be good."

Around the same time, I asked Elizabeth Rodriguez how the immersion into a saint's life had affected her. She had been raised in a Latino Catholic household that—like that of Yul Vázquez—readily mixed Santería and Catholicism. She prayed frequently as a child. "And I liked going to church, even by myself, for the peace that it gave me."

But her family's overemphasis on the saints turned her off so much that before the play she was uninterested in the lives of the saints. As an adult, she still prayed to God, but when it came to organized religion, she "didn't take a stand one way or another." Saint Monica's story, however, spoke to her, especially Monica's prayers and works on behalf of her son Augustine.

"Reading about Saint Monica gave me an insight into the mothering part of her," she explained. "And during the play I felt like I was becoming as unapologetic as she was about her truth. You know, I'm not a mother, but when I talk to my girlfriends they tell me that they would do *anything* for their kids. Monica felt that way about her son, and about Judas."

This idea of the saints—and, by extension, God—going to any lengths necessary to reach human beings has a long provenance in Christian theology. Francis Thompson's nineteenth-century poem "The Hound of Heaven," for example, describes a God who pursues us even as we flee. "I fled Him," begins his poem, "down the nights and down the days; / I fled Him, down the arches of the years; / I fled Him, down the labyrinthine ways / Of my own mind; and in the mist of tears."

The God who pursues is also at the heart of many of Jesus' parables, including the parables of the woman who sweeps her entire house to find a lost coin and, most famously, the shepherd who leaves the other ninety-nine sheep behind to find the one lost sheep. In these parables, God's pursuit of us can seem profligate, foolish, even reckless.

But Elizabeth's insight about a mother and her children has even more specific antecedents. In her book *She Who Is: The Mystery of God in Feminist Theological Discourse*, Elizabeth Johnson points to multiple images of God as mother in both the Old and the New Testaments, even though these metaphors have been "actively derogated and consciously erased from the repertoire of suitable images" by male commentators on Scripture. "Can a woman forget her nursing child?" asks the prophet Isaiah, speaking in the name of God. It is a powerful image of the all-embracing love of a mother who will stop at nothing to save her children.

"Monica felt that way about anyone who was treated unjustly," said Elizabeth. "I mean, as soon as she opens her mouth, she's like this *locomotive*! But all that ferocity came out of love."

For Elizabeth, the entire experience of the play was something she wouldn't fully understand until long after the show had ended. "When you're doing the play, it's all about being in the moment, and it's sometimes hard to be outside of yourself," she said. "Even during the run, when people would come up to me in the lobby crying and tell me how much it meant to them, even though I was really honored, it was hard to take it in."

But one evening, several months later, she saw the movie *Capote*, starring Phil Hoffman. Walking home afterward, she saw Phil. "And I thought how honored I was to be a part of the same business, and I thought how this guy directed me in this play, and what a great thing we were able to do together. And I just cried and cried. You know, I try to be grateful to God as much as I can. But sometimes it's hard to feel something special when you're *in* it, which is really unfortunate, isn't it?"

Of course I was curious about how playing Jesus would affect an actor. "Playing Jesus helped me to see what it was like to love someone unconditionally, to love someone as they are," said John Ortiz. "It also helped me to see how God loves us.

"And you know," he said, "during the run I started to feel like my life was beginning to get a little better. I was seeing that in relationships, and with myself, and with my career, too. Big changes were starting to happen: I bought a house and accepted a role in a big film. And the amazing thing was that I wasn't freaking out at all—and this would have been a good occasion for freaking out! I felt like things were happening for a reason. And I think it's because I'm more *aware* of all this stuff. My relationship to God and to Jesus has grown significantly; it's based more on communication, it's more open now, and it's great to be aware of that. I feel like everything is going to be okay now."

For Yul Vázquez, the play represented a "demystification" of the Gospels. "I've always thought that Jesus was God, but I never really had it explained to me." The theme of despair also made an impression on the actor. "You know, I've had these moments in life, especially when I was in the band, where I would wonder what I was doing with my life. Once, when I was playing guitar, I developed this awful tendonitis, and I thought, *If I can't play again, if my career ends, what will I do?* But you just have to continue. When Judas despairs, and Jesus tries to help him, you can see that it's just Judas getting in his own way. Jesus wants to help him, but Judas becomes a victim of his own ego."

Not surprisingly, Stephen Adly Guirgis's perspective on the spiritual life had been altered during the long process of creating the play. "For one thing, I pray more now," he said. "And I pray more for a willingness to be open. Before, I used to pray for results."

When I asked if he felt any differently about his Catholic faith, he offered a story that reached back to his childhood and his experience with the Dominican nuns at Corpus Christi School. When he was in the sixth grade, one of his teachers used to read one chapter of The Chronicles of Narnia to Stephen's class each day, as a sort of treat. C. S. Lewis's famous tale is both a children's adventure story and an allegory of Christian themes. "The sister would read it to the class and explain the imagery to us," Stephen explained. At the end of the series, the powerful Christlike figure Aslan, a wise lion, confronts his vanquished enemy.

"There was this evil prince," said Stephen, "who all the while had been fighting against Aslan and against the good guys. But when he was finally judged by Aslan, he was not condemned. And all of Aslan's followers were pretty upset. But Aslan said that though the evil prince was misguided, he was true to his motives."

Stephen remembered struggling with his faith during that time, and struggling with the notion of a good God condemning Judas. "Lewis's story taught me that maybe things were more like I thought they were, that God was merciful to everyone, even sinners. I felt like the story had opened a door for me when I was a child. But I didn't want to walk through it. There was still so much fear.

"With the play," he said, "I feel like I'm starting to walk through the door."

Sam Rockwell fell silent when I asked about his faith after the play. I was most curious about how the play had affected him because one of the first things he had told me was how little he knew about religion.

"I still don't know if I believe everything," he said tentatively. "But the play did inform my faith, and I think about Jesus in a different way. I think the message of Jesus is about love and forgiveness, and I feel closer to that, and I also feel like I know how to *talk* about it."

Then Sam warmed to the topic. "There's an important message in all those stories we talked about, and his message is still relevant, and it's still a challenge to the world. Jesus still challenges people. You know, like no one's better than anyone else, and let the one without sin cast the first stone." He paused. "But, you know, organized religion can be such a nightmare sometimes. Like, what does homophobia have to do with God? What does God have to do with any of *that*?"

For Sam, the whole experience of the play was, as he said, a "religious" one. He laughed as he listed some of the more bizarre happenings around the set—like the power outage on Easter Sunday. "There was always something, I don't know, *lurking* around that play."

"I guess I know more about Jesus and his message," he said, by way of summing up. "But I just hope I don't fake it or take it for granted now, because during these last few months there was this feeling in me, this feeling that I had just a little more faith."

✺

The weekend after closing night, I celebrated Mass at St. Ignatius Loyola Church, a local Jesuit parish. Some of the cast and crew, even some who weren't Catholic, said they wanted to come.

I very much hoped that Stephen would attend, as he had not been to Mass for some time. That morning, however, he called me with bad news. "Hey, Jim," he said. "I'm really sorry, but I don't think I'll be able to come to your Mass this morning. I think there's a leak in the apartment above me, and the superintendent isn't coming until ten. It's like a f----g *river*."

I told him I would pray to one of the stars of his play, Saint Monica. In my room I knelt down, lit a few candles for good measure, and said a prayer to her for a miracle: "So here I am, giving you a shout: let Stephen be able to come to Mass." It was hard not to think of her dressed like Elizabeth, with her silvery boots.

On my way to church in a cab, I called Stephen and told him I was praying for a miracle. "Well, I don't know," he said. "It doesn't look too hopeful. The super's not here yet."

Inside the church, I lit another candle and said another prayer to Saint Monica. By the time I reached the sacristy, I figured it was time for another call. "Any miracles yet?" I asked.

"You know, I think it's going to be okay," he said. "It's just a radiator leaking upstairs. I turned it off myself."

As I stood in the pulpit and began to read the Gospel, I looked toward the rear of the church and saw the great brass doors open. It was Stephen. He ambled in and took a seat in the last pew. I looked around and noticed for the first time that several cast members and their friends were scattered throughout the crowded church.

The Gospel reading for that Sunday was from the book of Luke. In the story, Jesus, after his Resurrection, appears to two of his disciples, who are traveling to a town called Emmaus. They are disconsolate at the death of their leader and friend. The risen Jesus comes to join them along the road, but at first they don't recognize him, even when he interprets Scripture for them and reminds them of the prophetic literature that foretold the suffering of the Messiah. He helps them, in essence, understand the meaning of his suffering. They invite him to stay the night at their home. And as they sit down to the evening meal and he breaks the bread and blesses it, their eyes are opened, as the Scripture says, and they recognize who it is who sits before them.

Later, the two wonder how they could not have recognized Jesus at first. "Were not our hearts burning within us," they ask themselves, " . . . while he was opening the scriptures to us?"

The story of the road to Emmaus is often used to explain how we can overlook the transcendent even when it's right in front of us, and how sometimes we notice God only after an experience has passed us by. In my homily, I talked about how human the disciples were, how even those who had been in the presence of Jesus could doubt, and how it's important to always look for signs of God's presence. And I talked about how my time with *Judas* was a real experience of grace, a wonderfully surprising gift from God, and how I hadn't fully understood that until closing night when I looked back on the whole experience. As I talked about this, I could see Mary Magdalene, Mother Teresa, Simon the Zealot, and Judas's mother listening intently.

Afterward, I greeted everyone on the steps of the church, in the open air, feeling the sun on my face, and I told them how grateful I was that they had come to Mass.

"You came to see *our* show," said Deborah Rush, to laughter. "How could we miss yours?"

FOR FURTHER READING

For readers interested in learning more about the historical Jesus, there are dozens of good books. Perhaps the best place to begin is Albert Nolan's *Jesus before Christianity*, which serves as a terrific brief introduction to life in first-century Palestine and provides an idea of what we can really know about Jesus of Nazareth. For a brief introduction to the content of the four Gospels, you might try *Who Is Jesus? Why Is He Important?*, by Daniel J. Harrington, SJ, a renowned Scripture scholar who brings his years of experience to bear in a book that is remarkably succinct. *Consider Jesus*, by Elizabeth Johnson, CSJ, is a look at Christology, that is, the process by which the church developed its theological understanding of Jesus Christ. In the book, readers will find discussions about, for example, the Christian concepts of the human and divine "natures" of Jesus Christ and the "self-knowledge" of Jesus. Like Nolan and Harrington, Johnson has also written a book that has the benefit of being short.

For the truly ambitious, the best overview of the historical Jesus is John Meier's magisterial multivolume work *A Marginal Jew: Rethinking the Historical Jesus*. In it you will find everything you could ever want to know about the historicity of various scenes from the Gospels and the historical evidence for incidents from the lives of Jesus and his followers. Meier's first volume, *The Roots of the Problem and the Person*, includes a fascinating look at the criteria used by contemporary Scripture scholars for determining what is historical and what may have been added by the Gospel writers. For a comprehensive overview of the Gospels in general, including some theological reflections, you might try *An*

Introduction to the New Testament, by Raymond E. Brown, SS, the work of an eminent scholar but accessible to the general reader.

Some of the best material about the historical Judas is found in the books mentioned above. But perhaps the best one-volume work on the betrayer of Jesus is *Judas: Images of the Lost Disciple*, by Kim Paffenroth, which not only seeks to place the man in a historical context but also looks at the way in which his story was used by subsequent generations, typically to suit their own purposes.

Most readers will, by this point, be interested in reading the final version of Stephen Adly Guirgis's play *The Last Days of Judas Iscariot*, published a few months after the play closed at the Public Theater. While I included some of my favorite scenes in this book, quoting the play selectively fails to do justice to the playwright's creativity. I encourage you to read the play in its entirety.

TALK-BACKS

At the late-night talk-backs after a few of the performances, the actors would invariably thank Phil, Stephen, and one another (and me). Now it's my turn.

I want to thank the cast, crew, and creative team of *The Last Days of Judas Iscariot*. They always made me feel welcome in their world, and the confidence they placed in me, both personally and profession-ally, was consistently touching. I appreciate their letting me use their personal stories and observations in these pages, and I hope that this book conveys some of the affection I feel for these men and women, even those who aren't mentioned by name. Special thanks go to Sam Rockwell, Stephen Adly Guirgis, Philip Seymour Hoffman, and John Ortiz for their initial invitation to participate in the production. Thanks also go to Abby Marcus, formerly of the LAByrinth Theater Company, and the wonderfully efficient staff at the Public Theater for their help, and for their patience in getting me (and my friends) complimentary tickets. And I'm grateful to LAB for inviting me to join their company the year after *Judas* closed. (I happily accepted.)

As for this book, I am grateful to Daniel J. Harrington, SJ, pro-fessor of New Testament at the Weston Jesuit School of Theology, in Cambridge, Massachusetts, for reviewing the manuscript and correcting any errors I made regarding the Gospel narratives. Father Harrington, a remarkable and sensitive teacher, has an astounding grasp of the New Testament and an amazing attention to detail. Another of my teachers in graduate school, Roger Haight, SJ, now professor of the-ology at Union Theological Seminary, provided a helpful review of my treatment of the various "Christological controversies" that split the early Christian church.

I am also thankful to Dave Gibson for his helpful comments and insights on ways of organizing the book, as well as to the many contemporary authors I have quoted throughout. John Meier's monumental multivolume work *A Marginal Jew*, Elizabeth Johnson's *Consider Jesus*, Raymond E. Brown's *Introduction to the New Testament*, Daniel J. Harrington's *Who Is Jesus? Why Is He Important?*, and Albert Nolan's *Jesus before Christianity* have been of particular value for my own education and in my own spiritual life, and they proved especially useful in this project. These authors' lives as serious scholars and faithful Christians have also served as powerful witnesses in my life. Joe MacDonnell, a Jesuit priest who died as this book was being written, and Rick Curry, a Jesuit brother, were both helpful in pointing me to sources on the history of Jesuit theater. Joe's book, *Companions of Jesuits*, was invaluable.

My friends at Loyola Press, including George Lane, SJ, Terry Locke, Tom McGrath, Joe Durepos, Matthew Diener, Jim Manney, and Michelle Halm have been enormously supportive in this project from the very beginning. Special thanks to the dedicated efforts of Vinita Wright and Heidi Hill, whose editing and copyediting skills are amazing. Their careful attention to detail is nothing short of astonishing, and I am deeply grateful for the care that they lavished on this manuscript.

I am grateful to my literary agent, Donald Cutler, for his early enthusiasm about this project as well as his usual astute observations and detailed comments, which greatly helped improve every aspect of this book. Don is not only a terrific agent, but he is also an excellent reader and a fine theologian to boot, who challenged me on some of my theological discussions and strengthened the book.

ABOUT THE AUTHOR

James Martin, SJ, is a Jesuit priest and an associate editor of *America*, a national Catholic magazine. A graduate of the University of Pennsylvania's Wharton School of Business, he worked for six years in corporate finance before entering the novitiate of the Society of Jesus in 1988. During his Jesuit training, Martin worked in a hospice for the sick and dying in Kingston, Jamaica; with street gang members in Chicago; as a prison chaplain in Boston; and for two years with the Jesuit Refugee Service in Nairobi, Kenya, where he helped East African refugees start their own small businesses. After completing his philosophy and theology studies, he was ordained a priest in 1999.

Father Martin's writing has appeared in a variety of newspapers, magazines, and Web sites, including the *New York Times*, the *Boston Globe*, *U.S. News & World Report*, and Slate.com. He is a frequent commentator in the media on issues of religion and spirituality, and he has appeared in venues as diverse as NPR, CNN, the Fox News Channel, PBS, Vatican Radio, and the BBC. Martin is the author or editor of several books, including *In Good Company: The Fast Track from the Corporate World to Poverty, Chastity, and Obedience* (Sheed & Ward) and *This Our Exile: A Spiritual Journey with the Refugees of East Africa* (Orbis), winner of a Catholic Press Association award. His books have been translated into Spanish, German, Polish, and Korean, and his writing has been selected for the Best Catholic Writing series (Loyola Press).

Martin's most recent book is *My Life with the Saints* (Loyola Press), which was named by *Publishers Weekly* as one of the Best Books of 2006 and was the winner of a Christopher Award. He lives in a Jesuit community in New York City and is an assisting priest at the Church of St. Ignatius Loyola. And, since 2006, he has been a member of the LAByrinth Theatre Company.

WHO ARE THE JESUITS, ANYWAY?

In *The First Jesuits*, the Jesuit scholar John W. O'Malley notes that while "reform of the church" and responding to Protestant Reformers are the agendas most commonly ascribed to Jesuits in both academic and popular literature, these ideas are virtually nonexistent in the early Jesuit documents. One phrase, however, is repeated on practically every page in these documents: *to help souls*. This deceptively simple idea would become their religious agenda.

After combing through the voluminous writings of Saint Ignatius of Loyola, who founded the Society of Jesus in 1540, O'Malley notes that no expression occurs more frequently. "In the *Autobiography*, *Constitutions*, and his correspondence Ignatius used it again and again to describe what motivated him and was to motivate the Society. His disciples seized upon it and tirelessly repeated it as the best and most succinct description of what they were trying to do."

By this phrase, the first Jesuits meant helping the whole person, not merely the "spiritual" aspects of the person's life. They could help souls in almost any way, and they did. "This is why," writes O'Malley, "their list of ministries was so long, why at first glance they seem to be without limits."

The Jesuit "way of proceeding," as Ignatius of Loyola liked to say, was based on a broad-minded spirituality that sought to find God in all things, in all peoples, and in all environments. This meant that the Jesuits' method of communicating their religious worldview was not confined to the more traditional works of priests and brothers. From the Society's earliest years, a Jesuit would not be surprised to find himself in the classroom during weekdays and in the pulpit on Sundays—or, as a few Jesuits did in Rome three years after their order was founded, working with reformed prostitutes on weekdays and preaching on Sundays.

As a consequence, Western history finds Jesuits almost everywhere and doing almost everything: running schools and parishes and retreat houses, of course; but also working as physicians, lawyers, social workers, astronomers, theologians, writers, painters, scientists, labor organizers, and architects, as well as explorers of uncharted territories. As the British historian Jonathan Wright notes in his book *God's Soldiers*, a history of the Jesuits with the piquant subtitle *Adventure, Politics, Intrigue, and Power*, Jesuit missionaries discovered the source of the Blue Nile in eastern Africa, charted land routes in China, and navigated the Orinoco, Amazon, and Mississippi rivers. While doing so, they also reported back to their European confreres, in long, detailed letters, about a new world of plants, animals, and drugs (among them, camellias, ginseng, and the antimalarial quinine, which was originally called "Jesuit's bark").

Much of the history of the first Europeans in North America comes from the prodigious letters of French Jesuits such as Isaac Jogues and Jean de Brébeuf. These seventeenth-century missionaries dutifully sent home their missives, called the *Relations*, on a regular basis to their religious superiors.

Jogues and Brébeuf, friends to the Hurons, were martyred along with several other Jesuits by members of the rival Mohawk and Iroquois nations and later named saints, a tale told more or less accurately in the 1991 film *Black Robe*. Another popular, though less accurate, movie about Jesuit missionaries, this time those who protected native peoples from slave traders in South America, is *The Mission*, starring "Father" Jeremy Irons and "Brother" Robert De Niro.

Some of the earliest written sources of Native American languages, in fact, are the dictionaries that the Jesuits compiled to help them converse with the indigenous peoples they encountered on their trips. The history of the missionary era is a controversial one, to be sure, replete with cultural imperialism and collusion with European political powers. But the actual letters show that the Jesuits' travels were one way in which they saw themselves as trying to "help souls," of peoples whose complicated lives and rich cultures they found fascinating—worthy not only of sincere and often fulsome praise but also of careful observation and detailed documentation.

Back home in Europe, the Jesuits of the sixteenth and seventeenth centuries kept busy advising monarchs (sometimes well, sometimes poorly), writing treatises and books on nearly every topic imaginable, and, well, doing just about anything else you might imagine a curious and well-educated person doing. It is impossible to summarize their wide-ranging works or their lasting influence on world history, but Jonathan Wright has fun trying:

> They have been urban courtiers in Paris, Peking and Prague, telling kings when to marry, when and how to go to war, serving as astronomers to Chinese emperors or as chaplains to Japanese armies invading Korea. As might be expected, they have dispensed sacraments and they have provided education to men as various as Voltaire, Castro, Hitchcock and Joyce. But they have also been sheep farmers in Quito, hacienda owners in Mexico, wine growers in Australia and plantation owners in antebellum United States. The Society would flourish in the worlds of letters, the arts, music and science, theorizing about dance, disease, and the laws of electricity and optics. Jesuits would

grapple with challenges of Copernicus, Descartes and
Newton, and thirty-five craters on the surface of the moon
would be named for Jesuit scientists.

During my philosophy studies as a Jesuit, one of my classmates was
an astrophysicist, a Jesuit who received his doctorate from MIT, and
now works in the Vatican observatory. His specialty is meteorites.

Thanks to these varied activities, the Jesuits have never lacked critics, both inside and outside the church. Until recently, for example,
the figure of the Jesuit was a stock character in Western literature and
drama: a villainous wraith, cloaked in a black cassock, skulking around
the corridors of power, always ready to dissemble and prevaricate. The
word *Jesuitical*, still found in most dictionaries, is used to mean slyly
twisting the truth to advance one's own ends. Because of their perceived
worldly influence, Jesuits have, since their founding, attracted the ire of
both conservative and liberal Catholics. And because of their ecclesial
orthodoxy, they found even more critics in writers and philosophers of
the Enlightenment.

The prize for the most virulent anti-Jesuit quote is hotly contested:
one can find barbed critiques of the Society of Jesus from the most esti-
mable figures in European and American history. My own favorite is a
zinger from John Adams, who wrote that "if any congregation of men
could merit eternal perdition on earth and in hell, it is this company
of Loyola."

At the same time, the Jesuits have attracted almost as many critics
inside the Catholic Church. Thanks in part to what was seen as their
undue influence in secular affairs (and in part to their defense of the
native populations in South America against the European slave traders), the Society of Jesus was for a time even formally abolished, or "suppressed," by a decree of Pope Clement XIV issued in 1773. According

to Jonathan Wright, Clement dissolved the society because "the secular powers of Catholic Europe left him with little choice." (The empress Catherine the Great, however, no fan of the pope, stubbornly refused to permit the decree to take effect in Russia.)

After the political winds changed in Europe, the society was restored by the Vatican in 1814. That decision prompted a fevered response from Adams, who wrote to Thomas Jefferson two years later, "I do not like the resurrection of the Jesuits. . . . [S]hall we not have swarms of them here, in as many shapes and disguises as ever a king of gypsies . . . himself assumed?"

In recent decades, the Jesuits have been criticized within the Catholic Church for being too liberal, too unorthodox, and, in general, too freethinking. Beginning in the late 1960s, under the leadership of the superior of the order, a Basque named Pedro Arrupe, the Society of Jesus committed itself to a "faith that does justice." In one of its most influential documents, the society's general congregation wrote in 1975: "The mission of the Society of Jesus today is the service of faith, of which the promotion of justice is an absolute requirement." It was a position based on the call enunciated by Jesus to care for the poor, and on the Catholic Church's more recent emphasis on a "preferential option for the poor." It spawned countless new works on behalf of the poor around the globe, most notably the Jesuit Refugee Service, founded in 1980.

Nonetheless, it was an approach that prompted charges of Marxism even by some of the society's most faithful supporters, who wondered why the Jesuits didn't stick to running high schools for the elite. After Arrupe suffered a debilitating stroke, the American Jesuit he named as interim head of the order was removed by Pope John Paul II, in a move widely interpreted as a rebuke to Arrupe and to the society's approach to "social justice."

The Jesuits' solidarity with the poor also led to the assassinations of a number of Jesuits working among the impoverished in Latin America, striving to free them not from slave traders, as did their forebears, but from the slavery of poverty and political injustice. In 1989, six Jesuit professors at the University of Central America, in El Salvador, were shot at point-blank range by government-backed soldiers because of their preaching against political oppression in that country. To remove doubt about the motivation, the assassins scooped the priests' brains from their skulls and deposited them on the grass beside their bodies.

Over the past five centuries, the Society of Jesus has also provided Catholicism with some of its most influential saints: Saint Ignatius of Loyola, of course, but also his best friend, the peripatetic Francis Xavier, whose wanderings took him from Lisbon to East Africa to India to Japan to just off the coast of China. Aloysius Gonzaga, a young Italian nobleman who, to the consternation of his family, relinquished the title of Marquis of Castiglione to enter the Jesuit novitiate, and who died at age twenty-three after ministering to plague victims in Rome. And Edmund Campion, the brilliant Oxford-educated scholar whose pamphlets posed a direct threat to Anglican Christianity in England, and who was captured, thrown into the Tower of London, tortured, and hanged for treason. At last count, there are forty-four saints who were members of the Society of Jesus.

More recent Jesuit notables include the nineteenth-century Englishman Gerard Manley Hopkins, whose poems are found in nearly every anthology of English poetry; the twentieth-century French geologist and theologian Pierre Teilhard de Chardin (the model for the main character in the novel and film *The Exorcist*, though more for his scientific bent than any experience with exorcising); Rupert Mayer, the German Jesuit whose anti-Nazi sermons landed him in a concentration camp; and the American social activist Daniel Berrigan, whose protests against the Vietnam War landed him, for a time, in a Pennsylvania jail, where he was visited by Pedro Arrupe, the superior general of the Jesuits.

Today the Jesuits, some 20,000 of them, still try to "help souls," still train men to assume a variety of odd jobs, and still draw criticism like a lightning rod. Among my own friends are a Jesuit physician working as a gerontologist at a Chicago hospital; a Jesuit who served as a chaplain with the Army Special Forces and saw action in Afghanistan (and who received a Purple Heart after his jeep was fired upon and he rescued a fellow soldier); a Jesuit who teaches gang members in inner-city Camden, New Jersey, how to design Web sites; and a Jesuit who works in a refugee camp in the deserts of northern Uganda, where I spent some time during my own Jesuit training.

So, given our history, the idea of a Jesuit priest working with an Off-Broadway acting company seems relatively tame.

BIBLIOGRAPHY

Armstrong, Karen. *Buddha*. New York: Penguin Books, 2001.

Saint Augustine. *Expositions of the Psalms: 121–150*. Translated by Maria Boulding. Hyde Park, New York: New City Press, 2004.

Bangert, William V. *A History of the Society of Jesus*. St. Louis: Institute of Jesuit Sources, 1972.

Barclay, William. *The Gospel of John*. Rev. ed. 2 vols. The New Daily Study Bible. Louisville, KY: Westminster John Knox, 2001.

———. *The Gospel of Luke*. Rev. ed. The New Daily Study Bible. Louisville, KY: Westminster John Knox, 2001.

———. *The Gospel of Mark*. The New Daily Study Bible. Louisville, KY: Westminster John Knox, 2001.

———. *The Gospel of Matthew*. Rev. ed. 2 vols. The New Daily Study Bible. Louisville, KY: Westminster John Knox, 2001.

Barry, William A. *Letting God Come Close: An Approach to the Ignatian Spiritual Exercises*. Chicago: Loyola Press, 2001.

Bergant, Dianne, and Robert J. Karris, eds. *The Collegeville Bible Commentary*. Collegeville, MN: Liturgical Press, 1989.

Bogosian, Eric. *Mall*. New York: Simon & Schuster, 2000.

Bokenkotter, Thomas. *A Concise History of the Catholic Church*. Rev. and exp. ed. New York: Image Books, 1990.

Brown, Peter. *Augustine of Hippo: A Biography*. Berkeley: University of California Press, 1969.

Brown, Raymond E. *The Death of the Messiah: From Gethsemane to the Grave; A Commentary on the Passion Narratives in the Four Gospels*. 2 vols. New York: Doubleday, 1994.

———— *An Introduction to the New Testament.* New York: Doubleday, 1997.

Brown, Raymond E., Joseph A. Fitzmyer, Roland E. Murphy, eds. *The New Jerome Biblical Commentary.* Englewood Cliffs, NJ: Prentice Hall, 1990.

Catechism of the Catholic Church. 2nd ed. New York: Doubleday, 1997.

Chadwick, Henry. *The Early Church.* Rev. ed. New York: Penguin, 1993.

Chilton, Bruce. *Mary Magdalene: A Biography.* New York: Doubleday, 2006.

Crace, Jim. *Quarantine.* New York: Picador, 1998.

Crossan, John Dominic. *The Historical Jesus: The Life of a Mediterranean Jewish Peasant.* San Francisco: HarperSanFrancisco, 1991.

Cunningham, Lawrence S. *A Brief History of Saints.* Oxford: Blackwell Publishing, 2005.

Downing, David C. *Into the Wardrobe: C. S. Lewis and the Narnia Chronicles.* San Francisco: Jossey-Bass, 2005.

Dulles, Avery Cardinal. *A History of Apologetics.* 2nd ed. San Francisco: Ignatius Press, 2005.

Ehrman, Bart D., ed. *Lost Scriptures: Books That Did Not Make It into the New Testament.* New York: Oxford University Press, 2003.

Ellsberg, Robert. *All Saints: Daily Reflections on Saints, Prophets, and Witnesses for Our Time.* New York: Crossroad, 1997.

Fink, Peter E., ed. *The New Dictionary of Sacramental Worship.* Collegeville, MN: Liturgical Press, 1990.

Fitzmyer, Joseph A. *A Christological Catechism: New Testament Answers.* New rev. and exp. ed. New York: Paulist Press, 1990.

Fülöp-Miller, René. *The Power and Secret of the Jesuits.* Translated by F. S. Flint and D. F. Tait. New York: Viking, 1930.

Ganss, George E. *The Spiritual Exercises of Saint Ignatius: A Translation and Commentary.* St. Louis: Institute of Jesuit Sources, 1992.

Guirgis, Stephen Adly. *The Last Days of Judas Iscariot.* New York: Faber & Faber, 2006.

———. *Our Lady of 121st Street; Jesus Hopped the A Train; In Arabia, We'd All Be Kings.* New York: Faber & Faber, 2003.

Gula, Richard M. *Reason Informed by Faith: Foundations of Catholic Morality.* New York: Paulist Press, 1989.

Haight, Roger. *Jesus, Symbol of God.* Maryknoll, NY: Orbis Books, 1999.

Hamilton, Edith. *The Roman Way.* New York: Avon Books, 1973.

Harrington, Daniel J. *Who Is Jesus? Why Is He Important?: An Invitation to the New Testament.* Franklin, WI: Sheed & Ward, 1999.

———. *How Do Catholics Read the Bible?* Lanham, MD: Rowman & Littlefield, 2005.

Hartnoll, Phyllis. *The Oxford Companion to the Theatre.* New York: Oxford University Press, 1951.

Kelly, J. N. D. *Early Christian Doctrines.* New York: Harper & Row, 1978.

Johnson, Elizabeth A. *Consider Jesus: Waves of Renewal in Christology.* New York: Crossroad, 1990.

———. *She Who Is: The Mystery of God in Feminist Theological Discourse.* New York: Crossroad, 2002.

Kasper, Walter. *The God of Jesus Christ.* Translated by Matthew J. O'Connell. New York: Crossroad, 1984.

Lacouture, Jean. *Jesuits: A Multibiography.* Translated by Jeremy Leggatt. Washington DC: Counterpoint, 1995.

Lewis, C. S. *The Chronicles of Narnia.* New York: HarperCollins, 2001.

———. *The Problem of Pain.* San Francisco: HarperSanFrancisco, 2001.

MacDonnell, Joseph F. *Companions of Jesuits: A Tradition of Ignatian Education* Fairfield, CT: Fairfield University Press, 1995.

Martin, Valerie. *Salvation: Scenes from the Life of St. Francis.* New York: Knopf, 2001.

Mays, James L., ed. *Harper's Bible Commentary.* San Francisco: Harper & Row, 1988.

McBrien, Richard P. *Catholicism.* Rev. ed. San Francisco: HarperSanFrancisco, 1994.

McBrien, Richard P., ed. *The HarperCollins Encyclopedia of Catholicism.* New York: HarperCollins, 1995.

McCabe, William H. *An Introduction to the Jesuit Theater.* St. Louis, MO: Institute of Jesuit Sources, 1983.

Meier, John P. *A Marginal Jew: Rethinking the Historical Jesus.* Vol. 1, *The Roots of the Problem and the Person.* New York: Doubleday, 1991.

———. *A Marginal Jew: Rethinking the Historical Jesus.* Vol. 2, *Mentor, Message, and Miracles.* New York: Doubleday, 1994.

———. *A Marginal Jew: Rethinking the Historical Jesus.* Vol. 3, *Companions and Competitors.* New York: Doubleday, 2001.

Merton, Thomas. *New Seeds of Contemplation.* Norfolk, CT: New Directions, 1961.

———. *No Man Is an Island.* New York: Harcourt Brace, 1955.

———. *The Seven Storey Mountain.* New York: Harcourt-Brace Jovanovich, 1976.

Metz, Johannes Baptist. *Poverty of Spirit.* Rev. ed. Translated by John Drury. New York: Paulist Press, 1998.

Metzger, Bruce M., and Roland E. Murphy, eds. *The New Oxford Annotated Bible: The New Revised Standard Version.* New York: Oxford University Press, 1994.

Morgan, Edmund S. *The Genuine Article: A Historian Looks at Early America.* New York: W. W. Norton, 2004.

Mott, Michael. *The Seven Mountains of Thomas Merton*. Boston: Houghton Mifflin, 1984.

Murphy-O'Connor, Jerome. *Paul: His Story*. New York: Oxford University Press, 2004.

Nolan, Albert. *Jesus before Christianity*. Maryknoll, NY: Orbis Books, 2001.

O'Malley, John W. *The First Jesuits*. Cambridge, MA: Harvard University Press, 1994.

Paffenroth, Kim. *Judas: Images of the Lost Disciple*. Louisville, KY: Westminster John Knox, 2001.

Pelikan, Jaroslav. *Credo: Historical and Theological Guide to Creeds and Confessions of Faith in the Christian Tradition*. New Haven, CT: Yale University Press, 2003.

Rahner, Karl. *Theological Investigations*. Vol. 3, *Theology of the Spiritual Life*. London: Darton, Longman & Todd, 1967.

Richardson, Cyril C., ed. *Early Christian Fathers*. New York: Simon & Schuster, 1996.

Rohr, Richard. *Soul Brothers: Men in the Bible Speak to Men Today*. Maryknoll, NY: Orbis Books, 2004.

Schaberg, Jane. *The Resurrection of Mary Magdalene: Legends, Apocrypha, and the Christian Testament*. New York: Continuum, 2002.

Schüssler Fiorenza, Elisabeth. *In Memory of Her: A Feminist Theological Reconstruction of Christian Origins*. New York: Crossroad, 1989.

Smith, Jonathan Z., ed. *The HarperCollins Dictionary of Religion*. With the American Academy of Religion. San Francisco: HarperSanFrancisco, 1995.

Spink, Kathryn. *Mother Teresa: A Complete Authorized Biography*. San Francisco: HarperSanFrancisco, 1998.

Staniforth, Maxwell, trans. *Early Christian Writings: The Apostolic Fathers*. New York: Penguin, 1987.

Mother Teresa. *In My Own Words.* Compiled by José Luis González-Balado. Liguori, MO: Liguori Publications, 1996.

Throckmorton, Burton H. *Gospel Parallels: A Comparison of the Synoptic Gospels.* 5th ed. Nashville: Thomas Nelson, 1992.

Thurston, Herbert J., and Donald Attwater, eds. *Butler's Lives of the Saints.* London: Burns & Oates, 1956.

Tylenda, Joseph N. *Jesuit Saints and Martyrs: Short Biographies of the Saints, Blessed, Venerables, and Servants of God of the Society of Jesus.* 2nd ed. Chicago: Loyola Press, 1998.

Wiersbe, Warren, W., ed. *Classic Sermons on Judas Iscariot.* Grand Rapids, MI: Kregel Publications, 1995.

Wright, Jonathan. *God's Soldiers: Adventure, Politics, Intrigue, and Power—A History of the Jesuits.* New York: Doubleday, 2004.

Wright, Vinita Hampton. *The Soul Tells a Story: Engaging Creativity with Spirituality in the Writing Life.* Downers Grove, IL: InterVarsity Press, 2005.

Wroe, Ann. *Pontius Pilate.* New York: Modern Library, 2001.